TWO
BUTTERFLIES
IN A FIELD

A Life and Times Story

TWO BUTTERFLIES IN A FIELD

ALICIA LINDSAY BOSWELL

www.aliciaboswell.com

GRATEFUL ACKNOWLEDGMENTS:
Charlie for the sub-title of this work, those cited in footnotes for the reference and reproduction of their work and all those (named or not) who were company along this journey.

ISBN: 978-1-7773267-0-8
Printed in USA

First Edition 2020
2 4 6 8 10 9 7 5 3 1

Cover photograph © 2011 Alicia Lindsay Boswell
Author photograph © 2020 Mariah Lewin
Graphic + Layout design by Colleen Keith
Edited by Nic Lachance

For all of you who loved me,

guided me

and wiped my many tears.

And for you B, merci d'exister.

You cracked me open to the journey.

You changed me as much as I changed you. ∞

NATURE LOVES COURAGE

You make the commitment and nature will respond to that

commitment by removing impossible obstacles.

Dream the impossible dream

and the world will not grind you under.

It will lift you up.

This is the trick, this is what all these teachers

and philosophers who really counted,

who really touched the alchemical gold.

This is what they understood.

This is the shamanic dance in the waterfall.

This is how magic is done.

By hurling yourself into the abyss

and discovering it's a feather bed.[1]

-Terrence McKenna

---

[1] Terrence McKenna, True Hallucinations: Being an Account of the Author's Extraordinary Adventures in the Devil's Paradise

CONTENTS

1	GIRL ON A BOAT	11
2	A FIRST DATE FOR THE BOOKS	14
3	SUMMER CARRIES ON	18
4	GIMME SHELTER	24
5	LIVING WITH EASY	30

TO ME

6	LOVE YOU TILL THE WHEELS COME OFF	45
7	BLEEDING HEARTS IN BLOOM	47
8	BOWEN LIVING	59
9	RIOT LOVE	69
10	TOFINO	73
11	HAVE LOVE WILL TRAVEL	80
12	HIGHS AND LOWS ON MUDGE	93
13	TAKING IT EASY ON EASY	98

BY ME

14	CHOOSING HAIDA GWAII	103
15	KABOOM	117
16	BOAT SINKING	123
17	EASY RETURNS	132
18	COMMUNICATION BREAKDOWNS	136
19	SHE'S BACK	141
20	HEART IN HAIDA GWAII	145
21	CORTES	148
22	TURNING 30	154
23	HELLO DESOLATION SOUND	157
24	THE MAPLE TREE	162
25	CORTES LIVING	165
26	PARADISE & BIRTHDAY	171
27	BEACH WALK	174
28	DECISION TIME	175
29	SAVED	177

30	EASY DOES IT	180
31	HOME COMING	182
32	IT'S ONGOING	185
33	BACK IN VAN	188
34	BREAKING POINT	201
35	BLACK	205
36	THE FALL OF CORTES	210
37	HEALING	214
38	HEARING MY OWN SCREAMS	219
39	SWAN SONG	224
40	RUNNING OUT OF GAS	227
41	FULL MOON MANIA	232
42	CHRISTMAS	234
43	DETOUR NATURE, HAIDA GWAII	237
44	FORESTS, BEACHES, THE ODD PERSON	241
45	PREPARE FOR LANDING	243
46	POLICE AND FIRE	246
47	HOUSE ARREST	249
48	JANUARY 12TH, 2012	259

THROUGH ME

49	ONE YEAR LATER	283
50	FEED THE EAGLES	290
51	DNA	294
52	THE RETURN OF B	296
53	KUUK	300
54	IT JUST KEEPS GOING	302
55	HAPPILY EVER AFTER IS A STATE OF MIND	304

AS ME

| 56 | 2020 IT IS WHAT IT IS | 308 |
| 57 | LOVE | 315 |

CHAPTER ONE

GIRL ON A BOAT

So I'm strumming along at work one day cut, copy, paste, printing enough future recycling to create a forest of dead trees around me. I worked as a legal secretary for a real hard ass trial lawyer in downtown Vancouver. You could say he was a type triple AAA whose morning exercise routine was biking from his home at the South Vancouver border to the top of Cypress and then back downtown to work, followed by swimming another few miles at Kits beach on his lunch breaks. He was intense with everything he did and he kept the environment so stressful that I learned to balance it by working on my own projects during work hours. That, Plenty of Fish and a bottle of vodka in the bottom drawer for a quick release at quitting time. Having just moved back to Vancouver spending the last six years in Montreal working in fine arts, antiques, high fashion, studying, partying my face off and eventually packing up pretty quickly to get away from a pushy boyfriend that didn't understand the word no. Summer of 2009 started off with a bang when one afternoon my girlfriend Cailey and I met for drinks on the Davie street Score patio which I had self proclaimed as the unofficial extension of my living room. She had also just moved back from Montreal and we were on a mission to plan out a fun summer. Looking closer at our recent relocation boating appeared to be the most obvious choice as we were already far too familiar with this no fun city.

I called the boat rental office and levelled with him. "I have a driver's license and a diver's each with a perfect record…can I rent one of your boats???" He laughed and said that as long as we could speak English he was OK renting us the boat. We finished our double short bloody mary's and probably had another while I chowed down on my habitual grilled cheese and pickle breakfast and we called around to our friends to see who wanted to join.

By the time our bill came we had shared our exciting plans with our server and so far it was going to be just Cailey and I on this boat and I could feel the gears turning inside my head and heart. *Just look at the map!* I thought to myself. We are surrounded with absolute gems of tiny islands and beachfronts! Hot boat guys, partying on boats…with the summer ahead of us how could we do anything else except explore this amazing place! It was the beginning hatchings of a summer which was termed *Girl On A Boat*, or later simply referred to as "the summer of oh-9."

For our first boating trip Cailey was rocking her Bruce Springsteen American flag bikini and me in a white crochet number that I had just picked up in English Bay. Instructions were easy, basically on, off and a kind of bumper car steering and we were good to go! For our first trip we went up Indian Arm since it looked cool and we should probably figure out where the party is up there! We set off with not much other than ourselves, phones and credit cards, figuring we could get anything we need out in the boating world. First on the list, liquor store… where is the liquor store? Boaters are drinkers so it has to be somewhere not too far, we thought. Our inquiry brought us right up to the end of Indian Arm to the one and only dock. OK, there has to be some kind of store or liquor store up here so we approached the dock but there wasn't really much space on the dock and it looked like all the boats had ropes to tie but our rental boat didn't actually come with anything to tie up a boat with either. Since we were just checking it out for a minute we decided Cailey would drive while I stood at the front and we just pulled in like a parking spot between the two docked boats 'Gangie style' like from Arrested Development.

There looked to be two cute guys we could party with but as we got closer they just sat on the dock, one kind of crossing his arms and both cringing and tipping their heads, looking at us like we were crazy and definitely not offering a warm welcome at all. I jumped off the front as Cailey nosed us in and tried to smile and ask these guys for the closest liquor store. Holding the nose of the boat while trying to look cute and keep it from hitting the adjacent docked boats while the waves came in didn't prove easy and these guys were giving a hard vibe that this was a private club, and no liquor was coming our way so we pushed off and looked for the next fun. Renting a power boat got old pretty quickly because they have these electronic shut offs if you cross the boundary lines so we couldn't really do much more exploring. To keep up the momentum of my summer mission *Girl on a Boat* I turned to Craigslist.

CHAPTER TWO

A FIRST DATE FOR THE BOOKS

Craigslist has always been good to me. Great deals out there, jobs, nice people and of course apartments. I was on the hunt for something fun to get me back on the water so I started perusing the boat section for the remote possibility that I would be able to find one for myself. The idea quickly turned to be overwhelming as I realized I know very little about boats and late June wasn't exactly a buyers market. OK fine then, so I turned to the personals. They have a couple categories like man for woman, woman for man etc. however you can search all of them at the same time with a keyword search: boat. A few different types of postings came up including things like "if you are in the same boat" or "whatever floats your boat" but then one posting really caught my eye. I don't remember what the subject line was but it was something quant and seemingly sincere. The post had a photograph of a sunset in Vancouver harbour and a long paragraph written by someone who had a boat and was looking for someone to hang out on it with them. I re-read it a couple times looking for the obvious psychopath red flags but even under close examination I got the sense of it being a genuine post. It said something like "I have a 17' Bayliner, spent a lot of time on the water having a blast with my friends but now I am looking to meet someone new, a female companion even to just hang out…we could go out for Canada day maybe go over to wreck beach or even to Bowen island and then just watch the fireworks." So I shot off an email making contact because if this was legit it sounded pretty nice. Within a few hours this guy emailed me back some photos and we found each other on g-chat. He was a ginger blond and looked nothing like the type of guys that I would say I was attracted to but he was polite and charming nonetheless so we chatted a bit and made a plan: I had a new bikini and his name was Bo and he was going to pick me up under the Burrard street bridge Canada Day early afternoon. I thought the idea was so great that I wanted to put a back up plan in place in case this guy turned sour so I put up my own ad "girl looking to *be* on a boat" which was basically just what it sounded like.

With my new bikini and tanned bod I was psyched for Canada Day. Like any smart online dater I had put up a few safety measures including telling my friends exactly what our plan was and who I was going to go out with (or as much as I knew at the time). I packed a small bag having known to be adventurously ready for nearly anything and walked my way over to the dog park under the bridge to get picked up. Bo called as I was standing there and said he was already there and that couldn't see me. He suggested that maybe I was under the wrong bridge and I was probably confusing the Burrard bridge with Granville. This was off to a bad start quickly and I snapped reminding myself and him that I was born and raised in this city and of course I know the difference between Granville and Burrard bridges. With that said he quickly appeared in view and started driving straight towards me standing on the dog beach. *How was I going to get on this boat now?* I asked myself, suddenly with it sinking in that I don't even know this guy. Before I knew it I had my sandals off and was thigh deep reaching for Bo's hand as I climbed over the bow and into the cockpit of his boat. The happy dog owners on the beach yelled and cursed at us both to get the boat off the dog beach which we quickly did. I looked back and one of the people yelling was an old lifeguard work friend… *at least someone saw me get on this boat if I go missing*, I thought.

"Hi... Alicia" I said, "Hi... Bo" he said, as he dropped the throttle to start our cruise away and I cranked my go to summer tune "Gimme Shelter" by the Stones. We decided to go hang out off of wreck beach first since it was the original plan we had discussed. The plan however had not factored in the messy seas but I think both of us were so nervous that we just went with it anyways. I was quickly impressed first of all with Bo being so much cuter than I had presumed, second for the stealth pick up and third for the cooler filled with crisp Stella beers. There was enough to be happy about that the messy waves hardly bothered me at all. The same could not be said for Bo however. Sitting in the back corner of the boat he was only a beer or two in before he turned green and hurled over the side. I was surprised but also assumed he was embarrassed so I tried to play it cool and offered him my toothbrush and toothpaste. I had no idea why I had packed that for an afternoon on the boat but as it turned out it was just the thing because he brushed his teeth and asked me to kiss him. *Kiss this pukey guy?? Well I guess I had just given him my toothbrush, plus he was just so uniquely cute* that I just couldn't help myself. We chatted for a bit and got real pretty quickly. He was from Ontario and worked in construction or something and I had just moved back from Montreal and was a little depressed about having to suddenly leave my life out there. Bo sympathized with my depression and mentioned he had some bipolar depression struggles in the past as well.

Once we had kissed and confessed our weaknesses we decided to abandon the messy shores off of wreck beach to give Bo's tummy a break and he suggested buzzing over to Bowen and maybe look for some fuel. The sun was shining and I had never been to Bowen so I was all over the idea fitting right into my *Girl On A Boat* summer. A few beers into it and we were getting along great. He was strong and seemed to have all the details taken care of and we were having fun! It turned out there was no fuel on Bowen or anywhere other than much further away at Gibsons or back in the city so we walked around on Bowen, bought some stuff at the General store and ended up running into my hard ass lawyer boss who had a cabin and weekended there. I felt a little off guard seeing as this was a blind date but quickly saw introducing them as a great safety net I could use in case things went sideways or something bad happened to me or us. We skipped through the afternoon together including swimming off the boat a little ways up Howe Sound and some making out. Back at the public dock on Bowen he made us dinner of a deluxe salad and home made pesto pasta. My ears perked and eyes squinted a little when he told me he had made the pesto by growing his own basil from seed and I wondered who the hell this guy was and if he was trying to impress me he was doing a mighty fine job.

Before we knew it 10pm was rolling in and it was fireworks time. I told him that they were in Coal Harbour for Canada Day but he insisted that he knew they were in English Bay. Even in my 26 years of watching Vancouver fireworks from my Grandma's *Ocean Towers* apartment couldn't convince him so we cruised into English Bay and ended up hearing the fireworks and only seeing a crackle or two above the highest buildings. It didn't end up mattering much because we both laughed and seemed pleased enough with each others company. A few more beers or maybe wine to chill the nerves and the hours just rolled passed us like the waves that we floated on. I was enjoying being on the water so much I commented on how great it could probably rock you to sleep and he snapped up the idea before I could even think about what I had just said. Bo suggested we anchor off of Kits beach and he would drop me off in the morning where he picked me up so that I could get myself to work. I was settling in with the waves and my drinking haze so nicely that it didn't take too much convincing. We were on a little speed boat though so there wasn't exactly a proper bedroom or even a bed. We folded up blankets and he may have even had a pillow or two and we curled into the v-berth cuddy and closed the door behind us. He tried the moves but I knew better for the sake of tomorrow morning than to get started with that so he offered me some melatonin and I tried to relax into some sleep. We held each other tight that night, hardly knowing each other and let the knocks of the waves rock us. I woke up utterly exhausted though, feeling like I had slept in a drum in addition to fending off all of Bo's pawing night moves. But still, overall the blind date was topping the charts so as he dropped me off at the little False Creek Ferry dock next to the beach he had just picked me up at the day before I climbed over the fence that they lock to keep people from using the dock and walked off to work, heart and smile beaming.

CHAPTER THREE

SUMMER CARRIES ON

I had a lot of steam to burn off that summer. Like I mentioned I had recently moved back from Montreal not exactly because I wanted to. This guy, my live in boyfriend at the time, had put me in the hospital twice trying to stop me from leaving- once for stitches and the other with a broken bone and I had been hiding it from everyone I knew thinking somehow I would be able to clean up the mess all on my own. It didn't work though and luckily some friends got wise and stood up to him which eventually allowed me to stand up to him and finally leave, taking nothing but my dog Isabelle and some red lipstick. Why that was an essential item I can't recall exactly except it made me feel more powerful and fabulous I guess. Months later with my sister and friends I returned to Montreal to pack up my apartment and it became pretty obvious that I was not safe to stay because even with a restraining order in place he proceeded to assault me after a chance run in on the street. I was on the fence about making the leap to New York since I was already so close and it had the art scene that I desired but it wasn't making sense so reluctantly back to Vancouver I went.

I landed on my feet pretty well and within a week or so had been hired at the most prestigious gallery of Canadian art, Heffel.

I had also started dating a super hot dude until everything started crashing down before my eyes. After only a week or so at Heffel they decided to let me go for no real reason they said, except it might have had something to do with the death stares I received from the other gallerinas as I towered passed them in my Montreal signature Yves St. Laurent velvet and patent leather platform pumps. The super hot dude also broke up with me a week or so in when I remembered to tell him that I had herpes. Rejection was smashing me down on me hard in all directions but in my defence I had never been in the situation to have that conversation with someone as I had been with the pushy boyfriend for a few years and it hadn't been an issue. Under all of the duress of dealing with police, lawyers, moving across the country, new job and trying to build my life back together it honestly didn't even cross my mind but nonetheless he freaked out and suddenly all my lottery winnings were taken back by the house. I wasn't going to take this lying down though so I landed that legal secretary job with zero experience or formal education which gave me barely enough money to rent an apartment, shared with one of my oldest childhood friends. It was brutal at the time in Vancouver with the market set at New York prices, not dog friendly at all and so competitive that people were bribing landlords and lining up by the dozens just to view unlisted rentals. My girlfriend and I had just moved downtown after my parties got us evicted from our previous landing spot on west 12th. With my companion Isabelle resting comfortably at my parents house, for now, I clung to my rich and famous lifestyle which was only crimped by the office day job required to survive it.

Meanwhile my *girl who wants to be on a boat* backup plan had a few bites! There were a handful of guys saying that they also want to be on a boat and would like to hang out thinking that would be enough for us to have in common. Two other guys surfaced one with a sailboat who wasn't attractive to me at all and another guy who was dark haired, cute and a professional diver with a SeaRay yacht. Dark haired guy and I went out one evening and watched the fireworks in English Bay. It was definitely not as much fun as I had had with Bo because this guy was super cautious of anything happening to his boat. We went out a couple times but the whole thing exploded pretty quickly because it turned out the rat had a wife and a child which he only told me about after his wife found my texts and got in touch to inquire. The Rat. I should have asked some pointed questions when I saw the diapers in the boat's washroom cupboard but I guess we ignore things we don't want to see. Serves me right for trying to play two hand at the same time and it also quickly gave this cute Bo guy the lead.

When I say lead it's because following the herpes rejection it seemed like I needed 100 non-rejections to let that one go. Let's say the number didn't get that high but between Plenty of Fish and Craigslist I was fresh meat and definitely had the upper hand in the dating scene. It was at least a few dates every week and sometimes more than just one in the same night where I would practice with confidence disclosing right upfront "you should know I have herpes" to which no one even batted an eye let alone think any less of me.

Dating was ocean centred as much as I could make it to maintain my mission to get on boats. Like the time when I rented a boat with this guy and spotted a freighter off of Belcarra Park with it's ladder down. Bikini and all I climbed up that ladder while the guy I barely knew held on to it at the bottom. I recall considering he might take off and my back up plan was to jump off the freighter if it came to that. Luckily the workers in their coveralls just froze, sat down and stared at me. I tried to make small talk but no one spoke English except the guy who came out and clearly said "you go now!" To which I did, lucky and pleased that my getaway buddy was still waiting at the bottom. I definitely got out on boats a lot that summer but in hindsight this highlight was only second to not dying or being kidnapped in some of my more reckless adventures. Even though it didn't seem related at the time we had also just found out my Dad was diagnosed with bladder cancer so I was running from a lot. To where? I don't know but playing party girl seemed to take the edge off and it didn't seem to matter whose arms I found myself in as long as we had fun and I wasn't alone.

My summer of dating and *Girl On A Boat* had a strong under-current of Bo throughout. He wasn't demanding and seemed to be confident enough that he wasn't bothered by my disclosures of playing the field. He got too drunk a few times which annoyed me enough to put him in purgatory for a few weeks but little did I know by the end of the summer he would win my heart.

We were spending a lot of time together even amongst my dating rampage. Our second or third weekend together was particularly dreamy when he picked my pup Isabelle and I up at our usual spot under the bridge. This time we headed from English Bay into more open ocean than I had ever seen from a small boat and it just got more beautiful by the minute as we left the land behind us. Well, except for the rolling whitecap waves that we were taking straight on. Isabelle and I bounced around so much that my beer was undrinkable for the fear of chipping a tooth on the bottle. "It's Ok, it will get better" Bo assured me. Unconvinced that the front of the boat would be easier as he suggested I crept to the back of the boat cowering with Belle in my arms waiting for the jolts to stop. Somewhere along the way it did get better but only long enough to realize we were racing the sunset to get to our destination. Or maybe it was planned that way because sure enough under a gorgeous pink and purple sky we finally beached our boat onto the white sandy beach of Thormanby and I crawled off the bow just in awe of the beauty to behold. I felt like an island princess discovering this new place and was convinced in that moment that this was the life for me. Belle loved it too and she showed us by rolling her face in the sand, eyes, ears and nose all filled as she log rolled herself around. I can't remember for sure if we had fresh crab that night because we did so many times that summer but I remember Bo cooking pasta in 1/3 sea water- a trick he had read about so we didn't have to add salt! The fresh pesto pasta never got old and his salads were to die for, all finely cut into small pieces because as he would say "I want many flavours in each bite." We drank too much to tidy up very well and sleeping in the cuddy was a little crowded with Isabelle but her enthusiasm made it worth while. Given the space and required 'pee bucket' for a crowded bed we were getting acquainted pretty quickly.

Bo became one of my late night go to calls when my priority dates fizzled flat. One night I was drunk enough that I even brought my Irish date out to meet him because the guy said he had never swam in the ocean before but my drunk idea made for threes a crowd pretty quickly and neither of them were into it at all. After the Irish left Bo and I took off to Bowen again, this time in the total dark which I remember clearly because my only job was to keep an eye out for the entry port lights as we approached the island and I remember him asking me to confirm what colour they were though I didn't think much of it at the time.

After the few weeks or so apart because he would get stupid drunk Bo had sent out a last ditch invite for me and some friends to take in an end of the summer weekend cruise and crab feast and with the encouragement of my friend Cailey I reluctantly agreed. "Why burn a bridge" she said, besides, it was one of those beautiful days in Vancouver where as the saying goes "like a cheating lover all is forgotten when the sun comes out" and a few hours later he picked us all up at the Coal Harbour public dock. Just as I remembered, hot guy, blond hair, tanned skin. We didn't have to talk much because as soon as we crossed under the Lions Gate it was full throttle over to Gabriola. He knew of a special spot called the galleries and we dropped the crab trap on the way in. Cailey, G Bo and I spent the afternoon cliff jumping in the blazing sun while my little dog Isabelle yapped at jumpers from the cliff's edge. We pulled up the crab trap and set up the Little Pal barbecue in the galleries to grill our crab and heat water for homemade pesto. The feast and sparkling light reflections were so good that we let the tide creep in much past our ankles while we continued to move the anchor to accommodate the rise. Bo and I caught up from the last few weeks of summer and I told him that my boating passion had turned to sailing after discovering Liza Copeland's *Cruising for Cowards*. With no hesitation he gestured at his Bayliner and said "If you want to sail I'll put this boat up for sale right now and get us a sailboat." I didn't really know what to make of that even though I admit it did make my heart jump. All I could commit to was that I already liked this guy a lot and didn't want our summer to end.

CHAPTER FOUR

GIMME SHELTER

A few weeks passed and our affection and infatuation for each other slowly grew. For my birthday Bo had surprised me with a most thoughtful and beautiful gift bag which included fresh Italian prune plums from his yard each individually wrapped in pretty tissue paper and a professional dive knife and headlamp for my newly hatched winter travel plans of heading to Thailand to live and scuba dive with my Montreal girlfriends. The following weekend he brought over a huge backpack of the remaining ripe prune plums and with his lead we made the most absolutely delicious walnut plum jam. This guy was killing me with the romance!

My lease was up at the end of September and my options were limited as I was splitting from my roommates likely due to my Kings of Leon/MGMT vodka fuelled dating rampage of a summer. I wanted to try and find an exchange where I could housekeep, cook/clean and live rent free before setting off to Thailand. I figured there must be someone in Vancouver proper who has an extra room and would enjoy the company for a few months. I had put a post on Craigslist and been interviewing people narrowing it down to only one real candidate, a guy from South Africa who actually had a spare room and was taking the lead even despite his slight sense of creep. With

Bo's help my apartment was nearly packed up and I shared my plan with him which was followed by this moment burned in my mind of watching his hand close my door while he said it was a terrible idea and that I should just move in with him. DONG (the sound I can hear in my head when something really strikes me). At first I had major resistance since were were not even that serious combined with fearing the idea of moving across the bridge out of downtown, likely emanating on some Sex and the City layover idea that it was taking me out of the action but I agreed to try it for a couple months because he said most of the people he lived with were away travelling.

Most everything from my downtown apartment went to my parents house except the basics required for the legal secretary work and what I would need for Thailand so together with one suitcase I moved into Bo's room at 1906 in Kitsilano. He chuckled and said I would need a little more room than just my bag on the floor and returned from the shed with his drill and a pole to put up for me to hang some clothes in the closet. We got rid of his single bed and put my double mattress on the floor under the window in its place.

It was remarkable to me how neat and tidy he was and how little he owned other than an entire workshop of wood tools. Turns out he was a finishing carpenter who was self employed and did specialized contract work throughout the city. He seemed to have a nice gig setting his own schedule and making enough to appear quite flush. Still, aside from flashing his bank account balance my way he had very little to his name including only one or two dress shirts, one belt, a few pairs of specially chosen shoes, little to no personal items except the boat and trailer, his work stuff, a wood desk he made while in university, an orange Navajo carpet hanging on the wall and a leather foot stool both purchased from a local Kits yard sale.

We lived in the main floor of this house with this guy Charlie who Bo knew from his childhood in Ontario. Charlie was a cool guy though he also didn't have more than a handful of possessions, he preferred sleeping on the floor and he didn't always get his words out. I guess he had ran away at some point and was on the street for a while before his family found him again. On the days we went to work Bo would wake him up and often asked him to do a few chores but mostly he was just encouraged to spend the day outside under Bo's best judgment to get him on a routine and not leave him alone all day in the house. Charlie's Aunt Kristen owned the house with her husband Nando, well kind of. They never got married per se but had been together for 20 years and Nando lives mostly in the Philippines now only coming back a few times a year and Kristen travels there, around and to India. It's actually Nando's house, also known as Nandostan. They are both original hippies and I learned later that they met somewhere in remote Afghanistan when naked Kristen and her long red dreadlocks jumped into Nando's VW van while Kristen was looking to get out of the sun and Nando was exploring for the world's best hash. Only after I had fully moved in did I ask Bo what he actually paid for rent, "nothing" he said as my jaw dropped "it's an exchange for taking care of the place." I couldn't believe he was already living exactly what I had set out to find! Ha!

For now it was just A, B + C kicking it and living large. Fall was super fun and filled with friends and romantic evenings by the fire, dancing in the living room, game nights and of course fine dining care of Bo's passion. He even made the effort to learn new vegetarian meals for me in favour of his strong preference for lamb and he would wake me up every morning with a coffee in bed, a sandwich to go and would drive me to work. That halloween we went to my sister's party down the street. I dressed up as a geisha (before knowing it was offensive) and Bo went as Bacchus in a borrowed costume care of Ellen who lived downstairs. We laughed, danced, enjoyed and partied together a lot...basically any chance we could.

Darker autumn days were starting to bring me down a bit but I mitigated my struggles at work, dreaming of my dreams barefoot and listening to Mishka's wave crashing "Coastline Journey" on repeat for most of my shift each passing day.

The relationship was still too new to know what was going on with us but we clearly enjoyed our adventures together and we had even discussed sailing around the world and having children in different countries while living aboard. I had been enamoured with Liza Copeland's books about homeschooling her three young boys while they sailed the globe and so was Bo. As our dreams grew my Thailand plans were slowly moving to the back burner and we would share links of other people sailing with children and discussed working up to the Vic-Maui regatta. Personal space was going to be limited at 1906 in the winter so we looked at renting a little spot over on Bowen to have a little retreat of our own. Bo was a Craigslist maven and had found a super cute treehouse type spot that was well finished and had a Murphy bed. I can't recall exactly why we didn't pursue it but likely it was a Mexico trip distraction and the choice to focus on sailing. He spent the next 3 months reading about sailboats and checking Craigslist every day first thing in the morning to see what was coming up boat wise and that became our main focus. His favourites were Cheoy Lee's but we both kept coming back to one of the first ones we liked. Looking back, he sent me the original posting on my birthday:

September 4, 2009
Bo
To me
Hinckley sloop
Fwd: Date: 2009-09-03, 2:22PM
Restored classic wooden boat Hinckley SouWester 34 ,mahogany over oak,35hp BMW diesel 1300hrs,sail covers,heater,elec anchor winch,3battery charger,solar panel,new upholstery,good sails,vhf,depth sounder,gps,autohelm,3 batteries,dingy,monel water and diesel tanks,holding tank,ready to cruise
I have put a lot of time and energy into Easy...she is a great cruiser for the coast..sails lovely with a blow...a lovely motion and sea kind....must sell...make an offer! will.....iarrh@yahoo.ca or 778...
¥Location: Ladner BC

In Bo's usual style we thought about it and continued to look around for months until Spring. In the meantime for Christmas he got us the Power and Sail Squadron course so we started studying like crazy and imagining our own circumnavigation one day. Christmas Eve is all about traditions with my family one being new pyjamas and this year we welcomed my man by playing a little trick and gifting him and my Dad (who was in on it) their own new pj's in the form scroogy looking flannel nightgowns. He went along like a champ and put it on for the fashion show even including the matching night cap and we all laughed and cheers'd ourselves to sleep.

As spring approached my blogger entry was as follows:

March 2010
First Visit to Easy: So we have been looking at this boat online for months and finally decided to take the drive out to LADNER!! to go and visit. I didn't want to say anything but I felt pretty quickly that it would be a nice fit. We had looked at others online and I just hated the idea of a v-berth that felt like a shoe box. Easy has two portholes that open, another two windows on either side and a glass hatch so there was lots of room to breath even though it was still a v-berth. The other sell-point for me was that someone had installed a small fireplace that Will had running before we got there. As we stepped into the boat in still winter-Vancouver, it felt warm and cozy and most certainly inviting. Of course, Bo looked through all of the (probably more important) aspects and it all seemed to check out well.
I am glad I took my camera along to capture our first visit to what would turn out to be our first boat.
Posted by Alicia Lindsay Boswell at 6:57 PM

We spent our first night on the boat in Ladner with my parents' dogs Winnie and my baby Isabelle. It only took one night to know that we didn't want to spend too much time driving out to Ladner and back let alone negotiating the dead head filled river so the following day Bo single handedly sailed her into English Bay. Coincidentally it was also the night of our Power and Sail Squadron exam which we ended up missing but we figured any real boating enthusiast would have done the same. I remember he called me as he came around UBC and his friend John and I bolted down to Kits beach to watch Bo sail her in. It was a choppy whitecap day and Bo had just seen another sailboat bottom out off of Spanish Banks so it took him a few attempts to feel confident about anchoring Easy, as she was named, in her new home- Kits harbour. Bo rowed out but the dinghy was a homemade salvage from a larger blue row boat that had been cut down so the proportions were all wrong and the oars kept hitting his knees as he tried to row. Still, I think Bo's excitement gave him all the energy he needed as he carved his way into shore until he couldn't row any further. John went in up to his knees to help exhausted Bo walk in the 150lb. dinghy and we tied her to the stairs near Kits pool and drove Bo home to a warm shower and stories about his sail in. I thought we were the luckiest kids in the world to be living in Vancouver and be able to walk just a few blocks to the beach, load into the dinghy and out to our 1947 Hinckley wood sailboat. The romance just killed me.

It turned out it wouldn't be the first time John helped us with our dinghy in that bay either. No matter what the conditions we used to go sleep on the boat after dinner and one morning woke to see our upgraded zodiac style dinghy washing up from choppy waves onto the beach. At 6am not many people would warmly receive a phone call to row our dinghy out to us except Bo's childhood friend, John. He was there in a flash and had to get soaked walking in to get her and bring her out to us. Not to mention that this was now the second time in March and cold as ever. The dinghy issues and transiting back and forth refugee style quickly got annoying so we were on the hunt for moorage, something highly sought after come Spring in Vancouver. Bo was at it again and checked Craigslist every morning until the perfect moorage came up. Actually at that point we were open to take almost anything but this one located in Coal Harbour just facing a dog park at the foot of Denman truly was the perfect fit.

CHAPTER FIVE

LIVING WITH EASY

What an incredible way to start the summer! Our first sail out together was a learning curve in and of itself. Bo was taking the lead since I was still totally novice and more concerned with things like hosting our guests aboard and which hand towels to use in the head. Friends came in their best whites for the occasion and we set off into English bay for a cruise. Even just a few months we had come a long way from being aboard like the first time when Bo changed tacks and both Cailey and I went flying from one side of the cockpit to the other, with drinks and snacks flying everywhere. This ensued me yelling at him saying things like "Bo you have to tell us if you are going to do that!!" To which he repeatedly replied in a dude voice "Babe, this is sailing." Our communication about the how to's of sailing never really took off. I was keen to learn and ready to rock but I felt overwhelmed being in charge of moving an object so large! Looking up her mast was 45 feet tall and below was a solid lead keel reaching another 5 feet down. Bo said it was the equivalent of a Toyota hanging off the bottom to reassure me we were not going to flip even when she heeled into strong winds.

Easy grabbed attention wherever she went. Like the first time we pulled around to the Coal Harbour public dock we had been at there for mere moments before an older sailor type guy and his wife walked down the dock to introduce themselves and let us know that they lived in one of the high-rises and had watched us come in. He said he "just had to come and see the wood sailboat with double spreaders." News to me that this was a thing but I agreed, she sure was pretty.

One of the first trips Bo took Easy out with some guy friends he came back disgruntled because one of the top spreaders had cracked in the wind. He hand made a bosun's chair to inspect the damage and being the genius at wood working that he was he was able to whittle up a new one in no time and finished it by buying cream coloured leather and hand sewing on the boots. I was thoroughly impressed.

Maintenance never takes a break on a wood boat we quickly learned. The varnish was wearing off on the mast and it was time to take her down for a refinish and we figured it was also a good time to take her out of the water for a bottom clean. The mast was refinished in no time and resetting her was fun. Bo let me paint a small heart on the top with red nail polish although I do recall us bickering a little because he wanted a sun face. A sun face reminded me too much of Karl Lagerfeld's 90's perfume so red heart it was.

It was a steep learning curve for old wooden boats but our passions and the romance kept us fuelled. Things like putting a coin down with the current year under the mast as it was re-footed and all of the friends we made at the dry dock left me enamoured and wanting more. It ended up taking us much longer than anticipated to get her back in the water. I was still working full time so Bo spent most days down at the Race Rocks dry docks with her in West Van and I would take the bus over to meet him after work whenever I could. John helped us sand off the bottom coat and they painted her fresh and pretty until something went awry... a crack in the hull with a small leak? Not quite the words you want to hear with a boat. I can't remember exactly how it developed but one of the keel bolts became Bo's nemesis as he couldn't get it off for the life of him. It had to be repaired though so he worked tirelessly day after day until the late hours. The pressure didn't really resonate with me at the time and

I recall us getting into a huge fight because I was still partying and calling him from the hot tub at Cailey's while he slaved away. "This is OUR boat" he would say. "Oooh...!" Good point I thought. So I committed further and ended up contributing any way I could which included hand painting her cove stripe from the current white to the Hinckley's signature golden yellow. A nice touch, I thought, very proud of myself. Friends came down with beers to help us and my parents even rolled up their sleeves in the same fashion. We ended up getting everything sorted and repaired as required and even changed the original bronze winches over to a ratcheting winch which Bo said would improve things greatly. Finally putting her back in the water brought a tear to my eyes. She really WAS our boat, elegant, well loved, hand tended and cared for.

It didn't take long to learn there isn't much wind up Indian Arm so we didn't spend too much time up there and instead went back and forth to Bowen a lot. Against my Dad's strong wishes we practiced navigating at night thinking it would better set us up for the Vic-Maui and sailing around the world. There is a lot to learn out there in the boating world and even though Bo had spent years windsurfing on Ontario lakes, we were pretty much brand spanking new to sailing.

One time friends joined us overnight for a cruise over to Bowen and wind was set to be getting good so we loosely discussed some plans for the next day's sail. By morning to my surprise Bo had woken up before everyone and quietly pushed us off from the dock. I'll never forget waking up to the sound of the waves, the blue skies and no land in site as we crossed the Strait of Georgia for the first time in Easy. We were not exactly prepared with provisions so breakfast was a warm beer but I was elated nonetheless to sit on the bow with Cailey just taking it all in. How far we had come...We found our way to Gabriola and anchored in a bay by nightfall while Bo used the bosun's chair to secure a hammock on the bow for Cailey to sleep in. She always loves sleeping under the stars and it was a warm enough night. Our sleeping quarters were comfortable also with a full hatch above our heads and what I liked most was that Bo had cut the berth slightly so we could actually walk into the cabin rather than crawl into it like a drawer which you see on so many boats with a v-berth.

Raising and lowering the anchor was usually my job and although Bo had toyed around with getting us a windlass we didn't want to compromise any space down below so for now it was just me doing it by hand. I was still very unclear as to how much line to put out so the method was mostly that I would just take vague directions from him on the fly from the cockpit. That wasn't nearly as nerve racking as it was trying to dock her at our moorage spot in Coal Harbour. It was a tight fit where we had to enter often in only a few feet of water with the dock on port side and all rocks starboard. The method was to slowly cruise in then make a sharp 90 degree turn when we reached our spot and direct the bow straight at the dock where I would stand leaning over the guardrail with the two 40' docking lines in hand ready to jump off just before we would hit the dock then quickly turn around to brace Easy and slow her down by the guardrail then run to the back of the boat to cleat her off then with both docking lines in hand I would gently negotiate her into the dock. Bo probably had to remind me 20 times to stop a boat by the back lines, a logic that came so naturally to him and not so much to me.

That wasn't the scariest part about docking though, in fact I would choose that role over holding the tiller any day. Though one time, the choice was taken from me. It was another one of those night navigations motoring to Bowen and I think Bo was trying to dock us singlehandedly which he had done many times however this time he jumped off and the line slipped through his hand leaving me alone on board to figure it out. I jumped to the tiller and luckily there was a lot of space on the dock to turn around and avoid any collisions. From the dock he started yelling directions at me of what to do and I was trying my best to follow. I turned Easy around and approached again but couldn't turn her sharp enough to get us close and turned her away again. I was so scared of hitting the dock I remember thinking I would just head us straight back to Vancouver before trying that again! Quickly it hit me that I would be faced with a much bigger challenge trying to dock in the city so with Bo's encouragement I tried bringing her in again. I guess our yelling back and forth was much louder than either of us realized because along came one of Bowen's summer livaboards to help grab the lines as he sarcastically grumbled at us with a slight sneer saying "great time of the night for docking practice."

Navigating between the freighters was also not one of my favourite things so I started searching youtube for videos of sailboats crashing into freighters. This infuriated Bo as he explained that was the opposite of overcoming fears but at the time I thought going deeper in them was the only way to satisfy it. I ended up resolving the issue by agreeing not to look at more scary videos and buying myself what I called "courage shoes" which were patent gold Sperry Topsiders like I had spotted on another girl one time at the dock in Secret Cove. She caught my eye because she came off of another Hinckley (rare to see on the west coast) but boy they looked classy and surely would give me all the strength I needed out on the water.

Communication wasn't exactly our strongest suit though we would get full points for trying. I recall meeting a guy once on Bowen who was offering sailing lessons which we considered but even just chatting with him was somewhat helpful because in his words "Guys and girls tend to see the boat differently. Guy's see it as a machine while girls see it as a living room." YES I thought, that is so true! I was always thinking about things like my outfit, the snacks and which cocktails to offer while Bo always had his head in the game for the mechanics of it all.

Inviting family and friends was one of our shared joys and I recall one folkfestful day having my Mom and my Aunt and Uncle out for an afternoon cruise, both experienced Ontario boaters and sailors. We were settling in getting ready to drop anchor amongst the other boats when my Mom said she couldn't hear the music and asked if we could get closer. In appeasing Bo tried to sneak us closer between two other sailboats meanwhile accidentally catching the adjacent boat's anchor line in the process. Everything looked fine at first but then the sailboat beside us started yelling "you have our line!!" as their boat started coming at us. Everyone rushed to the starboard side of our boat preparing to fend off the other sailboat as Bo continued to try and pilot us from hitting anything else. We were able to stop them from colliding but in the process having all passengers helping made it so that the masts were leaning into one another and our spreaders started knocking together. Fuck. We adjusted the weight to avoid more knocking but her line was still caught somewhere on Easy and we couldn't figure out where. After steadying positions someone lent us goggles and Bo ended up diving in to try and figure out how to unhook us. He found the spot under the keel where she was hooked but it was so tight nothing was working to untie us. Seeing as the other boat had a spare anchor line both captains finally decided the only thing to do was cut her loose so with my dive knife he went down to do it followed by writing a cheque to cover the damages. So many lessons learned that day including being prepared for unknown expenses at any moment.

Another time we invited friends out for a last minute afternoon winter cruise and decided to try something different and sail in Coal Harbour because there was finally enough wind to play around with. I was down below baking fresh bread for guests in our little gas oven and before I knew it I could hear everyone scrambling that the Coast Guard was coming and two of their boats approached us pretty quickly. I peeked my head out just in time to hear them yelling at us that we can't just tack away in the middle of the harbour that if we looked around there were freighters and sea buses and I think their exact words were "you can't just play around out here it's like a highway!" *Riiiight*, I though... excellent point.

One night coming back from a long day of sunbathing and chilling on Bowen we were transiting in the pitch dark of night. It was my job to stand on the foredeck as we approached the Lions Gate Bridge back to our moorage. I remember posting up and scratching my head at a tiny red light I could see ahead, but not being able to make sense of it because it was too high to be the port light on a boat, but it was definitely moving. In a flash it finally dawned on me that it was a fucking freighter coming basically straight at us in the dead of night, sure moving slow but they don't stop fast and even still their wake is HUGE. I screamed at Bo and he tacked towards Siwash rock to get us out of the way as quickly as possible. Sure, obstacle missed but the wake still was coming right at us. He turned so we would take it straight on and Easy rose uuuuUUUUPPP followed by a huge CRASH DOWN where everything including the boom smashed upon landing and it happened a couple more times before we were in the clear. Telling the story to friends later they said things like, uh, don't you use the radio or anything to know what's going on? It was a good point and I started taking safety much more seriously.

Bo was all about using the worst conditions to make us better. Against my nerves he would teach me that in the worst wind or rain the best thing to do was put up the mainsail so there I went cranking her up no matter what fears were getting in my way. I bought sailing gloves and started to feel more empowered with each practice, in fact raising the mainsail became my favourite thing, only second to sailing wing on wing.

The beauty of spinnakers would grab even non-boating enthusiasts but in Vancouver harbour we don't get the required wind very often. We did get to let her fly once or twice and let me tell you it was stunning even if we still had no idea what the hell we were doing.

It was party after party and sailing almost every weekend. When I say we sailed every weekend I mean we really took advantage of it. We lived on Easy as much as we could mostly spending weekends going to Bowen and back and she was starting to feel like home. With all of the antique mahogany and bronze, small propane fireplace, gimbled stove and so many windows I was gaining mega skills and step by step we were getting closer to living the dream.

My birthday that year was a real highlight as I had told Bo I wanted to do 29 as a bang instead of the approaching landmark of 30. He could feel my anxiety rising as I tried planning it and told me to step back and that he would take care of it. I didn't agree without a fight thinking there was no way this guy could plan the party I had in my mind but the joke was on me as it turned out to be one of the most memorable nights of my life. He held it on our sailboat at the dock with a mermaid and sailor theme inviting the coolest of our chic boating friends and my family who all dressed up to match. He rented carpets for the dock, tables with tablecloths to host a huge spread of food and a DJ to carry us through the night. Cailey made a slideshow of pics of all of our fun and they raised the mainsail to project it on as the sun set into the night. Bubbles were flowing and Tara made a huge mermaid themed rainbow birthday cake and it was an absolute delight of a party lasting until the early morning hours.

Deep in love and getting ahead of ourselves, it crashed out quickly because I had been concerned about not getting my period and Bo kept encouraging me to put off the inquiry. Sure enough we had been playing with fire and that morning I found out I was. I was terrified and panicked thinking things like I was not prepared financially, I had been drinking and was on Accutane not long ago (proven to cause birth defects) and how would I put my children in French immersion or hockey and what would they even look like realizing I had never even seen one photograph of Bo as a child or one member of his family. That was weird. I freaked, he was devastated and got angry that the efforts of the party and our amazing life had all instantly fallen to the wayside from my fears. We were so close to our dreams and falling in love with each other more each day but something held me back, something didn't feel quite right so with my lead and his reluctant support we closed that door thinking we could line the ducks up better and would revisit it again soon. Sadly we did revisit it a few months later. My Montreal girlfriends were in town at the time and one of them flat out confessed she thought something seemed *off* about Bo. She had been integral in helping me have the confidence to leave the pushy boyfriend not long ago so her concerns were taken straight to my heart and as badly as I wanted to take the leap to our dreams I didn't. We didn't... not yet I thought. Brutal, and we were never the same but we took comfort in that we had each other.

We were good at getting out of rough waters and stuck by each other as close as we could keeping focus on sailing, adventures and sharing it with friends as much as possible. One memorable trip was later referred to as "Sechelt in a day" whose return included a 4am waking to sail from Bowen to Vancouver so I could make it to work on time. Winds were nearly 50 knots and the dinghy was being thrown into the guardrail and the eight foot rolling waves behind her occasionally splashed into the cockpit. This proved to be yet another reason why I needed to get rid of the job thing, the sea doesn't work on such a regimented schedule and sailing took priority. By November 5, 2010 I had gotten myself out of credit card debt junk and officially quit my legal secretary job which I deemed as 'retired at 29.' The idea was to have some time and space to think and develop the skills and assets so that we could go on our sailing adventures as planned.

With the increasing skills and hours under our belt we decided our first big trip would be a sail to Desolation Sound and set it for the month of July 2011. It was to be exactly 2 years after first meeting that we were set to sail off into the first steps of realizing our dreams.

Leading up to the big trip we set up an interactive "to do" list that we could each access from our iPhones and cut and paste things weekly as we got closer to the set departure. My love for organization motivated our five week countdown along with loose ends that we would have to tie up and social events that we would have to incorporate before pushing off.

May 24, 2011
Alicia Lindsay Boswell
To Bo
Boat Note

5 weeks May 23rd (plant basil, file taxes,)
B ladder (8 hours)
A spinnaker pole (8 hours)
B dock hook (8 hours)
A finish tiny frame (1 hour)
Bmake bracket for transom (3 hours)
A research which gear oil to use d35 motor bmwmarine.net
A join seatow
A to research and prep for food
A put numbers on boat
A put EASY on boat
A research marking anchor line
*go to consign goods (oars, 2 sinks, tap, life ring, any stupid tools)
A research ditch kit

4 weeks   May 30th (Mom's birthday 4th)
B install motor mounts (6 hours)
A check charts
B change gear oil (2 hours)
A sail maintenance
A coat rotten wood on inside
B hang barometer and thermometer
B reroute water line in front and drill holes
B small 1/4 inch holes in floorboard so water drains
A marking anchor line
A take tiny frame for glass
A photocopy ID's/passports and leave copy on boat

3 weeks   June 6th (ALB trade show 10,11, 12)

2 weeks   June 13th (Father's day 19th)

1 week   June 20th

Final prep   June 27th (Black Keys concert 27th)

To buy:
-winch for boom
-outboard motor
-lifejackets x 2
-radar reflector $65
-sewing awl or needle and some sail thread
-new mirror for boat!!!!!
-longer line for towing dinghy
-longer bow line (right mariner)
-100 foot 1/2 inch rope
-yankee foresail (as per will's suggestion)
-life ring
-tubing
-condoms

Food:
-frozen meat
-preserved meat
-tuna
-salmon
-baked beans
-dried beans
-cereal
-flour
-yeast
-dried bean curd
-jam
-oils
-nuts
-

Bring:
-warm clothes (hoodies)
-extra tank of diesel
-gas for dinghy
-diesel oil
-coolant

Borrow:
-jet pack from dad
-winch

Life was going great. I was enjoying being 'retired' from a job that I didn't enjoy and was actively looking for the next step. With Bo's guidance I had weaned myself off all prescription drugs including Effexor and my depression/anxiety was not ruling my life as it had in Montreal. He had also been subtly influencing me to see things differently like reading the ingredients of the toxic deodorant that had been irritating my skin for years and special teas and natural remedies in favour of spending hundreds at shoppers drug mart. He encouraged me to wear a mask when I was painting my nails and he was cooking things like turkey and collard greens for the tryptophan and serotonin to boost my mood and feeding me almost all meals each day.

I had recently taken a part-time turned full time job for a holistic veterinarian who preferred dogs, lived part time in Hawaii and only saw new clients online via Skype.

Life at 1906 was a scene of bounty and beauty and Bo had just successfully remodelled the kitchen whose finishing touches included real Swarovski crystal drawer handles and Italian silestone countertops in a vibrant chartreuse that made pretty much anything and everything look absolutely brilliant. As the finishing touches were coming together we held an impromptu paint party in the kitchen one night with Andy which resulted in a sub floor mural that read "House of Equanimity," Bo's suggestion and a new word for me at the time.

Bo was in full swing checking things off our list starting with his own built to design wooden boat ladder so we could swim off Easy and not have to hurl ourselves like a beached whale into the dinghy to get back into the boat like we had last summer. I was so amazed at Bo's ability to push things forward and to be resourceful as well! He had researched boat ladders and looked around at options only to decide that he could design something better. It took him a few sketches but in no time his design came to fruition and my man built us a slick swim ladder that would get us through the summer complete with meticulously grooved steps that he hand stained blue to match Easy.

By the last weekend in May we knew we were heading into a crazy month of preparation but felt elated with the energy of spring sunshine coming our way. I had just seen my therapist Deena and the only thing I could come up with to talk about was my failed attempts to quit social smoking. She literally yawned and said "you'll quit when you want to" and we both laughed and smiled about my progress. We wished each other a good summer and I walked home feeling on top of the world. The following Sunday afternoon we took to party on the porch and moved the music outside and drank bubbles with the neighbours. It felt like the first days of summer where Vancouverites easily exchange nods and smiles as if to say yes, this is why we live here. We were sad to not have Nando home from the Philippines as he said he wanted to be back to see the massive 100 year old rhodo bloom this year. We danced and took photos of the one or two newly opened purple buds hoping to entice him to come back sooner. It was common for us to spend weekend days with a drink or few in hand. We worked hard and played hard and sometimes, like this particular afternoon, the party just invites you. We laughed at the luxurious indulgent lifestyle we were privileged enough to enjoy and as we tidied up the party Kristen said "Well this can't last!" DONG *What?* I wondered and asked. "This perfect harmony we have had going for so long, it just is too good," she said. Of course nothing lasts forever I thought, but what an odd thing to say and why jinx a good thing. It was a week later that I saw Bo for the last time.

FOUR STAGES

DR. MICHAEL BECKWITH

BY US	**THROUGH US**
Gain control	Give up control
Life supports our manifestations	Become a channel, life flows and guides us
TO US	**AS US**
No control	Co-creating
Life is doing something to us	One with ALL life

CHAPTER SIX

LOVE YOU TILL THE WHEELS COME OFF

Bo had been getting more and more irritable with people at work and told me he was ready to quit for a while so we could prepare for our trip. I thought it was an excellent idea because he had worked so hard for the last few years even doing weekly stints in Sechelt where he would work a day and do a commute that lasted 14-16 hours since we hated sleeping apart. He turned his plan into action and quit within a week. During his first days off we g-chatted while I was at work and he told me he was spending the afternoon writing music. *Writing music? Bo?!* I imagined him sitting with a yellow note pad tapping his pencil and a guitar on his knee but quickly corrected myself when I came home to see it was actually Bo sitting around with a scratchpad writing convoluted raps that I could barely understand. He had mentioned once or twice that he had done that in the past and I always supported artistic outlets especially since he was obviously getting frustrated with the precision and workload of his fine finishing carpentry work. The Fukushima Meltdown really seemed to rattle him. I was never one to really watch much news much but I remember him staring at the TV screen almost paralyzed repeating things like… "this isn't good…this reeeaaally isn't good." Other odd things had happened like him saying he never wanted to have children one night while we were making dinner. It caused an obvious rise out of me considering having children and sailing the world was our shared dream and my hormones were like a ticking clock. Later on I was sitting on our bed and remember him walking into the doorway apologizing for what he said and asked when I would like to have kids…"within a couple years?" I replied and he sort of glanced up sideways and said "mmmm…how about more like 4 or 5" which sounded like eons to me at the time and I couldn't really believe what I was hearing. One of the most peculiar things that happened early one morning was when he pulled out a box from the back of our closet that he had previously told me was private. He revealed his novel, yes novel, entitled North American Nomad, circa 2002-2003 Four square turned 12 in 3D. PSI Factors for Dancing Stage Actor's and told me he thought it could be neat to get it published. I was yet again thoroughly impressed that my man may know more of the 64 arts than I did and was falling more in love with him and his mystery by the minute.

The downside of these new sides was that he started getting more and more short and angry with me but would return quickly apologizing and explaining his irritability. I couldn't really stay angry because the affection and love we shared was growing intensely by the day. I was thrilled to have our plan unfolding right before our eyes and felt like champions of our own destiny. I had seen a funny poster on Facebook and Bo suggested we paste them around the neighbourhood. The city was on a rush since the Canucks were having such a good season and it was even a bit more than us non-hockey fans could take. It was certainly out of character for Bo to want to promote hockey culture but we rolled with it and both laughed at people's reaction and even had to explain the poster to a couple people, the poster said: Keep Calm and Trust the Gingers.

CHAPTER SEVEN

BLEEDING HEARTS IN BLOOM

The next morning we were set to head out for an early dinner at my parents house for my Mom's birthday. We got up in the morning and took an affectionate neighbourhood walk ending at Terra Breads. As we were leaving with our order I pointed out a girl's bob haircut that I liked and was in the middle of asking Bo if he thought it would suit me when I turned around and he had bolted right out of the bakery. I followed after him and immediately asked why he took off like that. He demanded that I drop it and asked me not to ask any questions. I was relentless and wanted to know what on earth could trigger him to walk out like that and he said "Didn't you see that guy looking at me and putting daggers at me with his eyes!?" So many weird things happening. I put my head in my hands and cried "Noooo, Bo I didn't." I walked home behind him trying to collect my thoughts. What the hell was he talking about and "daggers with his eyes??!" By the time I got to the door he was standing on the porch and apologized. He said he shouldn't have reacted the way he did and that he will try and explain himself better in the future. I maintained a state of utter confusion and walked into the kitchen with Kristen at the table. "Good morning" she said. I welled up with tears and said I don't understand but Bo is acting funny. She asked what I meant and I explained the dagger in the eyes detail and we sat in quiet with that for a minute. I walked out to the sunny porch to pick the brown leaves off of her geraniums and within a few moments Kristen followed behind me and said "I think you and I should talk." It sounded like a golden key to me! "YES!" I said. "If you have any idea what is bothering Bo please tell me."

We went upstairs to the Puja room where Kristen had put down some wool mats which we sat on. She kept the door open but there was a quietness in the room that had me on high alert. She took a breath, then paused, and said "Without labelling it, he is having an episode. It has happened before and everything goes back to normal but it lasts a while and he usually goes away for a while and then comes back." DONG My ears were ringing and I didn't know what to respond to first. "How long?!" I demanded. "A month, a couple months" she said. My brain completely refused that thought and I immediately told myself a week tops without really even knowing what we were talking about. "An episode??" I said. "Well yeah, maybe you guys can be like Michael and Rithea and find a way of communicating" she said. I had no idea how Michael and Rithea related to me or Bo except that we knew Michael as our artist friend, a local in Kits who had previously had manic breaks and his wife Rithea who often suffered from them. But Bo isn't acting anything like Michael, I thought and what is she talking about? The next few minutes were a blur where I could just feel my hands clawing at the wool mat beneath me looking for some ground. We were leaving on our sailing trip July 1st. How was this going to fit in?? Could we get him ship shape in no time? I tuned back in to hear Kristen saying "Sleep helps, he should sleep but he won't want to, and he REALLY shouldn't drive but he will want to." At some point during this flow of information Bo came upstairs and gently walked into the room. He was wearing his black hooded sweatshirt, jeans and was holding a coffee. His eyes looked glazed over and I couldn't tell if it was me and the new information, or not. "Hi guys," he said as I reached up and touched the back of his thigh. "Honey Kristen and I want to chat for a minute is that ok?" I said. He bent down and kissed me on the forehead and said "of course honey, I'll be downstairs." I didn't know where to take this. The words I was hearing sounded huge! Him "going away for a while'?!?" What did this mean? We hadn't spent more than a couple of nights apart for our entire relationship. And our trip!? We had been planning this for a year!!!

The afternoon was pressing on and Bo said earlier that he was too tired to come to Mom's birthday dinner. All the better considering the new information so I picked up my sister Alexis and broke the news. "So, apparently Bo is having a mental breakdown" I said. Sitting in the passenger seat she took a breath and said "Alicia, it's really important that you don't judge. Mental illness is all around us and we can get through this." I sighed a big sigh of relief, she was right. I myself had suffered from depression in the past and have an aunt with bi-polar and a cousin with schizophrenia so this was something I could deal with. Although the idea of him "going away for a while" still scared me I was determined to be strong and stand by my man.

"Happy birthday M--" "What's wrong" snapped my strongly intuitive mother and I sat down to explain to my parents that Bo was having a mental breakdown. "Can't you just take some pills for that" quipped my Dad. "No Dad, you don't understand, medicine isn't the solution for everything, he can apparently deal with this on his own and has done so in the past, medicine is toxic!" I replied. The afternoon went well and I only had to escape once pretending to be looking at the May flowers to cry as the information started sinking in. By the drive home it was 'all hand on deck' to do anything and everything to help Bo and be by his side through this. "It's no different than having diabetes" my Mom would say. *All Hands on Deck*.

Sleeping became the first really noticeable change. Bo was already a really light sleeper but now any sound or sometimes from nothing he would bolt upright and then have to go for a walk before being able to lie down again. One night my phone rang in the early morning from an unknown number and he demanded to have my phone and thought I was lying when I told him I didn't know who it was. He called the number back and yelled at the guy, Craig, that this was his girlfriend's number and not to call there. It was just insane and so unlike him to act jealous and the tension was rising. He would come back from walking the city and tell me about the neat things he had seen or found and apologize for any previous outbursts and then we would adore each other for a few moments. The adoration was bliss. We were constantly affectionate and minding each other and just so in love with being in love that anything else in the world didn't matter because we had each other. I thought it was possibly nature's way of making a hard time less hard. Like the increased affection and tenderness was to offset the escalating irritability and anger. Stand by my man.

He was acting really out of character in so many ways. One night at dinner he recounted how he had spent the day out at UBC asking to visit one of their science department where they let him take a tour of the nuclear technology that they were working on and he came back convinced that they had, quote "no idea what they were doing over there." He also started reciting by heart at the dinner table words from philosophers like Deleuze and Guattari on Kafka and (unknown to me at the time) their conjoined work on capitalism and schizophrenia. Again blowing my mind. I was having doubts though because he was also enamoured with things like binary and started printing posters that said "DANTES Academic INFERNO ASSYLUM" followed with "Leadheads should go Back to philosophy or psychology 101 and check themselves you're a drain on a healthy society. A TRIUMF of stoopidity" which was all right over my head.

Before bed one night he turned to me and said "Baby, I better give you my banking information." "Why on earth?" I thought and asked. "Oh, you know" he replied and logged in and saved the information on the computer so I could access his accounts. This was followed by a gentle "if I get lost will you come find me?" Pull at my heart strings why don't you "of course!" I replied follow by "you'll have to tell me where you are" and he smiled.

One morning he woke early and irritated again getting upset with me asking why he wasn't waking up to me doing yoga every morning. It was one of those DONG moments that stuck with me until I finally found myself actually doing it.

Within a few days Bo could no longer even try and sleep in our room. He said that one of our houseguests Jarred was giving him bad vibes so he wanted to try sleeping on the boat. "Anything baby, to help you get through this" and I packed an overnight bag for my man. We tried everything. Sleeping apart was so hard for both of us so we compromised by spending a bit of time at home and then he would move to the boat and sometimes a few hours later I would come down to meet him. I could hold him and brush his hair and almost will him to sleep but I would have to hold so still and breath so softly as not to wake him that I mostly kept myself awake in doing so. I would look at his ginger blond locks and they reminded me of antique roman sculptures just in the way that they held together in licks. It was enough to hold my attention. That and wrapping my body around behind him. I would mould my body behind his- knee to knee, heart to heart as best I could and rest my head on my one bent elbow and he would hold my other arm between both of his, in front of his heart. Since our first days together sleeping next to each other was one of our best assets. Nearly any space would do and we could just wrap into each other, almost balance each other from falling off an edge and didn't have to move much all night. Needless to say given the added tension of the situation sleeping apart was extra challenging. Night by night I was losing hours of sleep almost to the point of being awake every hour and Bo, try as he might, was just too jumpy and would wake at anything. One night he awoke suddenly and said he had to take a walk down to the boat because his neck was hurting. When I asked him why he said that it was "possibly the house or because I had been staring at it." I had been warned to expect delusions and paranoia but this was becoming sad to watch.

After he left I called the mental health hotline trying to get help for him, us, anything! They wouldn't even talk to me without me giving our full names and personal health information or so I recall. I don't know what I was looking for exactly but it felt useless and all they could offer was that he should see a doctor.

The next morning Bo had decided that the city was just too much for him to take right now. He wanted to get away, relax for a bit and clear his head. He said he was sure he would feel better on

Bowen island and it sounded like what he needed so I agreed to sail over with him. I told Kristen "Bo and I are going to sail to Bowen, he says he will feel better there and" "No he won't!" she said before the first sip of morning coffee. "Uh… well yeah but he says the city is too busy and thinks he will be able to sleep better on Bowen" I said. "He thinks that but it isn't true, but go! Go! Have fun" she encouraged. I felt nervous and confused but didn't really have any better ideas and it sounded like a great opportunity for us to talk about everything that was happening.

We packed up our bags and the two of us set sail to Bowen. I was happy for us to take our time thinking that by the time we got there it would be an easy turn around and sail back. The wind didn't pick up much that day even as we cruised through English Bay. I was sitting port staring out at the people crabbing off the dock on the pier in North Vancouver when Bo started explaining everything. He was telling me about how he can feel people's energy and read their thoughts as they come closer to him. That he is constantly filtering other people's energy and can poke around in their minds. I started breaking down inside thinking that my poor baby has completely lost his mind. I thought of the embarrassment he might feel when he re-hears the things he had been saying. He just looked at me and snapped "you don't get it babe, this is the NEW way! There ain't no going back and I'll tell you another thing there ain't going to be no two car garage either, do ya get it?" "Do ya get it!?" became one of his favourite lines to use when he would start tweaking out but at the time it just kept me at attention and ready to hear any explanation he could give me so I could be there for him. As we cruised around lighthouse point a large white yacht with an upper deck burned past us carving out a sloppy wake. Bo immediately jumped to his feet cursing and screaming at the "asshole Americans." I doubt they could hear us and I also doubt that they were American but some part of me thought he really did have a point. We were nicely cruising along using only wind power and taking our time to be crossed and get thrown around by a captain that only had his eye on the prize. The way those big plastic yachts bob around like a cork in the water and burn fuel like it is going out of style. It was hard to believe but in a short time I had already identified a firm preference for the simplicity and independence of sailing.

We got to Bowen by the afternoon and walked around the island. I noticed quickly that Bo was not much calmer than he had been in Vancouver and was beginning to feel exhausted from the sail and having slept so little in the last few days. By the time we had walked through the woods and through the local shops I thought it was a good idea if we figured out what we were doing and maybe try having a nap. It was getting late and I was getting anxious about what we were going to do for the evening. I had to go to work the next day in Vancouver and didn't want to leave Bo and Easy alone on Bowen in this state. I excused myself to the bathroom and called up our friends Tara and Andy who quickly said they would jump on the next water taxi from Granville island and come right over to sail back with us as they were both experienced sailors. We had rafted up next to another boat and tried to settle in to a short nap and I told Bo they were coming over to meet us. It was almost like having a baby to take care of because Bo was so jumpy and agitated that I had to cradle him and wait to hear his breathing changes as he fell asleep before I could try and get a wink myself otherwise he would jump up two minutes into it and begin some kind of project. Andy and Tara showed up about an hour later and after about a total of 14 minutes of sleep between the two of us combined. They climbed over the boat that we had rafted to and Andy with a big smile and half said "Mr. B! Can I offer you a drink or roll you a joint?" and I snapped at him and Tara with my eyes. Was he nuts? Had Tara not told him how deluded he already was? We would be lucky enough to get back in one piece let alone encouraging drinking and smoking while in this state! Bo had already pulled back on the drinking and was quite content to keep a tea going instead. On the way over I had noticed he kept trying to play Method Man and every time he did he would get worked up and it seemed to bring on anger and yelling. Tara and I sat at the bow of the boat while the boys sailed us back and I explained it to her. "I may have some of it figured out," I said "rap music seems to be a big trigger so lets keep it out of site and hope to get back safe."

I was nearly delirious by the time we were approaching the Lions Gate and Bo seemed to be amping up as we got closer to the city. We all switched places one by one so each of us got face time with the other. Tara could see that Bo wasn't quite right but Andy said he hadn't really seen anything funny with his own eyes. I knew enough to tell him this was serious but was so thankful to have him and Tara there to help us dock. Docking was always one of the nerve racking parts of sailing for me. Especially at our moorage site as previously described, it took some practice. Bo and I had gone through the procedure many times but I was always nervous for the both of us each time we made our approach but by now my nerves were almost shot.

June 6, 2011
Chat with Cailey

me: did you get my email?

Cailey: I did. Sent you a message this am.
How was Bowen?

me: i didnt get the reply. bowen was shitty

Cailey: ick. what happened?

me: Bo has had a mental breakdown

Cailey: it got worse?

me: he is currently not himself

Cailey: He still on Bowen? What could have possibly triggered this?

me: trauma from his life

Cailey: but why now?

me: well no one really knows. he says that things like it is seeing the world collapsing with nuclear meltdowns, tornados etc. he just got to a point where "his walls have broken down" and he goes in and out of whatever it is

Cailey: woaza. can't say i've ever dealt with something like this

me: he has hallucinations, uses a voice that is just not him... its been scary

Cailey: is he on drugs?

me: on the bright side i am the constant
no

Cailey: well that's good. so he stayed on Bowen, as per your email?
me: he is coping very very very well. no no. i was too afraid to leave him there. it wasn't a good place to be. even bowen was too busy and triggering it. power boats triggered outbursts. andy and tara took the first ferry over and helped us sail it back. b was so distracted he didnt even notice the sails were not up until we were half way home

June 7, 2011

I dont know what to make of all of this so I write to myself. Bo has gone through or is going through something. yesterday i was talking to antonio and i found that there was a voice in my head that was growing louder and louder so much that i could not focus on what he was saying. it wasn't exactly making sense but i could hear just bits of it and one of the things it was saying was what if Bo is picking up on 2012 and the end of the world. at that point i was freaking out so much that i excused myself from the convo and called tara to help calm me down. it helped calm me down for a while and then it came up again a bit after. i didnt know what to do so i sat down to talk to kristen. she listened, asked some questions and told me it sounded like an inner conflict. i thought about that and had a moment of realizing that through what happened with Bo i have done a few things and felt really really good about how i shifted to adjust to what was happening. the things included feeling strong and solid in myself, feeling strong and solid about being with Bo, and putting up boundaries (like the tel call from my mom on bowen when she said she was worried and i told her that i cant take on her being worried and that she needs to just hold that herself), and ...i feel like my jaw pain is gone, or i am outside of it. i told Bo about that and he smiled. we got to talking and he told me a lot of things. he said that when he was 15 in new york he had a moment with method man where they had a connection and read each others minds while staring at each other from a distance at a gas station as Bo was with his school kids from ontario. He said that it was acknowledged in a song by wu-tang written shortly after their first record deal. something about the line "my sue". he also told me about a time when he was at a rap concert and the guy yelled "who wants more" and Bo yelled "we dont want anymore" and the guy said "well you guys all seem to want more, i want everyone here to turn around and beat the shit out of that guy" he said that nothing happened. i dont know if it really happened. Bo said that he has inspired a lot of music with being able to connect with someone in their mind. he started telling me about all the gaps. and other times where he was "out of his mind" and the crazy things he would do (leaving a car and running for his life). we took a walk. at the dinner table the energy was running unbelievably high and the house was feeling weird. One houseguest got into a story about how he poisoned two pit bulls as revenge for them attacking him. jarred also told a weird story that i cant really remember anymore. after dinner i saw kristen with her head down on the table resting on her arm. I asked her if she was ok and she asked for some water. she said she just wasnt feeling well all of a sudden. i went outside to the porch and Bo was upset. i asked him what was going on and he said that he was "fucking sick of kristen not cooperating and acting like a baby." he said he has been trying to leave this house for years but she wont cooperate. he said she was cursed when she was travelling through india and that her guru is a bad bad man, the devil he said. i asked what happened and it was some kind of discussion while Bo was making the pie and he started pounding on the dough. i went inside and sat next to kristen and asked her again if she was ok. she said "i just feel an overwhelming pressure and like something is telling me to grow up kid" i told her that was what Bo was just saying to me outside. she calmly said "that is what Bo is saying, that i need to grow up" i said yes. she kind of chuckled and sat with it some more. she just sat in silence thinking about it. I asked Bo what he was trying to do with her and he said he was trying to help a friend. that she needs to understand that nando is not an idiot and that he deserves some respect. or something like that. he came in and out of the room saying what seemed like disjointed thoughts but since i had an idea of what he was doing I could see that they were not disjointed at all and in fact were provocative in place. at that point i was fairly shocked by what was going on. i started asking Bo questions. he told me that he is psychic. he said there are different kinds but his kind is that he remembers everything. he has an elephant brain that connects things and watches things react or come back. he also said he can see people's inner conflict and needs to help them "get to a place where they are ok... where they realize that they are ok and then see what is important, our earth." i asked him if he reads my mind sometimes and he said yes. ive felt it. he said i was his angel because he has finally found someone who can help him use this because i can ground him out. all of the above falls directly in line with the things he has been saying up until this point. the things that i thought were crazy. when we were on the boat and i was asking him when he thinks he would be coming out of this state of mind and he said "babe, you dont understand, there is no coming out of it. this is the new way. we will never go back." that is how it feels right now.

saturday at 530am i got a random text message that looked like a pocket dial of letters and numbers ending in ".glu" from a 604 number and Bo got angry and that is where this whole thing started spinning out of control. this morning, monday, i received a similar or possibly the same (i deleted the other one) message from a 604 number at 519am ending in ".glu". following that i received two blank messages. i dont even know how to send a blank message. i replied "?" but have got nothing.

Bo is calling the number. craig whitfield?[2] Bo said that it was an accident but he is on high alert.

Bo is saying our inside world affects the outside world that being diseased or chemically out of balanced is not healthy for our dna or for the world. and I can't write the rants down as fast as he speaks.

Bo is talking about how he has had this his entire life. he remembers his dad holding him up to a picture window and he said "its big" and his dad said "yes, it is big" meaning the world.

he says that we dont have a comprehension of the 3rd dimension of this earth. everyone sees the earth as flat. we cant comprehend in such distances. he said maybe tara is someone who can see but because of her work she has a hard time seeing passed it. she just has things being thrown at her and all of a sudden she has a pringles can. she carries a lot. she carries a lot of people in her head. they are all in her head. she walks around heavy in this world because of it. tara is an earth mother.

---

[2] turns out it was an old lifeguard friend who had pocket dialled me which happens often with my name beginning with A.

CHAPTER EIGHT

BOWEN LIVING

I was being bombarded at every waking moment, which were increasing by the day, with Bo's thoughts and insights and visions and on and on and on. I couldn't write them down as fast as I heard them and I certainly couldn't process them as fast as he would spit them out. I had never heard him speak this way before and felt my heart opening to this "new way" ready to embrace what I could and accept what I couldn't. Being around him was as volatile as it was uplifting. It was like he was seeing things that I couldn't see and his mind was racing making connections and filtering what seemed like an overload of information.

I came down to the boat after work the next day to hang out with Bo. At one point he called me a bitch and started getting really angry at me loud enough that everyone could hear. I wanted to test his anger to see if I should be fearing violence so I gently put my hand on his hands and tried to snuggle in for a hug but he was firmly angry. I got the sense that he just wanted me to go and was picking a fight so that I would. I think we sorted it out by text that evening but it was that was the last time we enjoyed our sweet spot in the city.

June 9, 2011
Chat with Cailey

Cailey: hey honey

me: ugh

Cailey: :(what's the word today?

me: im close to a burn out

so fucking close. ive been shaky all morning

Cailey: you at work?

me: yeah

Cailey: Have you been getting any sleep at all?

me: yesterday went fine so i tried sleeping at home. b slept 2 hours. i was woken about every 2 hours

Cailey: things still unchanged over there?

me: its in and out but since last night he has been totally worked up

Cailey: What do you think you will do for the weekend?

me: i think im going to look for an apartment. you know what it feels like?! its feels like...hey, lets watch Bo walk on the telephone wire just because he thinks he can

Cailey: but if you can't get him down, what are you supposed to do?

me: not look

Bo decided to push off to Bowen so he could clear his head and kept me posted with intermittent emails which he titled with things like "Vitamin B!" with photos that were sent upside-down or crooked, something that Mr. "attention to detail" would have never previously done.

With just a week gone by the rhodo out front was in full bloom. I walked around the house taking photos of things to remind Bo of me, and us and our life. I thought it would help keep him grounded while he worked through whatever it was he was working through. He was already beginning to look scruffy and thinner as K had said would happen.

Bo was spending his nights on Bowen and I drove over Sunday to spend the night with him and go to work on Monday. We had a lovely visit. I was happy to see that Easy was nicely tied up at dock and well taken care of. Bo was still highly irritable and needed to constantly keep moving or changing things and drinking coffee and smoking. It seemed like he had started making a home for himself and us on Bowen and I smiled at the idea of a new island life. His diet had gone into extreme vegan and he was completely revolted by any animal product. We had dinner that night at a new restaurant "Qi" and we had "Qi pour deux" which included 3 dishes each and tasty naan bread. He had to return his bread because they had buttered it and I think one of his dishes as well because of one of the contents. I laughed at the role reversal because for the duration of our relationship I had taken full role of the fussy eater. He was introducing me to his new friends as his wife. I was leery about jumping into that lingo but at the same time it filled my heart with what I had longed for from him for ages. We made friends on the dock with a new local who had moved from Alberta where he had worked as a used car salesman. Together with his wife they opened a second hand/antique shop on the dock in Snug Cove. Bo wanted to consign his crab and prawn traps, fishing rods (because he was done with eating anything with eyes) together with the second life ring I had picked up for us that turned out to be a decorative item and much too small. We made friends with his wife as well and someone suggested that the four of us have dinner on Thursday.

Monday morning Bo woke at 4am and let me sleep for as long as I could before the ferry. He would come into the v-berth and kiss me on the forehead, tuck the blankets around me and, as per usual, he woke me with some fresh coffee. We sat in the cockpit and took in the crisp morning. Waking up on the water was something we both loved. We had an affectionate morning and Bo packed me a lunch from our leftovers from last night. The day before I had brought him a salad or two, of the lentil variety for my new vegan man. As the ferry was pulling in we walked arm in arm, entangled, up the steep low-tide dock, got the bimmer (his nickname for his BMW that I was driving) and kissed goodbye. I walked to the bow of the ferry to look at him as we pulled away. A flash went through my mind of capturing that moment for fear of never seeing him again. DONG But we had plans on Thursday so I reminded myself I didn't have to fret yet. He stood at the top of the dock near the red ramp wearing his usual diesel jeans and black hoody but had adorned a handmade yellow and black Mexican messenger bag that used to kick around in our room. I was never crazy about it, or most 'crafts' for that matter and it was odd to see him wearing it especially across his body in a way I know he would have called feminine but I was in full support mode and now I couldn't care less about details like that anymore. I kissed my hand and blew it to him. Our hearts smiled to each other and I took in a deep breath of the fresh morning ocean air as the ferry pulled out. All things considered I felt blessed and excited about the changes and new opportunities that I could see lying ahead for us.

June 13, 2011
Alicia
To alexis, tara, mom, cailey, lal, andy
good update

just wanted to give my loved ones an update. went to bowen yesterday and Bo has really calmed down. he is staying at the dock, eating and sleeping and quite relaxed. still not in the clear but things seem to be improving at this point. i asked how it compared to the other times this has happened and he said normally he crashes out but he doesnt

see that happening this time because he feels grounded by having me.
(heart melts)

working away here today. im staying in the city tonight and might go
back on tuesday after work.
love to you. alicia

June 13, 2011
Alexis
to me
glad to hear it. I was talking to my favourite co worker who told me
that he is bi polar and about 6 years ago started medication and is
very happy about it. he used to go into the hospital. He told me that
in his opinion not treating it will only make it worse. I hope everything
goes well today.
xoxo

      June 13th and even as loving as we were I was slowly becoming resentful of Bo. We would talk on the phone and exchange emails and texts but he didn't seem to understand my position at all. He kept encouraging me to quit my job and be with him. My gut told me that with all of the unknowns in front of us that this was a terrible idea. I envisioned me working like a dog to support us while he recovered for a month or two after all of this. I needed to be responsible for the both of us, like he always was. It was what Bo would have wanted I thought. Sleeping alone in our room was hard. I couldn't sleep on my side of the bed and have the empty space of his next to me. I moved over to his command central side and we texted and talked goodnight.

A: Good?
B: Yes…Really appreciate the salad.
A: I'll bring more greens.
B: Wonderful!
A: So I guess I'll take the 530 ferry tomorrow baby?
B: Sweet!

A: Sound good hon? We can have a nice cuddle snuggle?
B: Yes babe

Which were followed by phone call from Bo laying into me again about quitting and being by his side followed by:

B: Trying to take the work stress away dear.
A: I'm learning the valuable lesson of making money saving money and having money. Let me learn and feel good about myself.
B: Ok…I need to wander a bit…Been on the grind to long…Tomorrow night is cool though.
B: Need incense…

I woke suddenly the next morning as if I had been punched in the stomach but I did't know why. I grabbed my phone, texted Bo that I felt sick and went straight to the shower. By the time I got out and had not heard from him I knew he had taken off. I panicked.

A: What is going on?
A: ??
A: Where are you? What is going on?
A: I can't take this disappearing act and having no idea if you are ok or not. It isn't fair to me.
A: Your phone is off or something has happened to you. You are hurting me so much.

June 14, 2011
Chat with Cailey

me: he's gone c

Cailey: Gone where?

me: no one knows. his phone is off. he has taken off

Cailey: as of when?

me: dont know. havent heard from him since last night

Cailey: what happened?

me: dont know c. i guess it was inevitable

Cailey: so just to be clear: last night he just took off for no
known reason and no one knows where to? that's fucked.
down at the boat or maybe he got a hotel somewhere to get
space (you and I have both done that

me: no he is on the boat and i think he has sailed over to
gabriola. or something like that

Cailey: oh ok

me: basically he is taking the trip we have planned for over a
year on his own. fml

June 14, 2011
I woke up this morning feeling sick. Thought I could shake it by going to
the shower but it just got worse. Seeing my own naked body, feeling like
I don't have much protecting me right now. My mind tosses and turns
ideas and what if's around like a room full of balloons. No matter which
direction I look all I feel is the swirl of being unsettled. I am amazed
at how "settled" I can feel when I feel the most unsettled. Why test it
though? It is extremely exhausting to maintain a false sense of ground.
I am like a deer teetering on a loose gravel ledge trying to make a home.

My boyfriend is bi-polar and is having the first manic episode I have
ever seen. He didn't tell me that he had this, no one did. His behav-
iour started to change over the course of a few days to an extreme level.
What seemed fun and outgoing quickly became scary and uncontrol-
lable. He couldn't ride in cars, and still can't speak on the phone due
to the overwhelming amount of information that his mind continues to
process minute by minute. He is distracted and becomes easily angry if
someone doesn't "look right". People and websites keep reminding me
that it is "not him" and that I have to remember to be supportive. I
have been doing those things but it has been a long 10 days of this. He

is gone now. He is sitting on our sailboat just counting the minutes for him to be able to take off. My heart breaks. I cannot reason with him. I have no one to reason with but myself. What does my reasoning say? Well I guess it would start off by saying, ouch. Brutal. WTF. One can be understanding and compassionate about this but how much can you expect from someone who hid this for 2 years? I have thought about how he probably prayed and wished it would not come back. But isn't that still him putting his own concerns before mine? God, I would be terrified of lying about something like this for fear of losing him and hurting him. Meanwhile when the shoe is on the other foot I turn around with support, love, kindness, compassion, concern...you name it. Talk about depleting. For over a year we have been planning a sailing trip this July. It is mid June. How can I realistically go and feel good about it? Part of his mania is not wanting to be controlled or something along those lines. He keeps telling me to quit my job and join him on the boat. I like my job. I don't even know who I am speaking to anymore but this person is not supportive. This person is self centred. This person doesn't care about anyone more than he cares about himself. This person is stubborn and vicious. This person is putting me through the wringer.

What can I do now? I always start with accepting the situation and starting from there. Ok so how is it leesh? My boyfriend has bipolar disorder. He didn't tell me he had this and instead I had to run the gamut of emotions including pure terror for days watching him onset and having no idea what was going on. I have stored that trauma now, just when I thought I had found a new plateau of peace. Bipolar disorder does not go away. You are born with it, and it stays. It can be managed. The big question here is medication. Wait, back to not telling me about this. It was family friends who finally told me what was going on. I sincerely question the relationship I thought we had because of this. The amount of trust I can put in him. Life is hard enough. Everyone has something. Proverbs are bandaids.

I am sad. I have a knot of energy in my back from bracing myself for the last few weeks with this. What have I gotten myself into? My only question is how cooperative is he going to be about trusting me and

getting treatment so this does not happen again. Is that my bottom line?
This cannot be left untreated? And what about when it does come back?
There has to be an action plan in place for me. I feel so scared, sad,
alone. No one can make these decisions for me.

I am also angry at him. I am angry for him dancing to his own song and
not even letting me know what was going on. This is not a relationship
that I trust. Can you ever really trust? I thought so...but maybe I am
wrong. I guess it is most difficult to tell when you are still in love.
I still feel sick.

June 15, 2011
Alicia Lindsay Boswell
To alexis, mom, andy, tara
some tracking
i can see on Bo's bank account that he was on gibsons yesterday. it
looks like he withdrew some cash and i think he bought a motor for the
dinghy (1600$ at a boat shop)
feeling really calm today. its like my worst nightmare has happened
but even still i feel ok and i do have confidence that he will be ok too.
much love.

June 15, 2011
Andy
To me
Hi luv,
I'm glad you are feeling better today! You are going through a very
traumatic time at the moment and Bo needs to understand that he can
not behave like this as you are worried sick. I think we should all have
a talk to him when he gets back, may be we still need to get him help.
What do you think?
Lots of love,
And

No one's words were comforting at this point. It really felt like we had passed the point of giving him a "talking to" although there still was something comforting about Andy's British voice as he constantly repeated "everything's going to be juuuuuust fine." I was clinging to those words.

CHAPTER NINE

RIOT LOVE

On top of the full moon, tonight was the chaos of the final Canucks game in Vancouver. The news had been playing video footage of the famous 1997 'Canuck riot' for weeks and hosting experts to predict how it would go this time around. To counter this brainwashing the police had brainstormed and came up with preventative measures including closing the government liquor stores hours before the game even started. Now tell me, how else is a grown adult supposed to react to something like that except with anger and frustration?! I ran into this myself and there was a news camera recording the after-work crew's reactions as they tried the locked liquor store door on Alberni and Bute. I guess in retrospect considering what happened that night people could say the prevention was spot on but it was fuel for a fire if you ask me. Like parents who lock up the liquor cabinet instead of raising children that they can trust and who think for themselves. The game was a total bust and made everyone who watched it sour. I felt glad that Bo had not been in the city for the game because really it was true that the energy was a lot to filter. One of the 'group think' effects that I noticed was my attention being oddly drawn to anything that had the blue or green of the Canucks colours. Psychology tricks everywhere and I chose to wear red.

Once the game had quite sadly wrapped up and people trickled back into their own lives I decided to take a walk seeing as the sun was still shining bright. I walked down the street from the bar we were at and wandered my way to our moorage spot. Luckily I barely knew anyone at our dock so I wouldn't have to field questions about where Easy was or what we were up to for the summer. Santorini who was moored behind us had some friends over and were taking in the last of the sun from their cockpit. I stood at our spot alone for just long enough to say a prayer for myself, Bo and Easy. I didn't want my mind to wander needlessly so I just once-overed the place and took a mental snapshot of my summer paradise spot. As I was leaving, Santorini's crew joked that the riot had started already. I heard them say something about a fire started and then finally recognized the humming noises of the helicopters that had been zooming around since I was on my walk. Felt like LA. I started walking up Denman and a guy in street clothes jogged passed me hissing "light something on fire!!!" I still didn't really have any idea what was going on because it just felt like another magical summer sunset but as I walked closer to Davie I started to see two distinct flows of people. One was sauntering in the sun just like I was and the other was speed walking towards the action with spiked slurpee's. I drove home and briefly watched the chaos unfold on TV.

I found out later from Bo that he was tweaking out too much even in Gibson's and pushed off to cross to Vancouver Island. He later told me he was completely out of his mind and that he spent the entire night awake by the light of the full moon crossing the ocean. He said there were 50-60 knot winds and Easy just cut through the waves like a champ.

It had been days of sadness not knowing where Bo was. I remember Crystine, a friend of the house coming by for a visit while I held my head in my hands at the kitchen table one afternoon. She had been through a lot in her life so I tuned in as soon as she tried to offer advice except that her advice was to let him go, that this was "his journey." I remember pursing my lips and feeling rage against that idea and that giving up was not in the cards for me even though my life was crumbling before my eyes. By the middle of June I had to really start recognizing that our July trip was likely not going to happen as planned, or possibly not at all. Charlie's brother Alex had recently come for a visit just as Kristen and I were teaming up with ideas of how to get medical intervention for Bo. We were both freaked about him, a lost bark, wandering by the light of the moon. Alex sat down, kind of watched our rants and then flat out told us that it was a terrible idea to call for medical intervention because Bo would just talk his way out of any help or authority. He assured us that he was one phone call away from the Coast Guard zoning in on him and that if we needed to he could get a call to the right guy and have him tracked. He laughed and said that anywhere between Vancouver, the Island and Desolation Sound was like being in a bathtub. He said there was no way you could get lost and in fact it was possibly the safest place for Bo at the time "unless he took off to Hawaii…" or worse, if he headed down south and get arrested for his previous manic escapades that left him with an outstanding warrant in Washington state. It was one of the first times where I really had to make the best of a terrible unknown situation and get on with things so rather than sit and cry over another weekend I decided to take off to Tofino a place I had heard so many great things about but not before writing myself another "venting into the ether" emails.

June 16, 2011

b? where are you. it is thursday, june 16, 2011 at 1pm. im at work. my stomach hurts. it has been upset for 2 days now. im sure you are fine but it still hurts. you just left. just what i thought my nightmare would be. im angry about it. i feel ditched. i feel let down. where are you right now? sitting in the glorious sun, loving life? or sailing away like we have dreamed about for 2 years? i feel torn apart. or maybe you are pulling out the charts thinking about the next adventure you can sail away to keep running away. good for you Bo. it is your boat, your life. just as i always said when push comes to shove you just cut me loose and carry on. all those hours spent arguing about how it is OUR boat.

what a fool i am. why do i think so low of myself to accept this? to accept that i am in love with a man that will walk away and let me burn.

this is not the kind of love that i give. my love runs deep and stays. stays too long i think. i can even love the people i hate because compassion is high in my body.

yesterday i had faith. today i have sickness. manifested stress and anger twisting my stomach into knots. today i feel like hurting you or seeing you cry because what i think you are actually doing is feeling elated. and it doesn't feel fair.

alicia comes last. Bo gets to do what Bo wants to do and alicia is left in the dust.

what would god tell me to do? move on. doing it. checked out the boat dock last night. nothing to check.

im going to go away this weekend. by myself. free to do whatever i want just as you are.

enjoy Bo. you have left quite a mess behind you.

CHAPTER TEN

TOFINO

I had never been up to Tofino and really needed to clear my head so I did a quick google search and booked a couple nights at the Whalers on the Point Guesthouse, inquired about some scuba diving and emailed myself a map so I could gps my way there in a jiffy if required. Ended up staying up quite late the night before after having my friend Matty over to load up my iPhone with tunes and roll me a couple joints seeing as my rolling capabilities had not yet progressed enough for me to rely on my own dexterity. Bo used to do it. I was still hesitant about going, still keeping one foot in the door so to speak incase anything happened with Bo. I awoke 6am to an encouraging text from a friend wondering how I was doing and that was all the boost I needed to get me up and out the door for the second ferry crossing to Nanaimo. As sad and down as I was about my love long lost, I relished in the romance that my boyfriend of two years was suffering a mental breakdown and had hit the high seas in our 1947 wood sailboat, leaving behind the memoir novel he had written and kept secret from me giving me insight into his madness by detailing a previous episode. I thought the least I could do was finish reading it so I spent the first hour and a bit reading and brought myself outside onto the foredeck for me to finish the last couple pages. I took deep breaths and I crossed through the words as we crossed through the waves. I looked out over to Bowen Island behind us and Vancouver Island in front of us. Any sailboat I saw triggered an instant heart pounding that was a confusing mix of alarm, anger, resentment, and a powerful desire to get aboard and sail into the sunset like we had planned. It is a funny thing the way the mind holds on to things from the past, ideas that never came to fruition. Logically I knew that us getting our vacation was highly unlikely but the mind, or maybe just the heart, could barely think about it not happening before things like rage, tears or total denial would fully envelop me. I took in the 360 and hugged Bo's novel into my heart trying to feel if he was around me or connecting at all. I texted him that I had finished it, thinking for a brief moment that him not answering his phone was possibly a ploy and that he would be so enticed that I finished his novel he would want to discuss it with me. A theme throughout it was him feeling like he was on his own, or "didn't have a friend in the world" and I was willing to challenge that idea with everything inside of me because I knew I loved him and was going to make sure he knew it. I left it at that and walked myself back inside the ferry intending to wander myself into the bathroom when my eyes caught with a familiar face, Charlie's Mom Lindsay.

I was thrilled to run into her at this low point and thought that she could offer some sage, experience based advice. Lindsay told me she was on her way to see about getting a kitten and we talked about how cute that would be while inside I was chomping at the bit to talk about the real stuff. Then I flat out asked her what she thought of everything that was going on, Bo missing etc. She told me she thought the stress of living at 1906 was really a contributing factor to Bo going mad. She said we had no space where we lived and that it wasn't the healthy calm environment that Bo needed. Right, I thought, had I KNOWN about Bo's past perhaps some of this could have been prevented. She said in no way has he 'peaked' yet and that things were going to get worse before they get better and that it will probably be pretty bad. I was not too fond of any of this and still had my back up thinking that Bo and I would get through this, we were strong enough and of course had love on our side. That in combination with my seemingly everlasting patience and compassion sounded like a no-lose situation for us. With that said Lindsay's words stuck with me because deeper inside I knew that my view was based on likely Disney inspired unbridled optimism for a perfect landing and hers was based on real life information and experience. Her advice was, "Move on. You guys can pick up if you can later but for now just move on" she said. I would think about it but for now could agree to make the best of the time on my own and keep marching forward. The 'return to vehicles' message came over the loudspeaker and Lindsay and I hugged and parted ways. I walked away excited for the little adventure ahead of me but also confident from this chance meeting that I was in the right place.

Running into Lindsay like that was just the little boost and reality check I needed to remind myself not to float away into hopefulville and make sure I was having fun and taking care of myself. The coincidence was a beginning of really feeling for signs and cues to let me know if I was on the right path and making the right choices. 'Right' being like a flow and whatever would help Bo and I get through this and with him incommunicado it meant that we were left to intuitive and energetic communication.

After arriving in Nanaimo I went straight to Best Buy and got gist directions and a phone connection lighter thing to play my music in the bimmer. The drive out to Tofino is one of the best parts of the trip and it was long enough to clear my mind from sad girlfriend into summer beach chick. Whalers on the Point took me in and I ditched my bags quickly, grabbed a joint and my coffee and hit to the streets to get on one of these amazing beaches I had heard so much about. With a total lack of direction I walked down a tiny road and smelled my way to the water. There were signs of private property but I couldn't see any better options so I trespassed on. I found myself a nice rock to nestle onto that was sort of on the edge for me to look down and watch the waves lapping onto other rocks. I wouldn't exactly call this a good beach and the view was really not much different than the waters in van but I sparked up and enjoyed the moment anyways. Along came three dudes walking with fishing gear in hand. As they approached closer I could hear the mumblings of a french accent. I was delighted for the reminder of the accent I had lived with for six years and reminded myself that things would probably be ok because I had never really felt threatened around the Quebecois.

These were the kind of odd changes that I was noticing in myself. When I was in the relationship with Bo I had not even recognized that I walked through the earth feeling safe and protected nearly all the time. I started noticing it that night of the Canucks game when I walked around and observed this creeping feeling of vulnerability without being with my man, a man. I had to look around corners or ahead on streets again by myself now and was surprised that I didn't notice my own 'security' when it existed.

The three guys zig zagged their way to the large rock just below me. They said a quick hello and said they were trying to find a good place to fish and that they were going to be having a joint just down below if I wanted to join. I said I would think about it and thanked them. I took in another few minutes by myself breathing in and out before I decided some company would be nice. I was curled up on a corner rock and could not get any further without turning into a mountain goat and I would have to walk past them anyways to get out. Two were off closer to the water baiting the fishing line and digging through their tackle box that they told me they had just received as a gift from an old Japanese fisherman who no longer used it. The most hippy looking one sat back with me. He had dreadlocks peeking out an orange wool beret and I offered him a beer. He took a few sips and we did the who are you thing for a few minutes while finishing our joints. He told me him and his friends had come out here as a last weekend get away before they set into cherry picking for the season and he told me about that. The youngest looking one was wearing mostly black and had a bit of a darkness around him but he moved really quick on the shaky uneven rocks so he was fun to watch. He hopped his way over to the low point of the rocks and noticed some minnow's. The long hair blond guy scampered over and encouraged me to do the same. I bum shuffled my way down and smiled at the bright coloured sea plumes, crabs and other crayola coloured sea life. Their fishing wasn't going as well as they had hoped and they said they wanted to try another beach not far from where we were and they asked if I would like to come. My friday evening literally had nothing else so far so I gave it some thought as we walked away from the shoreline. The guy in black came with me to the hostel. I still had to check in because they were busy when I first got there. I sorted it out including the parking and still didn't feel any major red flags so I agreed to wander over to this other beach with the guys. I grabbed a bottle of wine from my trunk and walked with them into town. We stopped at their 70's van culture type van. The dreadlocks guy was already in the back sorting things around and he offered me and the blond guy some tortilla chips. We stood there and chatted for a bit and they told me how the three of them rearrange things to be able to sleep, drive and cook in the same vehicle. Then the blond guy told me we would have to drive over to the beach they were talking about and I could see he noticed the unsure feeling in my face. He leaned in the sliding door and reached for a map behind the drivers seat to show me. It really was a short drive and he said a walk back would be ok but it would be better to get there sooner rather than later for the fishing. Tick tock left and right in my brain but he looked soft, I had this map and Tofino itself was not that large so why not, I thought.

As we drove I buckled up and giggled to myself about the balancing act that the potted plants were playing on the dashboard and in the cup holders. Fresh herbs bouncing along the dashboard it was hippy at its max and no one seemed bothered by them sliding along left and right with the turns. We arrived and the guys wanted to heat up a bite to eat. Some rush we are in, I thought. I unscrewed the wine, took a couple sips and passed it around. They seemed really pleased with their first sips as though they had not had wine in a while and were thankful for me sharing. Regularly a bottle or two a night among friends was how Bo and I drank for years and so did our social circle.

We finally made our way out and it was a long walk. The tide was not out very far and we were climbing over rocks to the point that I told the guys I wanted to go back but as I did one called out that there was a path just ahead. I glared with skepticism but he was right and we sat down on large rocks. We sat for a long while, quiet. The guys fished and I breathed. And thank goodness the black dressed guy brought sandwich stuff because it hadn't even occurred to me to bring food on this walk, sun, drinking tour. A sun tanner who ran out of sun wandered his way up and introduced himself as Bernard. We smiled to each other with our eyes and he said "you can feel it too can't you" and I said yes before even thinking about what we were talking about. Like pure bliss. I tagged off the fishing crew and decided to walk back with this Bernard guy who turned out to be going most of the way I was. We walked back just when the sun has that golden light and it was beginning to feel like summer camp. My mind quickly flipped the romance card wondering if this person was supposed to be something in my life, like scanning it to see if it projects forwards. I wondered if this was the magic that would counter it all and make all my pain seem 'right' again. He said he was going to go to the bar that night and I agreed to pass by to meet up having absolutely nothing better to do. I went to the Mackenna bar but he didn't show so I sat by myself with a beer watching this one girl falling over drunk. Like literally bones turning into jello as she tries to stand up, falling over. I can honestly say I have never seen someone so gently collapse to the floor repeatedly like that but she kept getting up and was she pretty and was trying to get people to hold her up or dance with her. She really didn't want to leave when they asked her to. I didn't either, though it was a good idea, because I knew watching her was imprinting a strong message in me even though I couldn't quite put my finger on it.

The rest of my Tofino trip was a score. I spent a day walking Chesterman beach and sitting on rocks. I got to make peace and think about a lot. I admitted that Bo still had my heart as the thoughts drifted through my mind. He held my interest with lines like "people know you are wearing a sweater and you are not really that big" when he would see my look of discomfort as I would try to catch a 360 of myself in my new thick Cowichan sweater. It was comments like these that would take me aback because it was like skipping a step! I hadn't even realized my discomfort and was still blaming the sweater until he pointed it out. Left field. When I was angry I would think about what must be driving him and where his compassion was for all the people he was hurting in this wake. Compunction came via dictionary word of the day. Compunctious... he has no compunction? he is compunctious? (strong unease caused by guilt). Either way I was constantly tossing around ideas and thoughts that tangled me more than when I started. The walk back on Chesterman was the best because I took my time and got to take it all in pausing at the break where north and south meet and walked out to Franck Island. The wind was coming sort of south east and ushering me from behind. Looking at the sand while I walked I was feeling this almost atmospheric flickering from dark to light and glanced around for the source. I looked up and it nearly knocked me off my feet like vertigo. The clouds were rushing overhead so fast passed the overhead sun that I just wanted to sit down and take in the rush. People passed me with the warmest gentle smiles almost exchanging with our eyes a feeling of YES, this is heaven on earth. I sat on drift wood to smoke and have another of my stow away drinks and was mesmerized by how quickly the sand was carried by the wind. It seemed to follow the natural grooves left over from the tide and just tons of these thin streams of sand kept whooshing by me challenging any sense of ground. I couldn't resist stripping down to my bikini to get into the ocean even though it was colder than I was used to it was a reset, soothing and refreshing.

It was an early night because I had set up scuba diving for Sunday and wanted to be in good shape. We did two dives and I was the only one in a wet suit. I was miffed we didn't see the octopus I had heard so much about but was chilled to the bone by the time we were finished our second dive and still had to make it back for Father's day dinner with papa. I tore through the drive back to the ferry and I was already one sailing behind and now had time to kill. Can't use the phone because I would be charged for using it out of local range and its just me, the bimmer and my thoughts. By the time we load the ferry I'm in a full blown funk and decide to spend the trip crying/sleeping in the back seat of the car. I did a good job because I didn't wake up once until someone (quite loudly!) banged on the window for me to wake up. Sure enough all cars ahead of me had cleared and I could feel the angst for me to get moving. I giggled a little about how I can fall asleep anywhere and when I got home called to settle the rain check Father's day plans with my Dad.

CHAPTER ELEVEN

HAVE LOVE WILL TRAVEL

It was about as rainy as it could be when you're sad in Vancouver but my transition to summer was pumped up to a soundtrack of the Black Keys "Have Love Will Travel" and I already had Tofino under my belt to start so figured going north might bring even more epicness! I had taken off another week making the best of being apart by going to the movies, visiting the local sex shop that used to make me kind of uneasy, doing all the laundry and all the stuff that people who sail every weekend don't get to. By the following Sunday I felt like I had put everything together, everything in its place. I had done a magnificent tidy of our room, washed the sheets, made the bed and put everything back as it should be as well as checked off various other things that had been otherwise put off for months on end. I walked out of our room feeling pleased but was stopped suddenly by the door as soon as I realized or remembered he was still not coming back. One week had turned to more and I was taking it as light as I could, making the best of it, expecting my patient to walk in the door any minute, but he wasn't coming. Then I noticed his bath robe and realized I had forgotten to include it in the wash, which turned into something like "of course it isn't time for him to come home yet, we're not quite ready!" In addition to this ludicrous logic, my summer was do or die. I could fall into some woe is me and spend my free waking hours in a coma (either sleep or otherwise induced) or take the bull by the horns, ride the wave, however you call it. July 1st was quickly approaching in my horizon and I knew it would be a tear jerker. So walking I went and the beach was a good place to start. Anytime I don't feel like going to the beach I remember Bo saying "you don't live blocks from the beach and not go to the beach" and it makes me giggle enough to agree and put one foot in front of the other.

One Kitsbeachful day me, my headphones and a couple beers took rest near some rocks next to one of the trees that grow out of the wall. I started talking to this extremely tanned beach guy in red shorts who frequently applied oil one of his friends Ash came and sat down with us just as the sun was starting to fade. We shared whatever beer, cigarettes and weed we had left and I blurted out that I had been thinking about going to Haida Gwaii. I hadn't actually thought about it for days because things with Bo were so off but sometimes on and it turned out Ash was from there and raved about the place. I asked him about a single girl, camping deal and he said it would be no problem at all. He said it was a magical place and the animals were everywhere. He told me all I needed to bring was a tarp and good shoes, he said everything else I could get there and that people would be really nice there. I was quite pumped on the idea having heard Ash's view on things. Though he did say he had not been back for nearly eight years or something so I was kind of skeptical as to if he was up to date on the state of things. I became increasingly more skeptical when I repeated his minimal packing list to family and friends. They didn't quite think that would cut it and some didn't think it was a good idea at all and I was still tentatively hanging on to my plans with Bo though he really wasn't interested in making a plan.

The timer was counting down and I was feeling pressed to decide not only what to do with my summer but how to turn Bo and my's original departure date into something other than emptiness. I wasn't really into playing my luck again with the Craigslist boat thing but figured I would feel it out and do a search. I connected with and met this Nick guy who posted that he was setting out for the long weekend up the coast with friends to see what we thought. He was in the neighbourhood so we met at a close coffee shop and we learned within a few minutes that he was actually setting off with my next door neighbours, the piano composer and his girlfriend who I had literally just seen packing the boat from the upstairs porch. I was quite thankful for the convenient coincidence because I didn't have to explain much more of my situation than the coles notes version about Bo going mad, plus everybody knew everybody. I think this still left Nick a little in the dark as to whether I was green or red and we wandered to get a beer at his buddy's place but it became clear when I bailed the scene later that evening. It wasn't really anything personal but I was having a vision of not making it back in time for work due to their loose plans. I didn't feel as though I was presented with a good enough lead to follow and more like a dead end as far as girl on a boat craigslist access…but a sweet little ending at that. Thank you universe.

The Black Keys concert we had tickets to was around the corner and clearly my date was no where to be found so Tara's boyfriend Andy took his place. I wanted to be happier but tension was bubbling inside of me. It was kind of a rainy day and it was being held outdoors at Deer Lake so many people brought umbrellas which were promptly confiscated at the door check along with any snacks people had brought forcing them to purchase any food indoors. I recall seeing what looked to be a European couple who had arrived with a woven basket, a bottle of wine, a baguette and who knows what else being so confused as to why it all had to be thrown in the garbage for an outdoor picnic style concert. The tipping point for me though was when the beer garden shut down before the main act had even reached the stage. Police no fun city! Sure pot wasn't legal and they didn't seem to mind the clouds of that around but alcohol was getting a huge crack down.

I was getting the feeling that if I didn't decide I would be taking no vacation at all. I had Haida Gwaii on the one side and a two week delayed to departure with my man on the other though, though he was still basically rogue. I had things to think about but in any event it was setting in that July 1st was not going to be the adventure I that had been planning for.

June 30, 2011
Chat with Cailey

me: hell

Cailey: hell-o? Not a good day love? it's early and there's a lot of time for it to turn around

me: yeah. some communication with Bo via email. NOT going well. he is still not out of it.

Cailey: well a conversation is a start

me: he is being an asshole, nasty jerk

Cailey: yikes

me: the conversation is come and meet me to leave for the trip as planned or see you later

Cailey: seriously?

me: well he is obviously not "normal"

in his dilusions he keeps attacking my boss

Cailey: even still

me: saying that i am more commited to him or something

Cailey: ha. logic is obv vacant

me: it is so painful to watch :(

i woke up this morning from a nightmare. it has almost never happened. i had a nightmare that my dads big toe just fell off

Cailey: jesus

me: it was totally gross, like a limb that had been cut off from circulation

and he freaked out and ran the other direction and wouldn't let us see or help

Cailey: weird

me: well its kind of how i feel in this situation

Cailey: yea the parallel is evident

me: i havent been handling the last few days very well. i thought something would change by now :(sleeping in my clothes. sleeping at 9pm-730am

Cailey: you should get out for the weekend
mis up your routine
mis = mix

me: well i just dont know what to do
im still about 1500$ in the hole on my cc so dont have much dough to go around
ive been racking my brain of how to shake it up

Cailey: it doesn't have to be $$

me: ideas?

Cailey: day trip to the fraser valley. check out some green houses or antique shops. Go for a hike, do the Grouse grind or one of the regional parks, pack a picnic, go to Jerico, take up paddleboarding me: paddleboarding...hm

Cailey: I am learning with my sister in law thin it would be a good fit for you

me: that is when you stand on the board right?

Cailey: yea

me: never really like the idea too much...although i do generally just love being on the water

Cailey: well try it. only have to do it once

me: diving could be cool too. the motivation is lacking i suppose :(

Cailey: http://www.windsure.com/
Well you'll have to dig deep to find the motivation.
it's either that or sleeping in your clothes and being miserable.
which life do you want?

me: yeah thats the tricky part about depression. you dont think logically like that.

Cailey: I know - that's why I just say it point blank

me: honestly c in the last few days ive just been feeling like i want to be touched. it is so painful.

Cailey: You are lonley and somewhat isolated, so that makes sense

Cailey: http://www.theweathernetwork.com/fourteenday/ cabc0308?ref=qlink_lt_14day Looking forward to that finally. All those little sunshines put a smile on my face just looking at them

me: ugh. its like salt in my wound. sail away Bo. have a blast

Cailey: you can't blame the weather for smiteing you.

me: im still very very very disappointed and angry about this trip being cancelled. wait all year for this. sanding the boat. FUCK

Cailey: my understaindind is that is was not cancelled? just moved up 2 weeks

me: he isnt going to be better in 2 weeks. he isnt going to be the Bo that we knew for months like maybe december
that is what i gather from kristen

Cailey: gotcha

me: i guess i dont know what to do with myself. all i want is to be going on this trip :(

Cailey: that has to be pretty taxing since you don't have anywhere to really direct your anger and disappointment

me: nope im back on cl looking for a boat to go on. my my how things have not changed. i think i need to get my own boat

Cailey: cool. what kinda of boat?

me: well probably sail
$

Cailey: I am interested in doing a boat-share with someone. but I am looking for a powerboat

me: yep. still a girl who wants to be on a boat

Cailey: well that's a good startingpoint

me: i would love it a hell of a lot more if i had a boat and could take off myself. sit on the docks, chat it up

Cailey: well there's a goal

me: i guess so but realisitically i wont have enough money till probably the end of this year for something like that
so the interim is still at hand

Cailey: yea, otherwise you'd need a loan

me: no way am i getting aloan for a boat

its like asking for an open wound!

Cailey: haha

me: also, ill need to sidle up to some male friends to get advice on what to buy as far as getting something that won't need repairs i cant do

urgh

me: man this bites

Cailey: oh man - I took page out of your book yesterday. T&T

me: huh?

Cailey: I got a parking ticket!

me: oh-t squared

Cailey: right

me: sucks balls

Cailey: i was pretty pissed. alas

me: how much

Cailey: well if I pay now 35$ if I wait 105$

me: the usual

Cailey: probably

me: believe me, its the usual ;)

Cailey: haha. you are an expert in the field

me: now they have 3 levels of payment. it is BRUTAL used to only go up to 75

Cailey: it's kinda strange

me: now they have a 3rd tier. its total bullshit

Cailey: it's like penalizing people for having a low cash flow and rewarding people with excess disposable income. doesn't seem fair

me: exactly! its total bullshit. there are places where these things are based on your personal income

Cailey: interesting

me: so the penatly fits the crime committer. for some 35$ is a dream for not having to worry about parking

Cailey: pretty much

me: i cant believe how much i am drifting away in all of this

Cailey: what do you mean?

me: i guess i just am still in shock. now finding myself thinking about "moving on". lately ive been thinking that if i met someone i liked and if something happened i wouldnt even feel guilty because of all of this. which scares me because i have never felt like that.

Cailey: well you've never been in a position like this before (at least not that I know of) so it's only natural for you to have unfamilar feelings/thoughts

me: yeah. on the inside i feel so hurt, abandoned, betrayed, angry and frustrated that somehow it removes me from feeling guilty over thinking about being with someone else :(as of the last few days at least

Cailey: I am sure there are probably a whole host of ever changing/evolving emotions that's why love is so fucking complicated and messy

me: i guess so. havent shared with anyone.

just feeling so alone in all of this. like when the fuck is the ride going to stop. would it be terrible to contact an old friend from the past...? bad idea. way too messy to invite visitors

Cailey: yea, I would think so. Might want to get through some stuff first

me: zing! first response invitation on a boat. haha

Cailey: did you post an ad?

me: yes!

Cailey: haha. ok - be careful.

me: i put it on stricly platonic and said "no monkey business, just fun on a boat" although i guess that leaves a lot of room for interpretation

Cailey: haha

me: i'm not about to jump on a boat just for the sake of getting on a boat it would have to be good and a decent human also

Cailey: well yes. pref with multiple people. don't like the thought of you (or anyone) on a boat alone with a potentially crazy stranger

me: well thats how i met b!

Cailey: I know and it made me nervous then

me: talk about the biggest craigslist scam ever!

Cailey: what?

me: Bo

Cailey: ha   I thought you were going to say someone from Nigeria wants to tranfer you 2.6 million dollars
me: well two responses "nick" who is going away with 2 other couples dont know the details yet or ron the 42 year old with a boat in richmond…richmond
mental note, make more friends with boats so to avoid choosing from strangers :P

me: now b says he isnt coming home

June 30, 2011
Bo
To Alicia Lindsay Boswell
We can meet wherever... Shant't be coming home. Should consider your priorities.
Sent from my iPhone

Chat with Cailey
Cailey: as in never? or was he planning on coming back until now?

me: he is mad and i dont mean angry this is the message: We can meet wherever... Shant't be coming home. Should consider your priorities.   people are right...it is good that he leaves! jerk

Cailey: "Shant be coming home".
?
personally, I question his priorities. or at the very least, that says more about his priorities than yours.

me: it is not real
he is mad
his mind has been firing on all cylinders for over a month now... not sleeping, not eating,. it isnt someone to talk logically to, sadly. on the bright side i am invited with this nick guy and 2 other couples to sunshine coast

hm....

Cailey: as long as you are safe, it would be more fun than just hangin in the city
long*

me: totally agreed

July 1, 2011
Alicia Lindsay Boswell
To Bo
Happy first day we met honey. Maybe one or two regrets but definitely a good ride. You have such a strong presence. I can't wait to have my man back.

July 1, 2011
Bo
To me
Yeah right happy happy.. I was just a toy then and you still haven't made me first in your life. Let me know when you are over your toys of the moment and ready to get real or get lost.

Sent from my iPhone

I was still delighted with any sort of dialogue that we could carry on. I thought that like a snake charmer our dialogue could seduce him out of his state and back into our world. Trying to correspond with Bo was like trying to hug a feral cat but even with the occasional slash my heart was guiding me strong. Until...

CHAPTER TWELVE

HIGHS AND LOWS ON MUDGE

Tension had been building with the hot and cold, back and forth. I continued with the email sonnets professing my equally strong love and hate for how things were going. I was baffled by his lack of empathy, and just clung to any acknowledgement that he would offer, using it as fuel to continue on. Another weekend was approaching and I was hitting my breaking point because Bo had dropped off communication again. After all of this my resentment was building. It was 100% disregarding me by dropping off like this. On top of this, Bo's friend Mark had ran into him at the Nitinat sauna was possibly going to meet him. Apparently going to Nitinat on a scooter is insane as in you blow a tire 50% of the time, and he had a rented scooter at that. Mark never gave a very wordy account as to how Bo was doing but everyone let me know that it was quite a feat. I had talked to Mark and told him how worried I was for Bo and was following up via text and his only response was "he's fine." GRRRrrrr. Was he clueless or what? Wounded soldier's wife over here…wanting to know how he is doing! Later he told me Bo had just tossed his iPhone over his shoulder into the ocean on a whim.

I had set my mind that this behaviour was unacceptable and that I would NOT be going over to see him this weekend. He would have to learn that keeping me in the loop is essential for this to work and I was looking forward to a weekend of curling up and mourning all of these losses. Later that night Charlie's mom Lindsay called and said that Bo had been anchored near her place on Mudge and wanted to see me. Lindsay said she did not want to be involved other than to say that he wanted to see me. She also said it would be ok if I came to visit and needed a place to stay. Well, as you may have guessed, my heart quickly went pitter patter at the idea of seeing Bo after all this time. It had been about a month since I had seen him, and at least two weeks since he first went missing. For us this was an unprecedented amount of time apart. Prior to this the only thing that could separate us was our own cataclysms, which usually couldn't last more than 24 hours for either of us.

I tried to keep a calm clear head as I packed my bag up but I admit at the same time I was imagining dreamily romantic scenarios where we would be reunited and all ends well. They were often followed by the reminding possibility that we may not even run into each other. Yes, he was anchored nearby but I had never actually been to Mudge, he was also completely erratic and Lindsay said she hadn't seen him in a few days so I prepared myself for both outcomes and set the bottom line at having a nice visit with Lindsay and getting away to the islands for the weekend. Reuniting with manic lost lover bag packed- check! Hair straightened and ready for my closeup with Mr. Bo.

Harbour Air was a delight. I had never flow in sea planes before so I arrived a smidge too late and was bumped to the next plane. I was quickly fine with that because these two guys were playing awesome reggae infused music that made me feel like I was in a Corona advertisement, sans Corona. Me and my gold boating shoes were going to put the nerves aside and just enjoy the sun and fun as best we could. When we got on the plane the pilot asked if anyone needed a taxi to wait on the other side. I put up my hand and said that I might need one, that I was going to Mudge but wasn't sure how to get there yet. The planes are tiny so everyone listens and can hear everything so I felt a little silly when the pilot responded with something like, well you can't take a taxi to Mudge. OBViously....just wondering if I needed one in the interim, friend. People smiled at that and probably at my beaming enthusiasm. Nearby sitting strangers helped me figure it out during our little flight over to Nanaimo and after getting my bag I straggled behind some flight mates who were going the same total direction. The next little leg was a ferry over to Gabriola, then somehow I had to hitchhike a ride across the island because the ferry takes us to one side of the island and the boat launch to get to Lindsay's is at another end of it. So yeah, ferry to Gabe, hitch-hike across island to the boat launch, then either wait or ask for a boat ride across to Mudge and then just ask people where Lindsay lives or wander around until I find something. That was the plan at hand keeping in mind that past the ferry dock on Gabe cell phones were fully out of range.

Ferry lineup for walk ons is the best. The ferry really isn't all that large just enough for a few cars and a little room with seats on both port and starboard sides. I was setting into a little adventure here! So far things were working out smooth and silky so I felt like I was on a good wave. I took a seat starboard side only long enough to spike myself a juice to get this weekend started. I was honing in on Bo and wanted to be prepared for anything, which included numbing thyself or at least having the capacity to do so at close hand. A couple deep breaths, everything in check and I stood up and decided to catch some sun and perch myself on the bow. One or two steps out the door and my eyes lock onto some familiar plaid shorts. Like one of those moments people talk about where everything is slow motion and you are almost outside of your body without thinking and I walked my way up to them and without a conscious thought I tapped the wearer on the shoulder. He turned around and looked prickly and said "There you are!" and leaned in to give me a kiss. I am sure I tipped my head away from it because I was so in shock by who and what I was seeing I just stood back for a minute to try and take it all in.

I was shaking almost instantly that I was actually with him again. Was this finally the beginning of the end to all of this?!!? But things seemed wrong. For one he had a metal cup hanging from a loop on his backpack and his feet were really scruffed up in these new ugly thick sandals. This guy looked like a bum and I didn't really get it. He was wearing a blue camo print baseball hat and Bo hated baseball hats and said he could never wear hats because they didn't look good on his head. He was wearing the grey shirt I had got him a few months ago that he didn't like and I admit it looked terrible. Fawn grey? What was I thinking! But I don't know if it was the blah grey that was getting to me or the fact that Kristen was right he was getting thinner for sure. A backpack? (He had only used his computer satchel up until now) Sunglasses held to a string with duct tape? …and really ugly sandals, good thing I straightened my hair, I poked at myself. "You look beautiful honey" he said, and smiled. I told him I needed a few minutes to process this and stepped away and plugged my ears with my iPod to sip my drink and adjust realities. My heart was flooded with everything I had wanted having reunited with him. Except the metal cup really bothered me. It would clink on everything or when moved and I think that was exactly what Bo liked about it but I said it would have to go and we negotiated other details over a couple beers at the local pub.

One of the major points of contention for me was him being incommunicado. We talked about that for a while and he apologized and seemed to be understanding. We were not exactly seeing eye to eye but he definitely seemed more relaxed than he was in Vancouver. I sent a little note off to let everyone know that we had triumphantly ran into each other on the ferry. What a great story I thought. What are the chances? And having missed my flight….this must be kismet. He told me he had gone over to Nanaimo looking for me, ah, the earlier flight, I thought as I became slowly seduced by my own love stories. A couple beers later and A and B were side by side again. We set off to hitchhike and ended up splitting the ride into a couple of legs. Bo said it was a lot easier to hitchhike with me with him and I was equally happy to not have had to do it unguided and on my own.

We got to the boat launch and I was doing everything I could to try and figure out how he was doing. The last time we saw each other taking photographs and iPhones really bothered him so before setting off to this island took a couple more photographs to test his reaction. Non reactive so we were off to Mudge. It is just a quick zip over from Gabe to Mudge at the boat launch but Bo was moored at the other side of the island so the dinghy ride was about four times as long or longer depending on the tide. Scanning the situation: Getting into a dinghy with a person I know is in and out of their mind, no cell phone, but he seemed calm and worse case scenario I leave everything in the dinghy and swim to a shoreline and find help. OK, plan in action and I asked Bo exactly where we were going. Looking at him straight in the eyes and showing him my fear and telling him that things will really be bad if he hurts me or anything goes wrong. He assured me that it would not happen and maintained a solid stance and told me step by step the lay of the land as he knows it while we zipped over to the boat.

CHAPTER THIRTEEN

TAKING IT EASY ON EASY

As soon as we turned the corner to get to the other side of Mudge Bo pointed out Easy sitting pretty. I couldn't quite make her out yet but appreciate him telling me what the deal was as we cruised along. We didn't stay long and turned around for a dinner at Lindsay's that night. She lives in this very white house with multiple french doors that are left open a lot and so many deer walk by that people find it annoying, though I didn't. It's next to her friends house who made an entire floor out of pennies. Dinner was great with wine and a couple other couples aside from Bo's snappy rants about meat or Walmart. After much drinking and smoking we dinghy'd ourselves back to Easy where I didn't move more than 34 feet in 24 hours. As blissed as I was to slow down to the rock of the waves, sit in the sun and watch a spiderweb quiver in the wind I had to keep batting down resentment. I really didn't appreciate being left in the dark all this time, working all this time, WORRYING all this time while Bo and Easy just blazed the summer days away without me! Things were seemingly on the mend so I tried to let go of those thoughts and focus on the positive.

July 9, 2011

I pick up this book because I am so inspired by watching a spider web between the life lines flutter in the wind. The light is golden this early morning. Waking up with the light and making love again with my man. He is different now. A beard and still shaky. The wind blows past my ears so softly as shhhh....We are sitting on Easy just behind Mudge. Just drifting around with the tide change. The tide is out and all of the rocks and land we were able to cruise over in the dinghy at one time are now exposed. Bo is showing his crusty side as well. We still have the rap music playing ladies and gentlemen. Last night after diner at Lindsays a deer walked around the house. Everyone is used to it there.

By evening we set off to visit friends on land again. Climbing over some slippery rocks from the shoreline he was ahead of me in those ugly sandals and I recall looking up from my own footing for a moment to glance at him and thinking *please don't fall* to which he instantly tripped and then snapped a glare at me over his shoulder at me criping "you did that!" DONG.

Dinner party number two and the misfires were increasing. A friend cooked salmon and I was starving after spending a day with Mr. non eating vegan but as soon as I started eating he started with the trash talk. It was a melange of radiation in the water and eating souls not being right which I agree with but at the same time was hungry and just told him to lay off. A few days into this and I was getting increasingly exhausted. By Sunday morning I snapped, I crunched my stuff into my bag, climbed in the dinghy and told Bo to take me to the shore and he zipped me to the nearby shoreline. I know neither of us wanted to leave each other but we just couldn't meet in the middle. I was overwhelmed with the negative ranting and what seemed like him trying to plant bad thoughts inside of me. We sarcastically yelled at each other as I stomped away and he corrected my direction towards the path. Now what.

I wandered my way through the island deciding what to do. It was about 6am and there was no way Lindsay was up so I wandered my way to the boat launch side of things. Someone had told me during our hitchhike on the way over that at low tide it is possible to walk across to Gabriola. I had nothing better to do and figured it would really be a feat if I could actually get out of there Jesus style so I scanned the scene for the best place to attempt my crossing. It took about half an hour of slipping on rocks and a broken flip flop later to concede that in fact the tide was ripping along and that this was a terrible, likely very dangerous idea so I went back to Lindsay's. She was still sleeping so I wrote her a note to let her know what was going on with me and also thought of my last attempt at relaying a message to Bo which was something along the lines of come get me in Vancouver when you get your shit together and she woke up so I told her in person. It was early but we made coffee and enjoyed a nice chat over her home made bread toasted with butter and then I was invited to have a bath. After all of this stress from the roller coaster that is life with Bo a bath was just what I needed. I fell asleep for a bit at some point and then slept more on her couch until visitors came by and I got tangled into catching a ride off island with them to venture back on to Vancouver. It was for the best, I thought. Things had not gone all that well in the last stretch with Bo and I could see that there was little I could do anyways about his state. He would have to get his shit together and then we would talk. Not a total loss however and I was thankful that at least this little episode got me over to visit Lindsay on Mudge. The roaming deer, the islands, Easy and my love but it was still time for me to go and the chances of us going on this trip were really eclipsing and it was decision time for me.

FOUR STAGES

DR. MICHAEL BECKWITH

BY US	THROUGH US
Gain control	Give up control
Life supports our manifestations	Become a channel, life flows and guides us
TO US	**AS US**
No control	Co-creating
Life is doing something to us	One with ALL life

CHAPTER FOURTEEN

CHOOSING HAIDA GWAII

I was getting my strength back. We had houseguest Martin with us who is a fellow virgo and stellar at getting people enthusiastically pumped up. He reminded me of my strengths and how beautiful the world is and encouraged my thoughts of pursuing Haida Gwaii. A backpacking trip seemed daunting but he kept me on track with assurance that I would be able to handle it so the only question at hand was Skidegate or Masset, where to fly and what to bring. Cailey topped the charts again by having readily available camping gear so I wouldn't have to go off and invest in stuff on my own. Pack, sleeping bag, thermarest and a loose floating compass and I was well on my way. My holiday time was quickly approaching and it was all systems north, total direction: adventure!

Martin and I hummed and hawed using the internet to try and figure out where I should fly into. After a couple beers one night it was as simple as looking at a map for me to decide where to go. The northwestern tip and Rose Island were drawing me in as far as what kind of spectacular view they might offer and I figured north was a good place to start, so from that Masset it was.

Martin took me shopping for hiking boots over at MEC which I had not really ever had since I was a kid. I recall trying them on and people oohing and awing asking where I was off to and the bizarre looks they gave me when I said I was leaving in a couple days to go to Haida Gwaii trying to imply that this a poor last minute purchase and rather something that needed much more time to 'break in.'

I was semi-realistic about going camping in Haida Gwaii and didn't want to bite off more than I could chew so staying a night, at least one, in a hotel or place sounded like a nice landing pad. Google search, second click in and the Copper Beech House had my name all over it and it was easily accessible from the airport.

Going to 3Vets for camping gear didn't exactly improve my confidence either when the clerk serving me while I was looking for a knife, flashlight and bear spray started calling his friends over to point out "the girl who is camping Haida Gwaii on her own." I did end up finding some pretty cool green fleece army pants that I was sure were going to help me along.

I was starting to notice that the more strength I gained the more in my face, angry and debilitating Bo became. He knew that my holidays were going to start soon and even though we had barely been in contact and he had chased me away like a scared lamb those things didn't seem to matter to him and he kept babbling another one of those rants of "woman! be by my side!" He tried everything including insulting me and the vet I worked for but I was firmly not going to jump how high like last time just because he decided to pop his head out again demanding I jump to be by his side.

I wanted my destination to be kept secret from B so I kept our conversations as loose and generalized as I could. I still didn't really know what I wanted to do even though time was ticking I was still open to the possibility of a miracle. However I didn't think our chances were very high considering he didn't seem to even have a grasp on what had brought us to this place. He kept saying that I was not honouring our plans giving no consideration to the loops and hoops I had been jumping through given all of these changes.

Possibly taking his cues from my vagueness Bo freed up 30k into cash. He was certainly acting angry and I had no idea where he was headed and what he would do next. He called me and freaked, yelling at me and telling me he was divorcing me. Sometimes I wondered why I even answered the phone but not for too long because I figured whatever he was working through was obviously all consuming and sticks and stones and all. He had done this before apparently, blown through everything. By Friday afternoon I was desperate to find a way to protect his money from himself but had no idea what lengths I could or should go to in order to do so. I transferred the maximum daily amount out of his account into mine, in trust.

Emotions were running high because I was scheduled to leave Saturday morning and by Friday afternoon I was depleted, exhausted and still not packed. I also didn't have a warm cushy bed to look forward to for more than a day and was sincerely reconsidering what I was taking on and thinking about a warmer shortcut down south. On top of this Bo had officially gone rogue and was a complete wild card that I was still contending with, verbal divorce or not. I registered Bo and Easy with Sea-Tow marine assistance and sent him the info because I wanted him to have it no matter what. I came to the realization that things were in fact, not going to work out as planned regardless of how hard I had tried and now faced with the last few moments before summer vacation started it was Alicia flying solo and sadly realizing we were at the place where one person takes a turn and the other doesn't.

I changed my flight to Wednesday so as to not be rushed and stressed and also so I had a couple of days on my own. I'd like to say I was gaining strength but in reality I was scared to make a leap and slept holding his shoe that night. Yep true story, one used shoe, because the other had already been lost somehow and I still thought it could be recovered when this was all over. I was woken that morning 5 minutes before my alarm by a raging call from Bo. Did he know I was leaving? What the hell? Seriously? Does he want to ruin everything? Bags were packed including everything except the lump I decided to carry in my throat. His raging call really gave me no material to work with. No matter how nervous I was for this trip I couldn't turn around and stay because of Bo because he was 100% asshole. I was nicely sent off by Kristen and Martin who waved at me from the porch as I loaded into the taxi. They were smiling as large as they could, probably hoping it would catch on because I was all nerves and anxiety. "You're going to Haida Gwaii!" she cheered and I glared. I had not thought this through, I thought, and had absolutely nothing to look forward to once I got there. Not a person or a thing, just an indoor cat heading into the wild and I comforted myself thinking I could turn around and come back whenever I wanted which gave me enough assurance to charge forth. Worst case scenario I'll get the heads up on where the radiation was at since Fukushima's nuclear meltdown because I heard they were getting washed up debris and were testing it up there and that would be enough for me to come home without feeling empty handed.

Things didn't exactly pick up at the airport. It wasn't like setting off for one of those down south stints where you can smell the party from the check in gate. Instead I was one of three, but only lone female, surrounded by Albertans and fishermen. I don't know who felt me out of place the most, me or everyone else, but none of us said anything about it except the stewardess. When our little plane touched down at the airport I was snapping photos like someone who cared and she leaned in and asked me if it was my first time to Masset. "Yes," I replied and she smiled and said "I think you will have a nice time, it's really nice". Skeptical for sure but I would take that at its full value! Thankyouverymuch. I was so grateful for her extending that. It was a good enough bandaid for me to calm my nerves long enough for the touchdown and unload.

The thing I like most about crowds is the ability to be lost within them. Now my fellow flight members and their pick up rides hardly make up a crowd but for Masset it could pass as one. I was relieved to have a few minutes to wait for our bags so I could try and decide what to do and I asked someone about calling a taxi. Walking could be an option as far as my map showed me but I really didn't know where I was going and I felt like everyone was looking at me which was fine but I wanted to know what I was doing because I was starting to feel vulnerable. Taxi arrives, a mini van, and he asks me where I am going. "Copper Beech House?" I say. "Whose house?" he replies and my city slicker eyes widen that this place could actually be small enough to give directions by someone's name. I fumbled with my papers to find out what the actual address is and we put 2 and 2 together and he drove me right there. There was no meter in the cab but that was fine. When he dropped me off I asked how much and he said five bucks. Was this guy kidding me!? In Vancouver it is $2.50 before your tires move an inch let alone an airport pick up. From a twenty he gave me paper and I tried to tip but he refused and said he enjoyed doing his job.

I walked in the Copper Beech door and was greeted with smiles and warmth from the young couple Kayley and Michael who were care taking. I was already fond of Kayley because she had the same name as my Cailey and Michael had really calmed my nerves when we had spoken on the phone earlier about the reservation and putting to rest my fears of coming up as a girl alone to camp in a place with bears etc. We talked for a bit and I was shown my corner room overlooking the water. There were a group or two milling about deciding what to do for their activity of the day. It was no bother to me because my eyes had enough to feast on between the collections of the Copper Beech House and the nature that fully surrounded it. I could see the differences quite quickly. Trees were larger, it smelled wetter and there were ravens everywhere. Not crows, ravens. Who caw differently and are noticeably larger. I decided to get my bearings by taking a walk and set off to wander. I had no plans so wandering through the town of Masset was the best I could come up with. First things- beach! And I walked along a pier taking in the fresh air. It was much colder than a sunny Vancouver day and I was beginning to doubt my decision not really understanding what this place had to do with me. My thoughts were halted when I spotted the bald eagle not far from the pier, standing on the rocks of the beach. We looked at each other and it was enough for me to drop all of the negative questioning and replace it with curiosity. A bald eagle just standing on the beach! Right time, right place I thought. I learned later that they were friends I would see often, and ravens too, both were all around me.

The town of Masset is really just a street or few and there wasn't exactly any crowd I could blend in with meaning everyone has an eye on the tourists as they come and go. Keeping it cool I thought

I would celebrate my touch down with a beer at the local bar. It certainly wasn't the average cocktail hour crowd and in fact I decided to keep to myself and cool off in their outdoor smoking area. The patio had some picnic tables surrounded by a fence and chicken wire on the upper. I didn't know what to make of the chicken wire but did observe how the enclosed space somehow made me feel better. Like if I was in the enclosed space I would have to think less about what I was doing or where I was going. A weird kind of comfort. I was joined shortly by some local Haida and we chit chatted with beers. Two of them invited me to smoke a joint round the corner which I was eager for so I agreed. On the way out another guy (possibly drunk) crossed the street staring at the three of us and he said to me "You're new aren't you." "Uhh..Yyyesss" I reluctantly replied (was it that obvious). "Don't go with those guys," he said "they hurt women" and I stopped. The two guys I was with walked on to smoke and left me standing with buddy. I wasn't exactly getting a straight up vibe from him but still didn't like what I was hearing. I ended up thanking him for the tip and told him I would be cautious and he said ok and stumbled on. I was certainly concerned but also didn't really trust the source so I continued on to the two guys and a joint. They asked me what he said and I recounted. They laughed and told me the half drunk guy had just been talked to by the police that morning for kicking one of their dogs. I couldn't really relate to this drama I had walked into so we just had the joint and kept the conversation light. One of the two asked me if he could offer a suggestion to me. I was completely on guard so I think I said something like mm, and he repeated his question as though he actually wanted permission from me before suggesting something. I admired the tiny moment and told him that yes he could and he showed me on my map a nice walk over to the bird sanctuary nearby. We walked back and finished our beers and I got to talking with another older man who told me he had lived in Vancouver and worked as a nurse for quite a while. I was more than pleased when I recounted the little interaction we had just had outside and this guy told me that the two guys I was with were the nicest outta the bunch and totally harmless. Bonus points for intuition! I thanked them all and made tentative see-you-next-time plans and went on the walk to the bird sanctuary.

The walk was the perfect suggestion because I could go as far in as I wanted and had time on my own in a path. I swear I didn't see one bird in that sanctuary but it was ok because my thoughts were enough to look at. I was still running the gamut of possibilities with all the Bo stuff followed by reminding myself that I was on my own now.

Luck was on my side again because I wasn't getting shuffled out the door from Copper Beech as quickly as I had thought. They had a cancellation and had space to house me for another night. Considering I was not exactly eager for the camping bit and still had little to no idea what I wanted to do up there I thought the idea was swell. Kayley and I got to spend some time together with the girl talk thing and we took her rescued young black dog Asha to the beach for a walk. We talked about things I could do and how beautiful it was up on the island and she mentioned this guy Dom we could go visit the next day. I don't actually know how many times she mentioned him but it was enough that my ears were perked up and I was curious who this guy was. Dom. Kayley had a friend arrive and the next day the three of us hopped into her car to do the rounds which included passing by Dom's. Dom's was not far by car and he was out working in the garden. He gave us a tour of his farm including chickens and goats and we all made nice talk and decided to take a walk on the beach with the dogs. The niceties were quickly replaced when Dom asked me what I was doing up there. I got the sense that he wanted a real answer so I told him my boyfriend has been suffering from a mental breakdown. I was a bit teary and he just said "you're going to have to cry a lot more than that." I don't know if I was taken aback more by his bluntness or accuracy but we kept walking and talking while the dogs ran the beach. When we got back to Dom's, Kayley mentioned that I was here and not really sure what I was doing and he told me if I needed a place to stay that his neighbour's cabin was open and that the woofers he hosts sometimes stay there, as an option. I thanked him and he invited us to share ice cream he had just made from the goats milk. The girls didn't want to stay so I went along with that, thanked Dom again and told him not to leave the ice cream in the sun as we started to walk away. "It's not in the sun" he rightly replied, the bowl was was in the shade, but what I meant was not to leave it out, and then I just stopped because I didn't even know why I was saying it but we smiled and I laughed inside a little.

By the next day Copper Beech was clearing out to get ready for a big crew of people and I had to decide what I was going to do. I couldn't feel any draw or pull inside of me in any direction and was feeling good in Masset so thought I would check out Dom's place as discussed. I tidied up what I could and gathered my things and it was just a local named Tripper and I kicking it at the Beech house. Lucky me again she was driving right past Dom's and offered to take me straight there. I asked if she would mind making a stop in town so I could get some things and she said no problem. I had no idea what to expect with this Dom guy but didn't think it right to arrive empty handed so thought I would bring enough to make us dinner and some wine to make it fun. Tripper and I took off down Toe Hill road and she dumped me off at the foot of his driveway. She also told me she lived down the road and kind of pointed it out and said if I needed anything I could wander my way down there. Wow, I thought. People are so nice up here! And with my backpack on and arms loaded with groceries I walked up the driveway and kind of snuck up on Mr. Dom who was working on the garden. "Hey," I said. "Hey," he said as he eyed the random city chick and all her gear now standing on his property. "So, uh, you said you have that place?" I started, and we awkwardly chuckled. He sat down on the bench and I sat down on the whale skull that he had found and retrieved on a recent kayak trip that was being used as a seat. I told him I had brought stuff to make us dinner and wine, hoping to sweeten the deal. He told me he didn't really drink but still thought the idea was ok and he showed me around to the neighbours place to drop my bags and then to his. Even through the immense clutter the charm of his cabin shone through. There were papers around and I noticed his name was written Dominic and I asked him why everyone calls him Dom. "I don't know," he replied. So Dominic it was.

Lasagne and wine turned into more fun than either of us thought. By nightfall I wanted to curl up in his loft but we kept the idea on ice, for a few nights at least. The cabin at the neighbours was small and had no electricity or water so it felt kind of like my childhood playhouse. There wasn't much inside of it either except I do remember Khalil Gibran's book The Prophet next to the bed where I would sit with my headlamp and journal for hours in the night. Days were spent walking on the beach and doing farm and goat things. I mostly felt on the mend and was trying to maintain a woofer cover. I agreed to make hay with Dominic at a nearby field just on the river. He had a sithe and I also took a go at it but I was clearly more useful collecting the cut hay. He had a little blue hatchback car and we just piled it inside and on the roof in a large sheet. It was really quite fun in the city slicker kind of way. City people keep their cars so clean they would never! Deelia (the one blue eyed princess mom dog with the cutest paws ever) frolicked around us while we worked on the riverside and I could hardly get the smile off of my face. Dominic told me that lots of city people like to come and do this kind of stuff. He said he gets doctors and professionals who want to sort of check out for a bit. Case in point, I thought. The best part though was giving it to the goats who would have clicked their heels if possible. As soon as they tasted the fresh hay they were climbing up the fence for more and they even wiggled their tails to my greatest delight.

I spent much time sitting, resting and sleeping as well. I felt like I had walked into a waiting room to heaven where I was safe, could relax and finally put down the bags that I had been carrying for both Bo and I for months. Dominic had a comfy Barcalounger facing a large window that I could shift left and right in for hours while he wrote music and played it till he got it right. The weather changes so quickly in Haida Gwaii that from one hour to the next you can get a new show and that was just the kind of stillness that I guess I had really been looking for. His clutter was slowly creeping up on me though. Imagine the climate is so damp that anything left outside even in summer can get rained on or wet just from the moisture in the air, meaning everything he owned had to be under cover. Plus getting rid of garbage is an issue since its a remote island. Anyways,

I was feeling like I could help since I am really good at organizing and helping people emotionally let go of shit and put in systems for new shit. Dominic was out working on digging the well (true story) so I took on prettying up his kitchen first. Parts were sincerely scary, for example open boxes with food with definite mice possibilities since they had not been stored properly or moved for years. With rolled up sleeves I dug in and turned overcrowded parts of his cabin into fully functioning spaces and new floor space! I was pleased that Dominic was so easy going about it and I think he was pleased to just have some help in places where he fell short. I could see in the little time we had spent together that chaos and clutter just didn't register much with him. He had a one track mind most of the time with his piano composing, playing, recording etc. He believes it takes a bit of chaos for creativity. The monotony of hearing a song over and over was soothing to say the least as a fellow piano player. I could tidy the clutter while he played and it was like time just didn't matter because my senses were satiated just by my surroundings. Given that, we were both careful to not let our hearts entangle though I would say Dominic put forth most effort. He explained some small town mentality of not wanting to explain things to people which I don't fully buy but went along with it anyways, considering turf, and kept any affection to a bare minimum.

Following his suggestion I decided to book a spot in the Moresby Explorers tours of the southern island, Gwaii Haanas. It was a pricy decision but it had been talked up by a few people as a once in a lifetime thing so I went for it. It seemed like it would work out well because Dominic said he could give me a ride down the island to catch the ferry to the south island. There was a gallery opening that we could go to and he would pick up some hay along the way. Lickity split and Friday came and I had my bag packed up again and ready to go. We had cleaned out a bus down the road from Dominic's that he had stored his stuff in or possibly lived in for a while when he first moved to the island. My wardrobe for the gallery opening came from that bus and I felt like a stray cat with a new collar. The drive down the island was more heaven. There is only one road and it is an all beach, all the time but with the crisp and freshness of the rainforest and wild horses starboard.

The show opening went well. It was a first for me to attend such a thing in rubber boots and wrinkled used holy clothing from a bus but I got mistaken for a local at least twice and my heart just loved it. It was an exhibition of photographs by Farah Nosh of the last 30 elders who can speak Haida. What was really nice about the opening was that there were families there and children running around. Something you don't normally see at these kinds of things. The space was full to the max with graces like a high school dance and even after everyone finished eating there was still almost an entire table left of pies. Generosity was something I was feeling a lot of up here. People always giving forward, making sure others have some when they have plenty kind of thing. How refreshing.

Dominic drove me the little stretch over to the ferry pick up and had a coupon for my ticket. We shared a held back kiss and he said nice things like I was on an adventure and it kept my momentum going. Waiting for the ferry was tricky. I was welling up inside, feeling vulnerable and alone again. I wanted to call my Mom from the payphone and then talked myself out of it because I didn't have much time and I didn't want to leave her thinking I was a mess. The deal was that the Moresby Explorer tour people were to pick people up in the morning just outside the ferry on the south island Gwaii Haanas or you could take a room at their camp and leave with the van on the way out. Dominic said it was important to ask around for a ride to their camp on the ferry ride and there was always a chance of there being no cars so he set me up with a hand drawn 'map' of a route to an abandoned cabin in the woods if I didn't get a ride to their camp and needed to wait for the ferry pick up till morning. I was leery on relying on this x-marks-the-spot sketch but he had drawn one for me before for a walk and it was pretty accurate so plan b was in place. Luckily the ferry people were hip to my situation and saw me looking around for a shotgun seat. A ferry worker suggested a car and by three I had found my ride. The ferry workers then invited me in for a coffee to their little kitchen and booth set up port side. I drifted in and out of conversation just taking it all in on this boat. Thinking about where

I was geographically, how remote, VAST and Strong it was, and being excited to see what was next. All with a lingering thought wondering if Bo was tuning in and could feel me.

Moresby camp had two sleeping options: one for hotel bucks in their new lodge that also offered breakfast in the morning, and the other as a shared room in their portable trailer home thing for cheap bucks. The girl also told me there was no one else in the portable so it was obviously the choice. I was told there was a beach party going on so I wandered down and was quenched to be offered a beer by the crew. They had a bonfire with entire huge logs on fire and made two pick up truck trips along the beach to get more wood but I had an early wake up so didn't stay out to watch it burn.

Morning was pure bliss. I woke up to the trail of a rainbow over the beach front view outside the huge front window. A sure sign I was right place right time and it only got better. We picked up the crew waiting at the ferry and set off down the logging road headed south and right into a full rainbow view. Double rainbow at times actually and I was snapping photos and raving like Paul Vasquez himself. It was just the icing on the cake as far as I was concerned because I already knew this place was the treasure. We set off to get geared up at a southern camp they had. Gear included layering the warmest clothes you can think of top and bottom, covered by Helly Hanson heavy duty foul weather gear, knee high rubber boots and a life jacket of course. One of the selling points of the Morex tours is that they are rugged meaning you crash through the waves in the same zodiacs as the Coast Guard, seated, but still holding on tight. I took a seat on the bow and we took off to the first site.

We saw three sites during my trip and went as far south as hot spring island, or Gandll K'in Gwaayaay (Haida for Hot-Water-Island). There were three outdoor hot spring baths to soak in and from two I watched a lone sailboat with heart's desire. It was a catamaran, the kind Bo had always talked about building and it looked to be an older couple. No wind for them, which I had been told to expect come late summer. I wondered about sailing from or around Haida Gwaii one day. Magik I imagine. I stayed as long as I could in the last spring looking over the ledge, until the crew leader wrangled me for the third time. I had a few more hours to soak in the beauty before having to figure out what to do next. I don't have enough words to describe how magical the Gwaii Haanas tour was. Each beach, each island had different sand, shells and life. There are watchmen who live on each island, two at a time for the summer season and their only company were people like us. They have guest books going back and stories to match. I think in three days, we saw only one other boat. Apparently you have to register with the government just to enter Gwaii Haanas, national park and all. Wildlife seen: the largest golden spruce still living on earth, two bears, many eagles and ravens but less than Masset, cotton candy jellyfish and we boated right into a feeding frenzy of hundreds of fish jumping like I had never seen before. It really was a sight of a lifetime and the tour guides were the best hosts.

The Moresby drop off was the same as the ferry pick up and I joined about three others on our way back to the North island. I didn't really have any way of staying on the south island and I don't even think there was a store. We took the ferry, while another girl and I had the same cordial ferry coffee chats as I did on the way over. By the time we docked I had lined up my ride and was set to make my way up to find a campsite near Charlotte City. There I camped by myself for a couple nights in this bay that gave me a clear example of what a 25 foot tide means. During the low tide you could walk across to what turned into full islands by high tide. It was also so close I had the waves in my dreams. It was a quiet bay and I could walk or hitchhike to town during the day for anything I needed or just to walk around. I made friends and toured around up and down island for a couple days. One highlight being balancing on balancing rock and slowing down so quietly that I could hear the difference in the wings of eagles or ravens as they flew overhead without even looking. Also bonus props to this indoor cat who has literally never set up a camp-site on her own and usually only camped in the high school days by sleeping in a truck. My dinner's got lame but it was easy to get to bed early. I had a nice fireside chat one night with a guy who came from Israel and had never seen forest like this. He told me how he arrived in Vancouver, bought his gear and a ticket to Haida Gwaii and went straight to Gwaii Haanas only to see for the first time what an actual wild forest is, no path or ground to walk through and he was bush-whacking trying to make it through barely able to get a foot on the ground. Him and his cute dog Moka.

CHAPTER FIFTEEN

KABOOM

Haida Gwaii had taken a firm grip on my heart and I felt like I had a new total direction and it was northbound and ocean centred. My life had been changed for the better and I could partially thank my trials and adversity for getting me to this blissful and strong state. Things took a turn once I boarded the plane. I could see the headlines in the newspaper bold all caps that the S&P in the USA had been downgraded. Not even really knowing what this meant it still felt like a very bad sign, and I was dreading that Bo's catastrophic predictions could slowly be coming true. I metaphorically kept my head down as long as I could on our flight back but by the time we were reaching Vancouver harbour my stomach started to sink. I felt like I was flying into interference and was clawing inside to stay where I was in my relaxed blissful relaxed Haida Gwaii mind. Millennium sky train fast tracked me back to reality. I closed my eyes in the taxi to try and limit what I was processing from the external world. No one I talked to on my way home had even heard of Haida Gwaii and I wondered how that was possible considering how beautiful and close it was. I was halfway up our stairs when Kristen opened the door, probably to take something to the recycling, and was a stunned bunny to see me walking in. "Alicia!" she said, "Call your mother" and it was another one of those ton of bricks moments where I have no idea what news is going to hit me but with that sense of urgency it can't be good. My descent into Vancouver was a stressful haze that was only lightened when my occasional enthusiasm flashback would kick in. I found out the sense of urgency to call my mother was because everyone thought I was coming home a week ago and that Bo had apparently "ditched the boat" and been missing for over a week.

The news was like being doused with cold water but my shoulders were broader now and posed and fuck him I thought. He wants to wander, fine! and I will continue to take care of things and I'll just sail our boat back to Vancouver myself. I know the old me would have been terrified of such an idea but not this girl. She just hitch hiked and backpacked Haida Gwaii and she will get Easy back, no prob. And at the same time, I was not going to jump and keep trying to cover his ass like I had in the past because I knew well enough by now that it would be a never ending story. I'm just going to settle back into my work, daydream about my trip and my piano man crush and I'll turn the ditched boat into another kind of adventure and bring her back on the weekend to our moorage. Things were quiet at home with just Charlie and I. Kristen was off looking for land to buy.

August 10, 2011
Chat with Kristen/Lal

me: hi kristen! how is the trip?

lal: Hi Alicia. Have Iyou heard from Lindsay this mornng

me: no, nothing

lal: the boat sank apparently

me: WHAT
WHAT
WHAT

lal: that is all I know...call her

me: do you know the number?

lal: 250....

me: ugh, no answer how did you hear?
holy fuck

lal: we are having a great trip otherwise..sorry about ba news

me: it can be recovered if done quickly

lal: she emailed me a few minutes ago,....keep calling and leaving messages and yr number she has gone on the line for a feew thousand dollars so she may be fixing it

me: fuck fuck
the policre are there
helicpotors
he has no insurance
she is FREAKING

lal: how dllid it sink????

me: no idea. she said she was dealing with it all night but i dont understand why she didnt call should i go over there?
jesus

lal: ask her she is on site

me: yeah she was running out the door for police

lal: police??

me: there are police there

lal: why??

me: charges maybe

lal: vandalism?

me: no idea

lal: is Bo around??

me: i have no word
nothing. i can check his banking when i get home
but other than that i dont know

lal: don't know what to say more

me: neither do i. ugh.
i am in shock. total total shock

lal: we shall have to speak later because there is nothing to be
done now

me: ok kristen. enjoy your trip

lal: so sorry about this...don't get too upset for now when there
is nothing to be done....

me: no i guess not

lal: I will call latr

me: ok

lal: Martin is here and we are all headed out to poke around

me: nice. please tell him i say hi and a hug

lal: he sends you a chaste kiss...grin
hugs from me. bye

    I panicked.

August 10, 2011
Alicia Lindsay Boswell
To Bo
URGENT
call Lindsay ASAP

August 10, 2011
Chat with Cailey

me: hey bud

Cailey: how are you feeling?

me: pretty overwhelmed i guess on the outside people would think i should just walk away and let everything burn but ive come to realize that these relationships are very valuable to me

Cailey: absolutely

me: so im just kind of sitting with that for a bit like it only hit me the other day how much it would affect charlie if i was to just take off for good

Cailey: I don't know that anyone is making any "should" judegements on your behalf.

me: im in a family here at nandostan

Cailey: i think everyone is equally stunned and clueless as to best course of action

me: last night it hit me that going through this may actually make a lifelong friendship between me and a lot of these people even Bo

Cailey: honey - it's your life. you need to do what feels good in your heart and for you.

me: having someone in his life who knows his shit and still accepts him could in turn give me a friend for life. well i also may be leaving for haida gwaii sooner than i thought

Cailey: can't wait til Jan eh?

me: there is possibly an opening at the guest house that i could do

Cailey: great

me: yeah. i would be ok with sticking it out iwht the vet for a bit but i have to honour that this is a LOT to take in a short period of time and i may not be able to keep up with it

Cailey: fair enough go at a pace that work
works. no need to add further stress

me: yeah. i mean. im really getting stretched here anyways, doing the best that i can. still helping him actually

if it wasnt for me today the gov't would have siezed it well, lindsay obviously took the lead but still.

Cailey: so update?

me: well it is currently at the bottom of the ocean and will be dragged up tomorrow morning the divers went down to salvage what they could. some personal possessions were salvaged. no idea what. still unsure why it sank but they will know more tomrrow

Cailey: holy fuck...

me: yeah, its done

Cailey: wow I can't even wrap my head around it

CHAPTER SIXTEEN

BOAT SINKING

Lindsay and I were exchanging frantic phone calls back and forth with the updates. The Coast Guard and a helicopter came to make sure no one was going down with the boat and after that they wanted someone to take responsibility or they would start pressing charges against Bo. Lindsay told me that she covered his ass before and he was happy about it so she would do her best this time to do the same even though she was pretty pissed. Apparently before taking off he had ruined her espresso machine which really is a bloody inconvenience for someone who lives on Mudge. She called in a friend, Captain Paul Grey and I tore through the city to transfer some money to cover the costs. Captain Paul Grey wanted a front of some money before getting in too deep on this pirate boat so I had to withdraw a bunch of cash to send in an envelope and trust that the ladies of Harbour Air would get it to the Captain tout suite. Meanwhile my Haida Gwaii friend Kayley was coming through town and I even kept my cool enough to sit down for some tea with her and a visit. I was freaking out about Easy going down but was still dead set to keep my centre.

August 11, 2011
Chat with Cailey

me: they found Bo on cortes
police will go tell him his boat sank and family looking for him
FML

Cailey: jesus who found him?

me: something to do with putting out a missing person report
and someone found him because someone reported a camper
acting iratically. guy who said he is from vancouver and ontario

Cailey: ha

me: cortes makes sense bc he did say he was going there so
the good news is he is alive

Cailey: that is indeed

me: and we will just wait to see the bad news lindsay and i
have beene quite a tag team in all of this

Relying on friends started taking priority and was bringing
me closer to many while separating me from others at the same time.
I felt driven to follow my heart not seeing much of another choice
before me.

August 11, 2011
Alicia Lindsay Boswell
To Rithea
Hi Rithea,
I certainly was healed in many ways on my trip. the place is utterly
magical and I intend on returning. Unfortuneately my peace was
disturbed only a few days after returning...our sailboat sunk yesterday
near Lindsay's place on Mudge. Don't know the details but it is being
pulled out today. Bo has been missing for weeks but I got word today

that they think he is on Cortes and someone is going to tell him about
the boat.
I think I may write a book.
Hugs to you, Alicia

August 12, 2011
Lindsay
To me
back at it today. THey did not get it up yesterday. Expect it to be @
Silva Bay by the end of today.

August 12, 2011
Alicia Lindsay Boswell
To Lindsay
man, that is a lot of time underwater and a lot of time getting it
up. thanks for the update.

August 12, 2011
Lindsay
To me
THe current was strong so it took longer to get the air bags in...and
the whole thing was totally locked tight, so they had to get in doing the
least damage. They got it all ready to lift @ low t
o raise and ide today. Then tow it to the Bay. It is just a big deal when
you raise them in tact rather than to dispose of.
It is taking longer thant they thoughht,due to sea conditions, but all is
fine. I will keep you posted. I have company from Toronto and Japan
arriving today, so will be out part of the dsayday. I will be on site @
11:00.
Hold tight, all will be well. Paul is the very best @ this.
Lin

August 12, 2011
Chat with Cailey

me: hey babe

Cailey: morning chica!

how was your eve?

me: lots of visitors but i was doing yoga in my room at about 930 so thats good
good bbq?

Cailey: good good yea, totally fun. the weather was spectac.
how are things today?

me: she is still underwater but expected to be on land by the end of today

Cailey: good news
police track down B?

me: sometimes i cant believe the words when they come out...
see above
anyways, no news on that

Cailey: yea it's not exactly something anyone prepares for

me: my jaw has been effing terrible

Cailey: ugh well no wonder

me: yeah. 3 weeks to relax and then this

Cailey: not ideal either way

me: lindsay told me after he "divorced me" he basically moved into her place because he couldnt be on the boat without me there

Cailey: did he ever try to get in touch with you after "the divorce"
me: yeah i could see on my phone about a week later that he had tried calling from lindsays multiple times but didnt leave any message and he called my mom a bunch of times

Cailey: i see

me: my raybands were stolen off the beach

Cailey: well curious to see what happens once he is tracked down

me: im in hate with "the city"

Cailey: shitty

me: the other night i could hear people fighting and yelling outside my window and locked the door
im not as tough as i used to be

Cailey: one day at a time chica

me: yeah, im ok with it
im just fragile for now

Cailey: you have plenty of reason to be shaken up

Cailey: G just asked me if you were sure about the Easy not having insurance he said to moo in coal harbour B would have had to provide insurance documents. we had to bring in the physical documents to our marina

me: well, i can see how he would think that but as far as i know there wasnt

Cailey: maybe check with harbour cruises and see if they have anything on file?

me: ugh. i dont really want to let them know what is going on...

Cailey: you don't have to just phone and ask if they have a copy of the insurance documents say you misplaced yours

me: ugh. lindsay wrote me to remind me that this is months away from being over

Cailey: nice
one day at a time

me: i feel like i am going to collapse. i see my therapist on the 29th
i just want an exit strategy fuck.

Cailey: why so far away?

me: it was an appointment i made with her a while ago
i just feel like i have to feel things out at 1906 still
see what k is up to
nando
and also my boss would be pretty blown if i just took off

Cailey: why don't you push it up?

me: push what up?

me: c i am having a wave
a wave of trying to get him into a hospital

Cailey: yea, that would probably be a good thing
 he definitely should see someone

me: at this point, with my heart drifting already, i dont see that i have much to loose also last night Krazy Crow (jeramyaa's mom) amped me up about it too

Cailey: only you can judge what is best for you

me: yeah its not even really about me i guess fuck i guess i may be going to cortes this weekend

Cailey: Are you coming out tonight for Brian's bday?
me: i was going to but now i dont think so
im just too down and out

Cailey: As you wish love
might do you some good to get a change of environment so you are not focussed on Bo issues though

me: i agree but being in a loud resto and drinking just doesnt sit easily with me right now.

Cailey: fair enough

me: "Pick the day. Enjoy it - to the hilt. The day as it comes. People as they come... The past, I think, has helped me appreciate the present, and I don't want to spoil any of it by fretting about the future." — Audrey Hepburn from my mom

August 12, 2011
Alicia Lindsay Boswell
To Krazy Crow
Hi Krazy Crow,

I wanted to write first to tell you that I heard about putting your dog down. I am sorry to hear that. John told me, remorsefully. Seems like a lot of people are going through tough times....

I have been thinking about calling the police and getting Bo into a hospital. On one shoulder people tell me not to get involved, that I will just look like the bad guy...etc. On the other shoulder I somehow feel like it is my responsibility since there is no one closer to him in the position to help.

I am so torn and so pressured by all of this. Lindsay told me from her experience that involving police or hospital would just make him angry and won't result in much because he will talk his way out of it and may react worse.

Inside I just want to collapse or run away.
Wondering what your thoughts are...?
Love Alicia

August 12, 2011
Krazy Crow
To me

i have another view,look at charlie,if he'd been hospitilized early,he may have a chance of more of a life,with presence of mind,look at john,yeah it was difficult to take him to the hospital,but he's gotta life,,,so i say a lot of people ar'ent being realistic,maybe cause it's too painful,i do'nt know,,i say fuck the anger and fuck what you look like,,if you feel in your heart you want to help,then do it,and if not then do'nt.

the question is if you want to,how are you gonna without bo's cooperation,he may just attract so much attention from the police,that he may end up in the hospital anyway,cause nows he's dissrupting other people,he got beaten up before from someone,i guess he pisses a lotta people off,he showed up here once,all dis combobulated,and bruised,so someone had enough of him,,when he's in these states

so thats the problem,also if your detaching yourself from the relation,i dont think you should take it on,theres too much emotioninal between you two.right now your pissed off at him too,for his dishonesty etc,and those feelings may come out while trying to help him,and then there would just be craziness,,sooooooo

if you want to run away your allways welcome here.

grampa used to say,do'nt try to help anyone,unless they ask for help,cause then,, it could end up putting the blame or anger or what-ever feelings come up,on the person who was trying to help,, if he gets in a space where he is clear there's several people he can ask for help,,,and if he dosent,sooner or later,help will be forced on him,if he keeps disrupting people,

*i'm just writing down things as they come out,and just re-read your
e-mail,if you call the police,is there any way you can do it,without
Bo knowing your the one who called,you can allways ask them,think
about these things and write me back when you feel like it.*

 *thanks for your thoughts on our dog millie,it was a sad day,but noth-
ing to compare from all the great days ,,she had a great life'and lived 14
years,shes at camp with tewa dog now.love yourself,and go easy,luvya,
Krazy Crow*

Conversations with so many family and friends revealed new
information to me that Bo and the other boys had all come from a
small town and they played together as young boys. More than half of
them ended up with similar mental illnesses that onset in their later
teenage years and the feeling at the time was that the local lakes had
been contaminated with former small mining operations. Lindsay,
Krazy Crow and Kristen had Erin Brockoviched it for their boys far
as they could but I presume the battle just became too steep to take
on any further.

August 13, 2011
Alicia Lindsay Boswell
To Bo

*today is the worst. i feel like you have died. i am writing an email to
no one. the person i knew has vanished or rather, self-imploded. i cant
hold back tears anymore. i cant pretend to be ok. i cant go outside.
sirens and busses and cars feel like they are driving over the top of
my head. my jaw tension is worse than ever. i dont know what you
expect to happen or how long you think i can wait through this. i have
no one to ask, no one to talk to. i am not ok anymore. the stress has
manifested physically and i am inches from my breaking point. all of
my dreams and everything we worked at together has been destroyed.
i cant carry on like this.*

CHAPTER SEVENTEEN

EASY RETURNS

After three days under water I was sent 27 photos of Easy and all her glorified damage. The highlight was the mast… completely covered with seaweed.

Everyone agreed that we thought it would look worse, that it kind of just looked wet and the reality was actually uplifting from the fears I was facing in my head.

August 16, 2011
Lindsay
To me
No it looks pretty good. Although it seemed like a long time under the water…it really was not. We acted really quickly and there is a good current there so .o do that extra work.o have the jewellery delivered, so sorry you need t
Alex was t ops, I will stop in today when on the other sidenot heard from the ct kept "flushing". The real damage comes from after it is out of the water, but I think you will be able to do some yourself as well the shipyard are pros.

Notice I sent the CC to Bo. In case he checks his e-mail...he will know.
I have bputer sucks! Hopefully on Wednesday I will have my new one
working!
Lindsay
Com

Mom sent me links about how to clean wooden boats after they have sank and Vicky from the shipyard confirmed that the boys in the yard were "still trying to stabilize her." Things looked so good I even emailed to ask if they could put aside the Mexican blankets that we had on board but Vicky confirmed that they went out with the garbage and all other diesel and salt water soaked items. I was so paranoid and out of my mind at the time I actually looked up the Gabriola island garbage schedule wondering if she was lying to me. Clinging to garbage at this point.

August 17, 2011
Chat with Cailey

me: morning hon

how was the boat party?

Cailey: hey chica!
just a bbq. hardly a party it was great. chill. just anchored at wreck and went swimming

me: ah wreck

Cailey: got some sun and packed 'er in before dark
we've been spending most our time off wreck because it's the closest to where we are moored and it fucking rocks, of course.

me: totally :)

Cailey: how are you?

me: im ok today

im still getting up in the morning and doing my yoga so im happy about that

Cailey: that's good - a great way to start the day just doing it at home? or going somewhere?

me: at home, in my room

Cailey: cool

me: just whatever i feel like with some structure

Cailey: that's good

me: so i think im around this weekend. what are you guys up to?

Cailey: good question. I don't think we have anything planned the forecast looks great - so probably will be spent on Serenity RFN.
no idea

me: what is the rfn detail?

Cailey: Right Fucking Now.

me: ha

Cailey: She came with the name Serenity, so we have to add our bit. It's pretty appropriate

me: ah, so nice

Cailey: Yea I got to find someone who can add the RFN on the back as a suprise for G

me: did i tell you i am going to a buddhist regreat? 10 days meditation 430am-9pm (with breaks) no talking for 10 days

Cailey: wow
where's that?
me: no communication ...only 1 hour per day if you book to talk
to an instructor
its called vipassana they have them all over the world

CHAPTER EIGHTEEN

COMMUNICATION BREAKDOWNS

August 17, 2011

Lindsay

To me

I got the package this afternoon @ Tofino. Thank you for sending the jewelry...sorry it was not delivered to you! I passed the envelopes on to Don and he is holding Paulsk in the Am.

the boat is not soo soo ba until he gets bac

d, damage for sure, but all things considered! He thinks it was the head as it was wide open when they checked. The stuff wnas pretty oily and asty from the toxin bloom, but coulkd have been worse!

I stipped inyt; rtjast co[show tiodayt to see if there awas any word on Bo, They said thay would let me know after 5:neo,ive out any other inf. All I will know is if they saw him...thay can not goight. If I hear anything I will of course let you knto

God Dam Fucking Computer!!!!!

Hope you can read this,

L

August 18, 2011
Alicia Lindsay Boswell
To Lindsay
Hi Lindsay, I think I get the gist of the email. I agree that it is not
as bad as I thought. I was re reading my journal last night and was
reminded that Bo's plan was actually to travel around the world for
years. He has been following his other "plans" as clockwork, next being
taking off to Ontario in September.
Talk to you later, Alicia

August 18, 2011
Chat with Cailey

me: im not feeling well :(

Cailey: as in coming down with something?

me: no
as in breaking down

Cailey: anything specific? are there new developments? or just
feeling the stress of it all?

me: i had a panic attack yetserday driving cant stop crying
finding it hard to concentrate

Cailey: you've bee really stong
strong
if you need to cry and have a bit of a freak out, you should

me: i just feel like i cant keep up anymore

Cailey: maybe you need to stop trying to then?

me: yep

Cailey: let go. and find the good in life

me: i guess i will move my stuff back to my parents and start from there?

Cailey: that is probably a very reasonable move

me: i dont see what else i can do

Cailey: well you could move to masset

me: or just go to masset

Cailey: or that
or go anywhere for that matter

me: save some money. in a couple months

Cailey: working towards that is a positive goal

me: problem is i am finding it increasingly difficult to work or do much for that matter

Cailey: well you need somehting to look forward to…make a plan and work torwards it. just going through the motions for no apparent reason is not inspiring for anyone

me: yeah i dont have a plan

Cailey: make one
or continue as is. those are your options.

me: well the plan was to go back to masset for a while which everyone keeps telling me is running away

Cailey: so what if it is
fuck - sometimes we need a break from life

me: now is a time i needa break from life

Cailey: no shit

go to masset, decompress, sort your head out, create a plan.
what's wrong with that?
Beats staying here with the ghost of Bo following you around,
causing you stress.

me: it is a ghost causing me stress
a lot of it

Cailey: exactly

me: so...ab going to masset then
i just have to make sure i buy a ticket out...just in case

Cailey: that'd be a good idea

me: just got a nice email from g :(

Cailey: why sad face?
nice emails usually have the opposite effect

me: it was sweet. makes me want to cry

Cailey: I don't think that was the response he was hoping for

me: the new blog: how to live on $20/hour in vancouver?

August 19, 2011
Lindsay
To me
*.B I think the dingey was located. It is on the beach @ Elveran
aeOTO It would be really good if I had a photo, or some identifying
information. I think it is his, I can have Scottbring it across and trailer
it to my place and have him it winterized or you can get a trailer and
get it back to Vancouver and have it winterized there. o to go, way to
stressed getting ready for the AM, and I need to go to bed,*
XOXO
L
G

August 20, 2011
Alicia Lindsay Boswell
To Lindsay
attached photo of part of the dinghy. Not sure what the condition is
like but it has a hole in the floor of it (the inside part, on one side) and
i think there may be a patch attempt on it as well. walker bay, and i
believe there is some red/rust colour paint that rubbed off while we had
it on dry dock before.
talk to you monday, have a nice weekend!

August 22, 2011
Alicia Lindsay Boswell
To Bo
my god i miss you so much today. my body cringes from the inside out.
it wants you on the inside. i want you back. i want to hold you. i feel
so sad.

      I was comforted by friends.

August 23, 2011
Michael
To Alicia Lindsay Boswell
Dear A l i c i a ,

I was moved to come across this picture of you two
when the dream was alive. I think you have been
doing brilliantly dealing with the changes.

It isn't easy.

I have new prints, lovely shots, of you and E l l e n
making music in the garden, and a porch shot
of you with the dough. I'll bring them by.
Soon,
M i c h a e l .

CHAPTER NINETEEN

SHE'S BACK

August 26, 2011
Chat with Cailey

me: hey girl i saw Easy yesterday

Cailey: Went to Gabriola (or whereever she is)?

me: yep

Cailey: and?

me: it was very very sad

Cailey: yea I bet

me: she looks dead

Cailey: well the pictures sure didn't look good

me: but the boat owner calmed me down
boat yard owner

Cailey: that's good

me: and he said in about 2 weeks he thinks it will be running and floating

Cailey: really?

me: structure is in good shape

Cailey: wow
that suprises me

me: hatch is torn apart, life lines all need to be replaced

Cailey: looked like a fucking lot of worked needed to be done to me from those pictures

me: well totally
i mean
electrical and on top of that everthing has been stripped out. its a clean slate

Cailey: wow

me: the walls would need to be scraped off and repainted anyways, lots of work but i left feeling much calmer about it and if i can actually motor/sail her back in 2 weeks time...wow

Cailey: I hate to say it but you will be able to knock me over with a feather if that boat is sailable in 2 weeks

me: how so?

Cailey: I don't know - it just seems like a pretty ambitious time-line but if that's the case, great
who is doing the work?

me: well a sailboat is a pretty simple machine
the hull and everything there is totally fine

the rudder has come off but he is charing me 200$ or so to get that fixed

Cailey: that is much cheaper than I would have guessed
thumbs up

me: well i mean to EVERYTHING is gone
so we are talking cushions
radio
gagets
inverter
batteries

Cailey: it's an empty shell basicallt

me: bare bones in a sense but i dont really care that much. i just was distraught to think of Easy being damaged but there isnt much to her
no cracks in the hull i dont think
even the hammock is still there and Bo's swim ladder stayed on as well
so i think im getting a scooter
http://vancouver.en.craigslist.ca/rds/mcy/2564327706.html
what are you up to this weekend?

Cailey: We are going to Gibsons with the 210 Fleet (Wilson's boat & our friend Donny's boat).

me: neat gibsons is quaint

Cailey: nenver been

me: you'll have fun

Cailey: we always do! ;)

me: i dont know what i am doing this weekend yet

Cailey: Nando's back?

me: not quite. this coming week

Cailey: ah

me: k was having a conniption the other day freaking on charles

Cailey: why?

me: he broke a 10k statue of hers

Cailey: jesus

me: nose off the beak of a carving

Cailey: fuck
bummer

me: pretty much
although i cant say it is his fault. i myself dropped the same statue on the beak and it didnt break
it is misleading bc it comes apart in a place where it doesnt look like it should
and i bet it was dropped 50 times before it finally broke

Cailey: alas
these things happen

CHAPTER TWENTY

HEART IN HAIDA GWAII

August 27, 2011
Dominic
To me

Hi Alicia, just got back from canoeing, am only home two days, going
kayaking on saturday for 8 days, back round sept 4th evening,
the canoeing trip was great, 250 km down the spatsizi and stikine river,
we were 4 people, 2 canoes,
all got along good,
was in a canoe with Sarah, this girl from hazelton/ smithers area, we
worked good together and had good chats,
was a different world, didn't see anyone, hiked in the alpine a bit too,
great to be on a river, lots of rapids the last few days were constant,
exciting,

brought home a new goat too, so I have 6 now, she's a sweet one, milk
is so rich and creamy,

what are you up to for the next bit in your life? are you staying around
in that house in Van?
any other leads/ / options coming to mind or feeling like you're headed
there slowly?
talk soon,
Dominic

Dominic and I were still in touch which was like having a life line in a friend. He shared with me a final recording of one of the songs he was working out while I was up visiting and kept me up to date with his goats and dog Deelia. I was trying to figure out what to do with my life thinking a vipassana might be the right step. It would be a huge step for me seeing as I was so addicted to talking but was wanting to quiet the mind.

A lot was changing around the house because Nando was coming back and Kristen was an inch away from buying her dream property, 160 acres in Lilooet so she could install some huge statues that were being supposedly being carved and shipped from India. The house was emptying quickly and still no sight of Bo. I was doing my best to wait things out, waiting for the right thing to come up. Still tossing around the idea of getting a scooter but as Dominic pointed out, they suck in Haida Gwaii so my leads were drying up faster than I could find them.

August 28, 2011
i can't get out of the pain today. kristen and i have cried on and off all
day. we have been trying to figure out your history and when you have
had these breaks in the past. i just can't get you out of my head today.
i miss you so terribly much. i broke an egg cup while cleaning. i keep
moving with total distraction in my head because part of me is with
you.

please come home. please be ok. Bo i love you, i am worried about
you and i miss you.
where can i find you? i want to hold you and kiss your head. and just
hold you.

August 28, 2011
Matty
To me
check check check checking in.
Matty

August 28, 2011
Alicia
To Matty
Nothing to report. Terribly worried about b these days. Kind of down and sleeping a lot. May go to Cortes next weekend. U?

August 28, 2011
Matty
To me
Craziness killed the cat, or in this case, sunk the boat.
Go to Cortes, get your wild woman on. Get some outdoor love.
In Brisbane, parents gone, doing laundry and booking hostels! Montreal done, Surfer's paradise next.
Yours in spirit.

CHAPTER TWENTY-ONE

CORTES

August 29, 2011
Alicia
To Mom
hi mom,

how are you? how was your dinner? yesterday was a pretty blue day for me. im meeting my therapist tonight, nando comes back tonight as well. kristen and i have been on and off crying for days now. i thnk i will go to cortes this weekend...to tell Bo i love him and that we all miss him or just to go for a visit to cortes since i have never been there and it is the closest easy place to get to near desolation sound.
maybe we can do a beach dog walk before i leave? wed?
love you. xoxo

August 29, 2011
Mom
To me
Is he still on Cortes, have there been sightings? Will you be taking the car? When you get a chance please call me it is so hard to communicate through email.
Love Mom

August 29, 2011
Chat with Cailey Murphy

me: hey boat babe

Cailey: hey chica

me: hey hon

Cailey: how was your weekend?

me: ok
how was the boat trip?

Cailey: fuck
so much fun

me: nice

Cailey: what did you get up to?

me: not much
slept a lot,
went paddleboarding on sat with john

Cailey: cool
how was that?

me: its a cinch to pick up

Cailey: haha
good to know. doesn't look overly complicated

me: it wasnt even excercise

Cailey: haha. alas
can't be for everyone

me: i guess im pretty blue c

Cailey: it too shall pass...what's on your mind?

me: just utter sadness, missing him

Cailey: I'm sorry babe.
any update on his whereabouts?

me: nope
i spent most of sunday trying to figure out when he had breaks
before and how long they have lasted
seems like it is about 6 months before he looks "ok" again

Cailey: how long has it been now?

me: 3 months

August 30, 2011
Chat with Cailey Murphy

me: fuckity fuck fuck
im really going to need a break soon

Cailey: what are your plans for the long weekend?

me: nothing solid. may go to cortes...but its like a $600 trip so
im not sure

Cailey: jesus that's kinda crazy expensive

me: 3 ferries and driving to campbell river

Cailey: my god

me: im including gas and everything

Cailey: fucking bc ferries is ridic

me: i think the ferries alone, with car are like 150 each way

Cailey: better off to fly to CR

me: but i need a car because you have to drive across quadra for the final ferry and there are no taxis or transport on cortes either

Cailey: rent one
it's probably cheaper

me: in nanaimo? then i have to bus from horshoe bay and back

Cailey: I was thinking fly to CR and rent one there

me: the logistics and only 4 days make it hard to figure out

Cailey: but I have spent exactly 4.5 seconds on the logistics of that

me: could do
any other ideas of what a girl could/should do for her 30th?

Cailey: Me, I'd spend it with friends.

me: i find it difficult to be with friends these days

Cailey: not sure babe. it's not really a headspace I can put myself in and give you a well thought out recommendation

me: gotcha

September 1, 2011
Chat with Cailey Murphy

me: morning hon

Cailey: hey honey!

how's it goi'?

me: pretty good

Cailey: good good

me: thanks for the text

Cailey: free tonight? have a pre-day drink with me?

me: :(nope. i woke at 6am this morning and decided to just go to the island straight from work. i even washed the car this morning!

Cailey: oh fek. so you are doing the cortes trip?

me: its ok. i haven't seen anyone/planned anything pre-birthday. i think it is something to do in sept when i get back

Cailey: ok - I told Emerson and G they were in charge in the event you stayed around. We can bump it to the next weekend maybe

me: aw thanks hon.

Cailey: what ferry are you catching?

me: yeah. i honestly didn't decide what to do until this morning. and g informed me a bit more about the drive so i decided against the scooter for this trip. to tofino it would make more sense i think, but not to cortes
ferry...not sure. i think ill leave work around 3?

Cailey: you leave from Horseshoe Bay right?

me: yeah then to nanaimo then drive to campbell river
then ferry to quadra then drive across quadra then ferry to cortes
its nuts

Cailey: yea, that is totally nuts

seriously wtf
you'd think they'd try to make it atleast a little more accessible

me: i think that is the whole point
keeps it desolate

CHAPTER TWENTY-TWO

TURNING 30

So it is the week leading up to my 30th birthday which this year falls on a Sunday, the best day to have it during a long weekend because it gives you a day of rest after and a full birthday week before. I am excited this year because I feel like I am ready for whatever 30 means including leaving all the speed bumps and guardrail crashes of the 20's behind me and into the smooth experience-based cruising. I have decided to do the Cortes trip and even though I haven't planned anything birthday I figure it will be something I can look forward to when I get back. I couldn't decide what to do until this morning and since G informed me a bit more about the drive I decided against the idea of taking a scooter for the trip…Tofino might make sense but not to Cortes. My ferry trip is three fold and I may not stay on Cortes that long, I haven't read very nice things about visiting. People say it is all private property and no beach access. I am not going there to look for Bo. I have wanted to go to Cortes for years and it is the closest thing to Desolation Sound that I can get to without a boat so that makes up more than half of my reason to go there. If B and I cross then good but I am not going to hunt him down. Yep, sounds like a plan. I don't even know if he is there for sure although I was wrong when I thought that he had taken out insurance, I don't think he even has wheels now.

I am just going to go and if I see him I will tell him I love him and that we all miss him. My bottom line is that I can't be in a relationship with him if he wants to continue this pattern. Scratch that, I don't WANT to be in a relationship... Far too difficult and I have reasoned it as being far too time consuming being worried about someone for 6 months! Come on. As always, I am flexible and I can accept a lot, especially when I believe that someone is trying their best but status quo of ignoring the issue doesn't fly with me. Ok, I have to leave work earlier than I thought. I am so proud of myself, I have really fallen in love with these solo adventures. I am not sure where I will be sleeping but I brought Cailey's bag and tent and it may be the car even, not sure yet. I feel really small lately. Small as in not thinking ahead too much, guiding myself by how I feel in the moment, not reaching or branching out but staying quiet, mostly sober. I could call it 'going inside.' It's like I fell and got the wind knocked out of me and I walk away from everyone to sit by myself for a few minutes to calm down and gather myself. I have a few minutes by myself before leaving work and my heart is starting to warm up. I don't know what I am going to find ahead of me on Cortes and Bo has been missing for weeks now and I don't even know if he knows about Easy sinking. I decide last minute to draft up a MISSING poster with the last photo I took of bearded Bo and I print out a few copies for the road.

I am tearing in the bimmer to make the 3pm ferry and finally squeeze into the starboard stern corner and put the emergency brake on. Hands on the wheel and I take it all in. By the time I am coming back I will be 30. Although, I want to give myself a safety net and decide that if everything turns to shit I will come back to Van and spend Sunday dancing it up with my friends like old times. I feel energy where I just want to turn up some music smile and laugh followed by intermittent blue waves wondering what will happen to Bo, Easy and I. I wish I had the nerve to roll a joint, or would have thought enough to bring a drink for the road and I decide to wander my way out of the vehicle deck and take a seat under the Queen's photo and take in the view. I can squint my eyes ever so slightly so that the sun reflecting off each wave begins to look like twinkling lights making the most fantastic patterns! I marvel at the tricks that our eyes can do that still cannot be replicated as easily with a camera and make a mental note of these magical sparkles. I am watching a young boy and his older brother climbing up and down part of the boat to get a view out the bow window. The younger one doesn't speak yet and keeps his fingers mostly curled up except for pointing. His brother proclaims to have spotted a whale and his mother says that he might have but that it is unlikely because the Captain would have announced it to everyone and I don't like her curbing suggestion. The longer I watch the two brothers coming back and forth, up and down at the window I have time to imagine Bo in that small form, so innocent, pure and wide eyed. One of the only stories he told me about about being small was one argument between his mom and dad and they each had one of his arms trying to pull him apart between each other over who he would go with. I think his father won that time.

I take a walk around to pick up paper paraphernalia required to get me up to my desolation destination and sit back down to chart my trip. Working backwards I quickly learn that getting to Cortes tonight is out of the question because the last ferry to get there leaves Quadra at 5 and the drive up island alone is two hours and more if I want to take the highly recommended ocean side route so I am a few hours behind. I take out the map to decide where I might want to spend the night and curiosity settles on Courtenay recalling one of my elementary school friends had relocated there years ago and it looked nice in pics. So I quickly fire off an email (can't believe it is working on the ferry!) to a hostel to line something up. My mind has enough material to keep me amused and occupied during our crossing and before I know it we are marching down to the vehicle deck and I turn back to pick up a green string, likely discarded for being torn off and half torn apart from whatever it was previously tied around. On my wrist I am still wearing the grey string that Bo darned and the brown threads that I have tied round to keep me connected and protecting Bo and Easy. Heading into this unknown weekend and unknown second third of my life I think it is time to have string like that for myself, Alicia, to stay connected and protected, and I tie it to my wrist with the others as we scrape our bow into the ferry terminal welcoming us to Nanaimo.

CHAPTER TWENTY-THREE

HELLO DESOLATION SOUND

I spent the night in Courtenay and my eyes bolt open suddenly as I wake up on my hostel top bunk and I feel the big day ahead of me. New territory, possibility of seeing/not seeing Bo and a definite 30th birthday coming straight at me on Sunday. After a few minutes of a slow rise I am gathered and out the door to find the first and only coffee shop open, and get directions to Campbell River and the ferry. The drive continues along the oceanside and I am feeling less than calm. Memories of the the movie Twister when Helen Hunt is driving like crazy into the tornado with her truck loaded up with ping pong balls kind of feeling. But I look around me and the sun is shining and the water is calm so I remind myself to keep it together and not spend time living the future of problems I have not yet even encountered. I will have a wonderful weekend alone on Cortes, worst case scenario (not bad!) The ferry from Campbell River to Quadra is slow and uneventful. I spend most of it trying to hold balancing yoga poses on the foredeck pretending I am floating on the water while we cruise and I look around me but don't see anyone that seems open to talking so I just go with it. The drive across Quadra is longer and twistier than

I thought and lacking some signage however even a novice would know well enough to stay with the convoy till the other side so I am fine and then we load the ferry. I know my nerves are getting to me now because I am biting at the skin around my nails, sometimes until it bleeds, and I know it is not much after 10am but I am fixing for a drink so I go to my trunk for the vodka stash. I am digging around in my bag for morning cocktail material when one of the ferry workers starts walking my way. Now I know they are not police or anything but still probably not a good idea to bring out the vodka so I grumble about it and then close the trunk on my little plan. He wants to make small talk and seems nice enough so I use it as the chance to tell my real story and pull out the missing poster and ask him if by chance he has seen this guy, Bo. I can see his eyes sort of widen probably with his brain as he sieves through his ferry traffic memories but doesn't come up with anything. He calls his worker friend over to take a look and they invite me upstairs to have a coffee. I love this about the BC Ferry workers! They were similarly hospitable on my ferry to Gwaii Haanas and I am cordially impressed. They fix me a coffee and then they invite me into the Captain's quarters so I can ask the other ferry worker's if they have seen him. The cockpit is kind of what you would typically expect, large wood wheel and all. I give them the coles notes about my crazy love story while we drink our coffees and take in the morning sun. At one point the wheel spins a little to one side and I instinctually reach out to control the ship and then quickly pull back thinking of how aggro they would react on an airplane or something if you tried to do that. Greg, my new ferry worker friend, kind of laughs and says it is ok if I want to hold the wheel for a bit and he points out the gadgets and meters that help me steer the course. Coffee down, two hands and I am driving the ferry to Cortes! I want to hold on as long as I can so I ask them about what wildlife they have seen during this crossing and we talk about whales and dolphins. Dolphins! I think. Bo saw dolphins during a ferry crossing once when he was working in Sechelt and my jealousy kicks in as I whine, "dolphins, really?" I can see the ferry landing dock now and start heading us in that direction wondering how long my friends will let me continue my debut as Miss Capitan and I guess Greg reads my mind because he nicely excuses himself back into position for landing and tells me I can't be in there while they dock. Considering all the problems BC Ferries has had in the past while I put up no fuss and thank him kindly for his time and concern. The other ferry worker hands me a map he just printed of Cortes with some highlights of how to get around and what is what. Greg tells me he has a camper near The Gorge and that I could wander over and find him if I needed to. The other ferry worker wishes me luck but laughs and says I will have no problem finding Bo and to just check with the store because on a small island like Cortes it is tough to hide.

I take that thought in my mind and repeat it, tough to hide, tough to hide, as I drive onto the island. Looking at the expansive dense forest and the size of the island, I begin to doubt this no-hiding idea because he could literally be camping in any of these woods! I have no plan at this point other than to follow my intuition and my first thought is to find the flow here by watching people for a while or going to the town centre. The missing posters are starting to get the best of me and I feel like I am in a scene from a dramatic movie (my mind repeats, I can't believe I am putting up missing posters of my boyfriend!) as I watch myself go through these motions. I take my first intuitive turn and get to a dead end with a dock and decide to put up my first poster. I mean, he is missing right? No one has heard from him or seen him in a month and we know he is going through something heavy…does he even know that   our boat sank? I assure myself, tack it up with four corners and as I am walking back to my car I notice four women in their car and ask them for some guidance to the centre of town. One thing leads to another and they ask me about the sign I just put up and slight concern comes into their faces and they tell me a good place to try next. I park the car, missing poster in the rear dash, and try to get my bearings. By now the desolation of this place is starting to sink in and I have nothing lined up and I am kicking myself for not putting together a better plan B. I sit on a rock in the parking lot and watch people mill around me as they are getting ready for the Saturday market. I am getting really angry in my head and start hating Cortes and everything about it. I tell myself that no one would walk past me crying on a rock if I was in Haida Gwaii!

Here everyone glances at you then quickly away, like in the city, so I have a smoke and cry on a rock, for a while. The only lead I have is that I know Pawl, one of Kristen and Nando's long time friends, lives on Cortes and he was one of the people who saw Bo and a girl in the community centre says that she knows Pawl and writes down his number for me. I am relieved when Pawl picks up the call until says he hasn't seen him but says that he could come find me and show me where he did see him last. He tries to describe how to get to the old maple tree over the phone but it quickly gets hazy so I agree to meet and hang up.

Hearing that Bo was here and seeing how small it was I walked over to the Co-op to see if I could get any more information. I walked into the grocery store side and sort of felt my way around looking for the right person to ask and I wandered my way through the saloon doors into the cafe side. It is quiet and I am afraid to really even say anything because even through the music I think everyone can hear everyone. Before I have a moment to let that sink in the girl behind the counter says "can I help you" and it turns the key into my heart. I pull out the missing sign and tell her that I am here looking for my boyfriend who is having a mental breakdown and the chef comes over to take a look as well. It takes her only a moment and she presses her lips with her index finger and says that she has seen him. "Bo," he says, "YES," I say. She says she saw him down at the old maple tree only a day or two ago. My mind starts racing (a day or two!) to get any information I can and the chef tells me that he has seen him too, and leans in to softly tell me that he has not been well. I tell him that is exactly why he got here and why I was there and that he is suffering from a manic episode and that he is normally a wonderful loving man. I ask him what was 'not well' about him and Chef tells me that in the summer he was talked to by the police about screaming at children (about what?) screaming that he would kill them, he said with big eyes. "And he doesn't like Americans, thats for sure" says Chef. I nod and tell him that is consistent with how he was before he left Vancouver and they tell me how to find him. "It isn't easy to find," she said "but if you drive down the end of this road and take it all the way to the end, walk down the path and when you see the prayer flags go to your right and you will end up at the maple tree." Sounds easy enough and I am hugging them for giving me a lead and putting up with Bo's antics all this time. And Chef tells me he was really acting weird (how?) he was wearing garlic on a string on his neck for vampires, he says. And Chef looks down and asks if I have any other shoes than my flip flops because the path down to the beach can get kind pretty mucky but I would go barefoot at this point and my mind is racing. Bo? here? now? only moments away? And as my racing heart starts leading me towards the door the guy pauses me by telling me that when she walked there the other day and saw him, "he looked peaceful," she said. Peaceful, started resonating in my mind. "He looked really at peace," she followed. And it was enough for me to drop the mixed emotions and just open my heart with acceptance and love and I was off.

CHAPTER TWENTY-FOUR

THE MAPLE TREE

I am jazzed to hear that Bo had been spotted only days ago so even though Pawl is on his way I can't wait around and risk the chance I could miss him. Besides, take a right at the prayer flags, how tough can it be? So I drive to the end of the road and end up looping through a driveway and can't find the path. Ok, try the other end I think and it is a driveway as well. I am looking left and right and my mind is turning it over about which way to go and a pick-up truck starts heading my way. I lean onto his window and ask him where the path to this Maple tree is. "It's Native Land," he tells me. I know, I know, I lie and tell him I am meeting a friend who may be camping there and he makes sure to tell me there is no camping allowed on the land there but that the path is down in the corner at the end of the road and he points behind him with his thumb. "Thanks!" and I'm off parking the car just in front of the no parking sign at the dead end. With my history and nickname tickets and towing or t-squared for short, I can hear my Dad's voice reprimanding me for it but I reason that it would take ages to get a tow truck here and leave it at that. And I am walking through this path and start remembering that they said it was difficult to get to and it is taking longer than I had thought. Prayer flags, looking for prayer flags, and at the same time I feel Bo all around me, all through the path and breath in where he did and walk where he did. And then I get a call from Kristen (I can't believe my phone is working in these woods!) and yammer off that I had touched in with Pawl and just talked to someone who saw Bo two days ago and she wishes me luck and suggests we both go to Hollyhock for a long hot stone massage once we find each other. I am not sure she really gets the fact that I am tearing through unknown woods to find my boyfriend who has been missing for a month but the suggestion is nice and under regular circumstances quite fitting. And thank goodness I have a good eye for prayer flags because they were much more tattered than I was looking for and they were fairly miniature not to mention that they are hanging at waist level, anyways I spot the prayer flags and take the right. I am gaining speed now, adrenaline fuelled and my phone rings again! This time it is a jumbled up number and I wonder if it is someone responding to my MISSING poster so I answer and it is my friend Nadia calling from Germany on Skype. I react with laughter at the terrible timing of her call knowing that we haven't spoken for months and there is no way I can catch her up now. Sorry Nadia, bad timing but I love you and I hang up. I can smell the water now and my heart is racing. I know he has been here and after three months of this shit and now one month of not even knowing where he is I feel it welling up inside of me. If I get to this beach and he is not here and I spend the weekend crying my eyes out for my birthday I just don't…and I start screaming his name. Bo! (I am surprised to hear my own voice) Bo!!!! (where the hell are you!!???) BooOOOUUUH!!!!!!!!!!! (I don't care who hears me, I am screaming this for the universe to hear!) and I get to a fork in the road. Left looks like more woods, right looks more direct to the beach, hum, haw, and I bolt right and my feet get to the sand and I am catching my breath. Standing on the beach I quickly scan the horizon and take two steps to my left and he is standing there. I stop as if walking into a glass wall, frozen by this sight before my eyes…that I had dreamed about for months. Bo, in the flesh and I can't believe it. Just as Kristen had predicted when this all started, he is thinner and now has a full beard and is dressed differently. He is wearing an off-white shell of a jacket that looks like it is yellowing at the seams, long black shorts that are falling off of his hips and duct taped ankle strap sandals and has a backpack that he is clenching to his shoulder with one hand and he just looks stunned. Stunned as if someone just lifted the veil on his Truman show.

"What's in the bag" he pressed. "You want to know what is in my bag!" I say stomping my way through the sand over to it..."here! This is what is in my bag" I say pulling out the missing poster sign and handing it to him and I feel him flinch as I even come that close to him so I pull back then try to get close again and try to touch him with my hand but he pulls away. I pull back again and move my bag further away in the sand and stand there with my hands on my hips having simply no idea what to do next and he sits down on his beach perch log. I need to reset this scene so I strip my tube dress over my head, slip my under ware off, noticing but giving little mind to Bo's eyes shamefully looking away as though he had not seen me naked so many times and I walk my skinny-dipping self into the clear, still, almost fresh water and as soon as I get in up to my knees I dive in head first, open my eyes and let it wash over me and cool me inside and out and I swish around like that a few times until I feel cleansed enough to walk back out.

CHAPTER TWENTY-FIVE

CORTES LIVING

I still couldn't get much closer than a few feet from Bo without him getting agitated and I kneeled in the sand, ran it through my fingers and watched him sit on his wood seat occasionally holding his head looking at me, the ground and his view across the water to Campbell River. I could hear in my heart his worlds colliding as he tried to gather himself back to our concept of time and space. "How did you find me?" he finally said. And I sort of told him the story including driving the ferry over but when I heard myself laughing, I quickly withdrew from telling him much more without knowing how he was and I asked him for some water. He directed me to a bottle by the log next to the grass just behind us and told me it was the last that he had of water. He told me it was ok though because he would just collect more down the beach from one of the trees in the woods. "Where?" I asked him, feeling eager to clear my head for a minute. "Way down the beach, you have to go over fallen trees, and there is a flat rock and you can just hear it," he said, "I would be pretty surprised if you found it!" he laughed. Naturally taking it as a challenge I set off thinking what the hell does he know, I was just in Haida Gwaii. It was a long walk down the beach, long enough that I turned back and took a photo to remember the point he was at. I climbed under, over and through the water around a few fallen trees and then just like he said I could hear it, the water trickling sound in my ear opposite the ocean. I filled the bottles and tried to come up with a plan. It didn't get very far because I needed to know more about Bo and my heart started racing at the idea of spending time WITH Bo, instead of just thinking of him. *Why was he looking away at my body like that? What if he won't let me touch him?* and I walked back. He chuckled at my successful water run and offered to make me a coffee. Yes please, it felt like him. He had a cracking voice that would break like he had not used it or had used it too much and he semi-sheepishly pointed out his coffee prep method which was boiling water in a large coconut water can, like a soda can, on a rock or in the fire. When it was too hot to touch he would move it around by picking it up with a twig through the loop in the metal flip tab and then pour it into a pre-used tea filter bag filled with store-ground coffee. The filter's were each pierced twice by the ends of a twig with enough over hang that the twig would rest on the mouth of the mason jars he used as cups. And he had coffee easily ready for two and told me he had one or two people join him for a coffee. Let's not forget this is the man who was so enthusiastic for superb coffee he was ahead of the curve when the Hario v60 craze hit Vancouver and now we're using grocery store pre-ground and a tin can. While we waited for the water to boil we didn't say much and would look at each other and sort of smile and look away. He said he was going to make some bread as well. I had been working on finding a good bread recipe for a couple months now including the one John had shared with me from Bo's Mom. He walked back and forth from his cardboard boxed stash behind some logs under a garbage bag next to the grass and the fire first taking out a shallow pot, then three kinds of flour and cornmeal, yeast and some coconut oil. He said he had come up with a nice easy recipe and had been making it nearly every day. He poured in the flours and cornmeal, some warmed water and the yeast and gently blended it with a wooden spatula until he could blend it with his hands into the perfect ball. I half paid attention and more used his preparation as a time to assess the scene.

So, OK he looks like a homeless person, has been living on this beach, eats food that he stores in a cardboard box under some logs, and… uh, wait a minute it's BEaUtiful here! What the fuck!? He has turned away from all the pressures in the world to live on the beach, baking bread and watching the sunsets next to a fire in paradise! All this time I was worried and here he is doing exactly what I want to be doing! As I looked around I noticed the Maple tree in the grass behind us, a dinky little thing that was only about a few inches in diameter and I thought wow people are sensitive to their trees here. Not too shortly after I finally noticed the magnificent widow maker, an entirely dead old maple tree set just off the sand that reached way into the sky. I was surprised that I had not even noticed such the powerful tree and laughed at my previous thought regarding the dinky tree. I sort of took it as a checkpoint to be careful and stay in touch with my environment and not get lost in all of this but also I completely wanted to get lost in all of this.

My brain is processing things fast and working in alert mode trying to absorb as much information as possible and after a few minutes of silence we slowly started talking. "I can't believe you found me," Bo kept saying moving from sentimental to surprised. I asked him why he was out of contact, why he didn't tell me where he was and he told me he thought I had left him by now. My heart sunk to my ankles and I said "left you! My god I spend every single day looking for you or crying for you or worrying about you." I think to myself it is clear we have a lot of catching up to do. He won't let me touch him even when I try to put a hand on his back or just gently touch his face or hand. He just pulls his arms in and gently cringes and makes a "mm" sound. I feel helpless. I want to touch him, to soothe him so badly, to take him in my arms. But at the same time we were meeting for the first time and so smells were different or just unfamiliar and he had a beard now and I had been to Haida Gwaii and everything was coming and going in my mind so quickly as we sat there. I stood up to change positions to avoid smoke from the fire and from a few feet back Bo said "boy you sure have seen a lot of people, you have a LOT of people on your back" and it felt like we were throwing fireballs and I turned around and glared at him. I hated this new part of Bo that would talk about things I couldn't see but admired that some things resonated true and I felt envy to see for myself. We asked each other a few questions and fumbled our way through the last few months into the present together as we sipped our coffee. The bread buns seemed to be ready in no time and he handed me half with a chunk of melting coconut oil. Fresh baked bread from the fire, beach in paradise, with Bo and I have an entire long weekend ahead of me to figure out what will happen next, I thought as I took it all in. "Bo did you know it is my birthday this weekend?" I asked, and he looked down and admitted that he had not known that and started recounting dates to try and figure out what day it was then he gestured to a piece of driftwood leaning on his windbreak built up from stones. He reached over and showed me his driftwood etched with markings (month across the top and a running stream of sequential numbers) to keep track of the days. We were slowly able to get close enough and touch hands for a little bit. He leaned over and kissed me on the forehead and I froze it like a snapshot. We both had a lot of questions but kept it light while we danced around each other in our minds.

The sun was moving on and even though I kept my phone fully out of sight fearing his response, I couldn't resist stealing one shot of my survivor man in his woven cedar hat while I took a pee from behind the swaying grasslands before the dreamy sunsetting sky. It was as close as I could get.

I was pressed to figure out where I would be sleeping that night. "You can sleep out here with me," he said. My god how many nights have I cried myself to sleep wishing I could hear him say those words and here we are, together, really? He said he usually sleeps under a small fig tree on a patch of flattened grass but I was scared. I didn't know what kind of a state he was in and what if I needed help during the night or needed to run away and was lost I tossed around, but decided to think about it. Either way I didn't want to leave the car where it was overnight so we decided to take the path back to the car and Bo really wanted to see it. I saw him noticing me clutching my keys and purse from his reach and warmed that he was respecting how freaked out I was. No sudden movements from either of us kind of thing. We tidied up the beach/living room and started our way up to the car. Bo pointed out a log bench that he made and positioned ever so slightly to get coverage from the forest branches when it rains. He showed me how he puts his backpack on his chest, crosses his ankles, rests his head in his hands and looks up at the forest canopy for hours and I was jealous he had all of this time to meditate with raindrops and leaves. Not much further up the path he showed me that over there was the path I took when I was first coming down here and he told me he heard his name yelled the first time he stood up but by the third time he thought someone had discovered a dead body from the fear in the voice. "You could hear the fear in my voice?" I said. "Yes honey it was from the bottom of you." It WAS from the bottom of me, I thought while falling in love with his words. As we walked further up the path, we got to a bridge, where Bo points out that he built it all from material gathered from the beach and that the hand railing still needs some tweaking. This brings me back to the beach in front of his rain bench, where I noticed a full size garbage can with a wooden stick and a paper plate taped to it. There is a smiling face on the paper plate and it reads "Karma can carry up the hill for good karma." And now I am really getting a little miffed here because I wish I was living on the beach coming up with ideas like Karma cans! Anyways, I follow Bo, closely at first then at my own speed. I keep flushing the idea in my head that we were actually in each others presence and had some time to spend together. Aside from my prevailing anxiety and nerves, nothing could have made me happier in that moment. I wasn't even attached as to how I wanted Bo to be, think or feel. I remained with my previous thoughts about loving him and wishing him well but not expecting or wanting more than that.

He was happy to see the car in good shape and I was happy to hear him sound like the guy I knew. I moved the bimmer just a bit from where it was. I fussed through the trunk and the backseat trying to make my final decision about spending the night at the beach, but who was I kidding I didn't want to be anywhere else in the world so I grabbed a few things and made sure it was no more than I could carry back up the path if I had to tear out of there for some reason. We walked back down to the beach like two in a pod. Our hearts dancing in our own happiness of having each other despite having no idea of our outcome. I don't think we stayed up too late that night but we would never know because it was irrelevant for both of us. When it was cold and dark Bo went ahead and combined our bed rolls, zipping our sleeping bags together and laying them on a spread out heavy duty garbage bag. We had a final smoke by the fire and together walked the little path towards our made bed when we were suddenly startled by an animal breaking some twigs with their steps. I think she was as surprised as we were and in the dark we heard her hooves bounce as the deer galloped back into the woods. We could hear her brush past us and we locked our eyes together with excitement. Sleeping together was making us both nervous so it was like a first date except that we held each other so closely there wasn't even room for air between us. Under the stars, among deer and not a care in the world I thanked my god for getting me here. I couldn't see as far ahead as morning but I prayed to hold Bo in my arms again and to be held it was pure bliss and I was grateful, even if we were on a garbage bag.

CHAPTER TWENTY-SIX

PARADISE & BIRTHDAY

I awoke the next morning to the familiar comfort of an empty bed and B most likely making coffee. I had taken his word on the fig tree but when I looked up in the daylight, there it was, with two green figs ever so gently placed above us. The romance was enveloping me. I stumbled my way down to the beach to see my man on his perch tending to the fire. He smiled like we were meeting each other in heaven and I sat down for my coffee. I dozed in and out of the morning being blinded and soothed by the growing sun overhead. I awoke once to Bo preparing more bread but this time filled with a squeeze each of agave syrup and blackberries picked from the bushes behind us. The romance. We spent some time exploring the island. To my dislike, Bo encouraged me to take a break from sun-sleeping and see more of the island, "so I would feel safe and know where I am" he said. Place by place he took me around, I drove, and we would stop and take breaks, walk around. We just kept talking about everything and both of us were entirely calm and honest. Bo was able to explain to me some of the things he has seen in the last few months including faces, scary terrible faces in rocks and colours and energies and visions. At one point when my pointed questions were starting to annoy him he said "Just think of me as a Shaman ok babe." Bo? a

Shaman?! Give me a little room here ok!? One day all of a sudden my boyfriend declares he is a Shaman?! We laughed and continued the back-and-forth. Bo told me a story about the wolves nearby on the beach that came by one night and took his sandal off his foot while he was sleeping. He said the wolf was young and looked like a trickster who sort of smiled and then took off into the woods with it. Another wolf tried to grab his knapsack as well but didn't and the shoe was later found by a passerby in the woods, who was taking a walk on the beach.

The only people we really talked to were people who came walking along the beach. One, maybe two in a day. They all knew Bo by name and he knew theirs. A few had dogs and Bo would put out lentils, or at least water, for each one. He also kept a bird offering on driftwood that the dogs would occasionally find. One of the passersby's came along with two black labs one old and one young. He said the younger one was schizo maybe from being scared by a wolf when she was young. She was the most adorable though. And the older one brought them to the treats. The passersby seemed pleased to see me and see someone there caring for Bo, or so he noted. I was just mostly delighted with every moment and criss cross of affection shared between us.

My birthday morning started with a clean slate and was filled with my attempt at making a bread bun this time adding apples freshly picked from the trees behind us and I set the intention of getting some yoga in as well. A few hours of morning coffee at the fire and I stepped off to the side to begin my yoga. Not more than a few moments in I was holding my downward dog, loosen the back and really feeling the ground. I notice, looking through my legs, something scoot across the top of the water and then saw it again, something like a fin but too small to be a whale and then all of a sudden they started jumping. There were six dolphins all dancing together only meters away from us on the beach putting on a full show. Bo and I sat on the wood perch and couldn't believe our eyes, he said he had never seen dolphins out there before. He thought it was a good idea if we kept talking because they like the vibrations, so we did. They swam away a little bit and gathered again for an encore and I think I was too excited to continue my yoga for much longer. I felt like the universe was blessing me, blessing us and wondered if this was literally the beginning of a happy ending for us together. I would try to let the thoughts drift, being cautious to not get too caught up in the dream but it was proving difficult as I bounced between dolphins, my man, the beach, living under the stars, fresh coffee and baked fruit bread.

I was elated and he said I saved him by finding him out there. He remembered asking me if I would come find him, I remembered too and here we were. We still hadn't decided what was going to happen next but were enjoying each day and moment, as it came.

We drove into town in the afternoon because Bo wanted to make me a veggie dinner but he wasn't allowed into the Co-op grocery store since they banned him because someone called the police over from Quadra after he screamed at some children. We took the long way to town and decided to take a walk first …at the end of our forest walk we stopped sharp in our tracks stunned to see a white owl perched on a branch just over eye level! She stared at us as we did to her and she blinked a few times. With the shape of their faces and HUGE orange eyes it's pretty unforgettable and now I was really getting suspicious of how much fun Bo had been having all this time but he assured me he had never been so lucky himself with these animal messengers. He said that the wolves and him made friends, and that the other day he had a fawn come up to his knee after sitting still in the woods for a while but he said he had never seen a white owl, barn owl before and neither had I.

CHAPTER TWENTY-SEVEN

BEACH WALK

We took a walk along one of the more public beaches and looked for a nice place to nestle and have a joint and our coffee. Bo pointed out that people come at low tide to hit golf balls and we could watch one or two guys doing just that. There were still a lot of people sunning in the remaining light but with so many crevices and boulders to tuck in next to the beach still felt just like our own. We climbed up a grassy mound and sat in the tall grass catching some shade from a nearby tree. Birds were gently zooming overhead and we talked about our life together. I looked at him, his eyes more like slivers peeking out from his woven hat and this new bushy red and blond beard. It was different, but so was I. Words were exchanged but underneath that our hearts married each other. After everything we had been through losing and then finding each other what we had was strong enough to fight anything. We talked about how much we had in front of us and how hard it was going to be but agreed that with our commitment to each other we would find any strength we need. This moment became a blur and I well up crying now just trying to write this. I don't really even remember exactly what happened while we sat on that grass but it was a memory burned into my mind of us committing our hearts to one another.

CHAPTER TWENTY-EIGHT

DECISION TIME

We were falling more in love with each passing moment. In a matter of a few days we had managed to find our groove in the butterfly dance and our hearts were intertwining with the fact that we had found each other again and were even more in love than when we had parted. Bo told me more about seeing scary faces in nature around him, about me arguing with him for leaving me and him saying that he did everything he could to not run.

Even though four days had seemed to slow down to a crawl, my long weekend was quickly coming to an end. My heart and my head were in paradise and I didn't want to budge an inch but I had said I would return to work on Tuesday. I felt like it was in my best interest to keep some kind of structure in my life because life with Bo was easy and breezy but it was also withdrawing me more from the commitments of everyday life. As much as I wanted to grab his hand and continue on our new life chapter, something in my gut didn't quite believe it would be that easy. I told Bo I thought it would be better if he stayed on Cortes and we could keep in touch and I would come back up as soon as I could for another visit. At first he agreed but then after some squatting by the fire he said he wanted to come with me and go see Easy who was on dry dock on Gabriola. I told him to think about it and still encouraged him to stay in his calm place on the beach and ease back into society but he insisted that he was ready and wanted to go so the next morning we did. Before leaving Bo almost ceremonially closed his site by hiding his food in a box way up the hill in the woods and tidying up the beach front living room fire pit…leaving everything tidy and accessible he wrote on the driftwood that was the calendar that he would be away X X X days and expected to return on the Friday and a note that read: Please use and enjoy! and he had drawn a sun and I added a butterfly. We had our bags packed and the beach had been cleaned up. We had even improved the place by collecting oyster shells and using them to line the path from the woods to the beach to use the light of the moon to guide you in the dark like I had seen in Haida Gwaii. And Bo had built that bridge with a handrail and had started building a teepee tent but only had gotten so far as the frame. No joke in the middle of the grassy area, behind us if we were sitting on the beach, he had built this tepee, it probably stood about 12 feet high and it was incredible. You could walk into the middle and look through the centre hole that was an absolute perfect circle. Now tell me how you would do that using only found driftwood and rope but boy it was sturdy. He must have had to tie it on the ground and then raise it up? I just don't know but it was impressive it pleased me he was still my woodworking man at heart. We were doing the final sweep before heading up the hill to leave and I asked Bo if he wanted to sort of, take a minute alone to let it all sink in and say goodbye to this place that had saved him this summer and he took about a second and was eager and ready to march on.

CHAPTER TWENTY-NINE

SAVED

We drove through town and Bo wanted to take down the MISSING signs that I had put up when I got there. We took the one down near the dock and he smiled and said "wow you came here looking for me!" Then we went to take the one down at the community centre and someone had coloured red over the little heart after the text. Bo smiled when he saw that and seemed touched that someone would do that, and not do something like tear it down considering the trouble he got into this summer. This place took him in and they really let him exist in his form with a lot of compassion and understanding. He was going to take a look at Easy and come right back up to his spot on the beach and we were going to keep in touch, talk and I was considering moving up there. We were going to talk. Two or three of the same ferry workers were there when we drove onto the first ferry, including Greg who had said I could visit him if things didn't work out with Bo. He spotted us as we were taking off from the dock and came over to my window. Bo was sitting in the front seat wearing my holy toast coloured sweater from the bus with his hat kept low and hands on his lap. He kind of looked like either a criminal in hiding or someone who is really not feeling well but still sort of smiled and met Greg. "So you found him!" he boasted while I lowered the window.

"I sure did," I said. He invited me up for a coffee. Bo wanted a coffee too so I followed him leaving B in the car. Greg and his other worker buddies told me they had their eyes out over the long weekend and we chatted a bit about what was going on and I said I was considering moving up there and everyone cheered that idea especially with cold weather coming on. They were thrilled to hear that things were working out with Bo and Greg passed me his email address so we could keep in touch. Thanks to him and the missing poster, everyone that took the ferry over the long weekend had my email address and phone number.

Intensity was slowly growing as we ferry'd and drove our way to Campbell River. I kept checking with Bo, asking him if he was ok. I didn't realize it at the time but thinking back I had been living on little sleep, a lot of pot and tied to the hip with a very manic person and I was almost obsessively checking with him if he was ok and reminding myself that I am ok too. I used to do that sometimes with Bo when we were out on the boat and I was nervous. Things were feeling good though because he and I were getting on like mad and even though the details had not been sorted yet we knew we had a baseline, a foundation that we were together. He seemed to have no problem riding in cars which was a drastic improvement over the last time we were trying to ride in a car. Crazy scary intense kind of reactions that I was pleased now had passed. We stopped a few places along the way and Bo told me how he took the bus up this way and how he stayed in Tofino and how we both stayed in Courtenay on the way up. We pulled over at a jam packed second hand/antique store and picked up a sourdough bread starter clay or porcelain container. I remember wondering if my children would pick it up one day and ask me where it came from and I would be able to recount this magical story of how we were reunited and how it was one of the first things we picked up for *our* home. These thoughts always seem to come in a flash, almost like the mind taking a quick snapshot wondering if it will return back or not but saving it either way. I tried to keep the remainder of the journey as low key as possible watching to see if Bo was getting wound up or not. He assured me he was feeling alright and asked that I let him drive for a bit. He did seem to be doing well so I switched over.

As we were pulling out of the parking lot he wanted to pick up a hitch-hiker across the street and after all of my good karma in Haida Gwaii I thought it was ok. We picked up a 22 year old guy who had spent the summer up around and had been waiting at that spot since 9am. He had come up for a girl but it didn't really work out so we was on his way back down to Victoria to get on with his Fall. The guys discussed where the best place in Nanaimo would be to drop him off and before jumping out Bo said if he wanted any luck he should add a little pink to his cardboard sign so I handed him a marker in the back seat and he added some hints of colour. We pulled over safely to let him out, he thanked us and smiled ear to ear as he went on his way. We drove off thinking he should cross the street from where he was so a car could have room to pull over if he wanted to get picked up and I thought about how easy that is for Bo and I to see, how obvious it seems to be, and how our road friend seemed to be what you could call blissfully ignorant. Neither one better than the other, just different.

The first sign of intolerance came while waiting in the lineup to get on the ferry from Nanaimo to Gabriola. Things had been going so well I was starting to decrease my alertness level but didn't get too far before Bo started getting visibly worked up. Chain smoking, angry, starting to lay into my boss or other seemingly random tangents. Nothing got too far out of hand and was easily overcome with a simple walk. It was as though the volume of cars and people were just too much and with the busy road and city spanning behind us he had no space around him. Like his vibrations were bouncing around everyone else around us and he was easily overcrowded and over-whelmed. We carried on and talked about how we had met on this ferry only months earlier. Happy to be putting that behind us and grateful to see how far we have come since then.

CHAPTER THIRTY

EASY DOES IT

We decided to start Gabriola like we did the last time and grab a beer. Bo knew a place we could camp for the night and it was only a walk away from where Easy was dry docked. Dusk was upon us so we went to the camp site to settle in. The man at the desk took our money, me for a night and Bo for two, and asked us to sign in the guest book. I signed under "Bo, Cortes Isle" as "Alicia, undecided" and laughed about it going to sleep that night. Was he serious? Cortes Isle? Either way it sure does sound cool. We took the shortcut path that Bo knew and walked over to the Silva Bay boat yard and Bo listened as I recounted my emotional trip here after she first sank. He told me that this was a deciding factor for him to leave Cortes to come take a look. He said that he thought if I could take it- whatever *it* was- that he was sure he would be able to as well and we held hands and walked there together. Someone was getting their mast lifted so there was a guy on the big machine and another few of them standing around. We walked past them and Bo went straight over to Easy. "Ok, ok," he kept saying but not much more than that. He walked around the hull and then up the ladder and to see inside. Inside wasn't a lot cleaner than what it was when I had seen it a few weeks ago. "Ok, not bad," said Bo and we climbed down to look at the outside again. The guy working the lift walked over and asked us if he could help us. "This is my boat" said Bo and the guy's face just lit up. "Bo!?" he said "Man, I heard everyone's been looking for you, this boat was quite a site!!" He laughed and said that she was down for three days with the top of the mast just COVered in seaweed. "Everyone was out taking photos we were expecting a pirate to come out…actually, someone kind of like you!" he chuckled. "You have photos of that?" I eagerly asked and he said "oh I bet there are photos all up and down the coast, everyone was out there taking photos!" B and I kind of looked at each other sheepishly but smiling. "Hey are you interested in selling?" he asked. "Not really" Bo said. "Yeah I wouldn't either if I were you, I can't believe she came up without a scratch! It's like she just….got wet" he said. We all laughed at the sweetness of it all. Don't get me wrong there were repairs to be done for sure, all electrical for one would have to be torn out but Bo said it was a rats nest anyways and had only been installed about 30 years ago. We were both keen to see her lose the 70's and 80's modifications in favour for the original 40's classic simplicity. So the guys talked about that for a while and then he showed us the pile of our stuff that had been lifted out with the salvage and we went through it taking out some of the things we could save and some kitchen stuff to use to make dinner tonight and coffee in the morning.

We laughed ourselves to sleep that night. We couldn't believe how lucky we were to have each other, to have lost and found each other again and then to have lost and recovered this boat all with little to no irreplaceable damage done. We made love that night really for the first time since reconnecting. I had never felt him so present and in tune with my body. I had flashes that I was making love with Jesus himself because he was such an overwhelming representation of man. To triumphantly overcome the hardships and become such a strong multi-talented and unique person. This intense attraction was definitely going both ways and if I didn't partially have my head partially screwed on I would have wanted to make a baby that night. We had way too much ahead of us that needed to be sorted out before that was even a remote possibility and by morning that was even clearer.

CHAPTER THIRTY-ONE

HOME COMING

I barely had a few sips of my morning coffee before Bo started in with the verbal diarrhoea. It was a melange of him hating my boss and telling me that everyone back in Vancouver is going to try and get me to stay and that they take me over and tear me apart by consuming me. We didn't even say goodbye when I left to go back to the city. The idea was I would come back over on the weekend and we would chat when we could in the mean time. He would have to call me because he still didn't have any other mode of contact having abandoned his email and throwing his phone overboard. We bickered a bit and I tried to reason with him again but the morning just went sour and I slammed the car door and drove off watching him walk away from me. Not even turning back once, I thought. He had been getting upset, wanting me to promise that I was moving to Cortes with him and that I was going back to quit my job. I couldn't promise that, but said I would give it serious thought while we worked out the other much more important things such as getting him back 'to normal.' I expressed that it simply wouldn't work for me to have a boyfriend that won't step a foot in the city. Considering my friends and family were all there it was something that would need to get worked out, but I was willing to give it some time and had wonderful images of us having our own retreat on Cortes in the winter. Time for both of us to heal, recoup and get on with planing our life! And we could live on Easy…how romantic.

I spent the entire ferry home from Gabriola to Nanaimo then to Horseshoe Bay actively tossing the idea of moving to Cortes around. I wrote it down in my notebook, Alicia Boswell Cortes Island. I thought about how I had wanted to move to New York in my 20's and how I regretted not taking that leap even if it didn't quite make sense at the time. I wrote down pro's and con's and looked around at fellow passengers wanting to make small talk so I could hear what it sounds like to say I am inches from moving to Cortes. I walked around and had a smoke outside and thought about moving all of my stuff up there, setting up a home, all of the wonderful walks, sailing and community life we would have up there. Friends who could come and visit. I had said that IF I was going to move up there I insisted that we had a place where friends or family could stay and Bo wanted to make sure that I had a place of my own in case he was too intense. My mind was racing from one thought to the next and I felt like I was hitting overload as far as processing emotions. It had been a roller coaster of a summer including some of the saddest moments in my life and I had just been reconnected with my love and now possibly moving to Cortes island. I texted my boss, the vet, that I wouldn't be able to make it in that day. I was already one ferry later than I had wanted to catch and I just felt full to the brim. I needed some space to unwind before I could take in another thought, project, decision or question.

My boss called me frantically but I wasn't about to pick it up and start arguing in the middle of this sunny peaceful ferry ride. I used to love not having caller ID on my phone. It was like having a phone that could only make outgoing calls and there was no guilt when you missed the incoming call because you are not on the hook to call back. I took my time driving home wondering if I took an extra turn or two if it would get me any closer to making a decision. I was sure feeling rushed but like Bo had said moving is hard and people always try and get you to stay because they want you to. I got home and was thankful that both Kristen and Nando were there to greet me.

I quickly sat down at the table and told them all about the wonderful time and then quickly got to my new conundrum about moving or not. I could hear the words coming out of my mouth as I tried to relay what seemed to have happened in one world to another. I could see things were getting lost in translation. They heard me out about the boat, we would rent a place etc. etc. and Kristen paused me when she said "sorry if I am missing something here but, but what's the rush?" It struck me that she was right. It was only five days ago last week when I was loving my job and happy with my life and now I am moving to Cortes? I started to worry that I had lost a bit of perspective having spent those days with Bo. I was reminded about how spending time with him when his episode started always took a toll on me and would take a day or two to wear off. I felt duped again like I had lost my footing and led astray in Bo's world again, but then again I loved the idea of living on Cortes and double loved it with Bo and our sailboat. We had agreed to rename her Cloud 10 and he said I could paint her any colour I want and we would redecorate.

Before I knew he was going mad, Bo had made picture frames for some magnificent art cards that we had of Kent Crawford that we were going to hang in Easy's gallery and some blue stain rubbed off from his fingers on it. I was shocked and asked him what happened because it seemed so out of character for him to make even a tiny slip like that let alone not fix it. He said he liked the little touch of colour and I thought he was messing with me so I said oh yeah and why don't we start adding touches of colour on a wall of two of the boat knowing he would take it as a joke but the joke was now a new reality for me and my technicolour dream man.

CHAPTER THIRTY-TWO

IT'S ONGOING

Breaking way into Fall, I continued living on cloud 10 myself. I was proud of my own ability to go into the flame and come out and continue marching along as I was and pleased to have had successfully reunited my man and our boat. Bo was camping near the boat dry dock on Gabriola and we would chat whenever he could remember, was not angry or could get to a phone. There was a pay phone nearby and sometimes when he would call and start on a rant I could only imagine the sight on the other end of the phone of this lunatic red head and wondered if anyone thought to sympathize with whoever he was screaming at on the other end. I would usually just hang up as if to suggest it was the wrong number or try again. Sometimes it would work and overall I was feeling a steady climb up in our favour and I wondered if we would come full circle. I daydreamed about my man surprising me by bringing Easy/Cloud 10 back to our moorage to pick me up and how maybe we could finally sail her off into the sunset to start the rest of our lives together as we discussed. My dreams kept me satiated while I waited to see how things unfolded with Bo meanwhile making my best efforts to keep the other man in my life on track. Being a full time assistant to an extremely intelligent and engrossing holistic vet was starting to wear me thin. It wasn't that I didn't want to be there, I loved my work but I was slowly finding it less possible to maintain a full time assistant to two grown men without completely losing touch with my own needs. It may sound dramatic but most mornings I would wake up and within moments feel claustrophobic when I would think about all the things I was holding up, helping to support, holding on to and being responsible for. On one side I had the love of my life coming in and out of reality and clinging to me as a touchstone and on the other I had a (not afraid to dream) visionary/ vet who had ambitions of making the world a better place starting by reforming our healthcare system. It was like being split down the middle dogs, improve the world, YES, Bo- the strongest man I know needing my help, YES! But even with his best efforts we still weren't in the clear.

Against all plans, Bo took off on the boat leaving me behind, again. I was getting increasingly anxious at work and decided to call the boat yard to ask Vickey and Don how things were going and when I did she quickly said they were putting her back in the water and that Bo was right there and I could speak to him. I could tell by the tone in her voice she wanted little to nothing to do with Bo. He had not told me that was what they were doing and just as before, he slipped through my fingers and took off again-this time with Easy- leaving me alone in the wake.

September 15, 2011
Bo is gone

i dont want to to get up today. i have been awake for nearly 2 hours in bed just lying here trying to wrap my head around the things that i keep forgetting. that Bo is gone. that he says he isnt coming back. that he doesn't look back. i have so much tension in my jaw right now. i just dont know how to ease this other than carrying on. but i dont want to carry on. i have so much anger and pain and hurt inside. how would i ever get passed this? when will i start loving myself enough to not put up with shit like this. no one is afraid of hurting me because i let them. they can just say whatever they want, push me around, hurt me, call me names and say whatever they want because i will take it and probably with a smile. im really sad today. i am really sad for myself.

no one is afraid of hurting me because i forgive. i listen with compassion. not so bad but i really should apply those things first and foremost to myself..?!? forgive myself. have compassion for myself.

The week didn't get much better from there. The bimmer was acting up and wouldn't change out of first gear which I would have been fine with for city driving except I wasn't keen to commute in a rickety car over the Lions Gate and on top of that I had been noticing some peculiar chest pains.

I guess it kind of worked out ironically because I just as I had realized I was too overworked from the double full time jobs it wasn't long before I was suddenly left empty handed with neither. After Bo took off on Easy without telling me my boss reluctantly fired me because I think it was obvious I was having a hard time keeping up and I had a lot on my plate. He said that maybe I should go to New York or back to Haida Gwaii for a bit because he said he thought I changed since I was there and that maybe I liked it. I was not interested in what he or anyone thought I should do at this point, I sunk.

I recounted my losses for the month: love, boat, car, job, and now possibly health. It felt like as fast as you see people win and lose in a casino. My birthday weekend love affair was a jackpot hit but now I had just as quickly started to landslide and couldn't see the bottom yet but I knew I had started my decent.

CHAPTER THIRTY-THREE

BACK IN VAN

When I got home, K read my face and asked me what happened, "fired" I said. "Let's be honest, you asked for it" she said.

I really had Bo on my mind after a few days of not knowing where he had sailed off to. One night, Charlie and I were alone for dinner so I decide we would change it up a bit and go for a bite at a resto that had just renovated down the street. We had just enough time to order some our drinks when in called Bo. "Hello," I answer. "Do you know who this is" he says, "Bo?" I say, "Do you hate me?" he pipes in and my heart was flooded again hearing the distant cry from my love. He told me he had brought the boat up to Cortes and he said that he was thinking of tearing through Vancouver to pick up a few things, including me. I chuckled and told him I wasn't going to move faster than I was ready but would love to have him come back to Vancouver.

His trip in was lining up with my last day of work and things were coming together better than I would have thought. I don't know what it is but I take utter delight in seeing seemingly unrelated things intertwining/fusing/coming to a head. Having everything slip through my fingers only a week ago I was still hesitant to take the leap with my heart again so soon. I had put things back in their place as best I could to prepare for this reunion but wasn't about to pretend it into a fairytale like I had so many times. I reminded myself to be practical, and also to keep in mind how intense he can be and how I have lost my footing in the past. I looked around our room for my vulnerabilities and grabbed Bo's computer which held two years of my photos and music. I started it on a backup while I added other things to my in case of emergency evacuation "to grab" list. I realized the irony that I was preparing myself for an emergency at the same time as I was getting ready to see someone who I claimed to call my love. In the meantime I was so nervous to have him come back that I couldn't do much more than grab my guitar and post up on the porch to strum away time or my nerves. The one song I knew at the time was Don MacLean's *American Pie,* which I was learning because my Dad told me that was the first song he ever learned.

My first clue that things were not going very well was when Bo stomped up the stairs and marched right past me over my outstretched leg as I continued to strum the guitar I was playing. It was so odd that I didn't really take it personally and didn't follow him either. He stomped back out and said something arrogant enough that I ignored it and said "hello to you too" which softened him enough to lean down and kiss me on the head followed by "ok so let's go babe, we have half an hour for a turnaround." Remaining calm I said "No way! If you want to leave, you are more than free to do so but I am not jumping like this OK!" He kind of chuckled and kept moving. I just played the guitar. He went into the bedroom and was tossing things around so I followed and posted up on the bed so I could monitor. First thing out was a large green folding suitcase full of my clothes that I thought I had given away or fully lost. Bonus for finding my clothes, I thought and he says "ok so this one's good to go?!" "No Bo this one is not *good to go* what the hell am I going to do with something like a tulle skirt while living on a boat in Cortes?!? There isn't even enough storage for all of this shit! I am not *good to go*, this stuff needs to be sorted." So he dumps all of my clothes onto the bed and with no more than two handfuls he grabs his entire wardrobe, hangers and all and dumps it into this folding green suitcase. He slowly returns the hangers one by one to the closet and leaves his

Hugo Boss suit in its bag with the baby blue Burberry tie I bought him that he never wore. I had never seen him wear the suit either but I have a feeling that it was from his father's funeral. I had first come to learn of it when we started dating and I shared my dream of sailing around the world and having amazing yacht black tie parties to go to as we cruised through different marinas. "I have a suit!" he said, when I was describing the imagine if scenarios. Fabulous, I thought, dreaming of a heavily varnished wood locker with bronze hardware with his grey suit and my various gowns hanging next to one another like a couple asleep.

So he hung the suit back and draped the tie over the rod. I am certain to him leaving it behind had as much to do with it not being a vibrant colour as it did with it being a symbol of everything wrong in the world. He continued putting back his hangers and stumbled on a gingham Lacoste dress shirt which got plucked from the pile and quickly identified as being one of those things that is not like the others. It was promptly removed and placed hanging with its discarded mates. The shirt was given to him by our friend Emerson and it was always a little snug. It's ironic though I think, considering how easily putting it on now would instantly change his current skeletal frame and bushy face into a hot modern LA hobo chic. Sigh.

He heads outside and I am thinking, yeah good luck going to try to get your old work van started, you will *really* have to snap into reality to focus enough to fix that van up. Nope! Within 15 minutes he had broken into the van, having lost his keys, the hood is up and he's got it running. I look at the time and think, ok it's nearly 3pm and he has no insurance surely he can't leave tonight we will have to go the insurance office and they have bank hours and will be closed by 5pm. Wrong again, he pops in and says "Let's go to London Drugs, they have insurance." Fuck.

We go to wait in line and he asks Grace, the clerk, for renewal on both the van and the bimmer. Papers are flying getting flipped back between the three of us as we try and sort out what is even what. We decide the van will get regular insurance and she asks who is the primary driver for the BMW. "Me" he says. "Why don't we transfer the car to you? Gift it, I mean, lets save the taxes." What? Give me the car? Are you sure? How does this work? So we step away from Grace to discuss our very own 'marriage/contractual agreement' in front of the people in line and agree that a car is something I would need in Cortes in order to be able to take off if I needed to.

"Oh it's not air cared" she said asking if we could take it in tomorrow. I can see Bo's face furrow at that idea for it taking too long or being too tedious and he says "naw, lets just throw a few days on it get it up to Cortes and then it won't matter"... *uh...what?* I think. "Yeah you don't have to air care it in areas that don't have the facility to check for it so we will just change the address to Cortes and it won't matter." I look at Grace and she says "actually he's right, you could do that." Fuck, how does he come up with this shit?

We continue to shuffle papers around and Grace asks me to fill out the transfer papers. This ancient process basically consists of me transcribing 25 digits of numbers and letters and all of our residence information from one paper to another for her to then read and transcribe back onto their computer system. Great! I thought, we can waste tons of time doing this. Bo gets up to excuse himself for the washroom and I glance back at the guy waiting behind us in line. He is near furious and quickly darts his eyes to the floor to not display to me his extreme discomfort with our process moving like molasses. A few too many minutes go by waiting for Bo and I tell her I am going to go find out where he is. I see him wandering from the bathroom into the electronics section. He doesn't seem that interested in actually looking at anything on the racks and instead walks up to some people and says "Hey!" As if he knows them. It's as if he wanted them to react funny so he could talk about how he is moving to Cortes. I call out "Bo!" And he turns around and remembers that he knows me. "Hi honey," he says and I point towards the car insurance section and his face lights up with recognition of what he is in the middle of and we walk back. He sits down for a few more minutes and we shuffle around more papers. It's time for me to sit down and shuffle papers so Bo gets up wanting to find some chocolate to pass the time. "Ok" I said, "I'll just sit here honey." He comes back munching on a 99% cocoa dark bar and hands me a broken chunk. No more than three chomps in and the crude dirt taste overwhelms my dry mouth with disgust. It is so obvious that Grace asks me if I am OK. "Yes" I say "this is just so gross, its disgusting" and I look around for the garbage. Crap, nothing. So I try to swallow it again. We continue shuffling papers and I just can't take it anymore so emotionally exhausted I am heading for my own burn out.

The rest of the day was a blur trying to find the middle way. Bo was full speed ahead moving mode while I was trying to keep my feet on the ground in what felt like a tornado cutting through. I woke at about 5am and turned in bed subsequently moving my leg which barely scratched against his big toenail and he jolted awake. He let out a moan and snapped "How could you do this to me, you know the morning is my worst time!!" He bolted out of bed and wailed "now I have to break up your parents" and stormed out. I looked at the clock, fuck 5am, "OK Bo, time for a walk. TIME FOR A WALK....NOW!" As I stood in the kitchen nearly nude in my nearly transparent sleep shirt. Charlie yells "simmer down out there!" from the living room floor and Bo picks up a stool in the hallway and jams it breaking the drywall then comes up and shakes my shoulders and screams something I can't remember in my face. Poor Charlie, I think. I go back to the bedroom and lock the door. Bo paced from the kitchen to front door and back, over and over. Then he would come to the door and yell how much of a whore I am and how I am nothing without him, or how he saved me from being a whore. I screamed "GET OUT NOW!!! TAKE A BREAK Bo, TAKE A BREAK!!!!" And by now Ellen calls from downstairs. He answers and just muddles off more of his nonsense about how the place is sinking into a hole and how I have to get up and leave with him this instant. I can hear him say that I am not coming to the phone and he hangs up. I am still locked in the bedroom and demand again. "Bo, leave!" At the same time I can hear Ellen outside in the yard yelling to the porch for Bo so I open the bedroom door and he charges in at me kicking the door at the same time. I bolt out to the porch and say to Ellen "He is fucking nuts!!! We have to call the cops!!!" She says "Alicia we can't let this go on, the neighbours will wake up!" Somehow I find myself sitting on the bed again with the door locked and on the phone with Ellen deciding if we should call the police or not. He rants again and pounds on the door. The decision is made and Ellen calls. Waiting for them feels like an eternity as it usually does. Lesson learned- call the cops when you first think you should.

I sat on the bed behind the locked door with my knees crouched in holding my phone which was on record. I looked down and watched the seconds tick, tick. Man, has it only been 5 minutes?! 7 minutes? Finally a knock on the door and Bo answers. A cop voice says "Uh, hello, do you realize the neighbours have been complaining?" And the other cop comes in to check the house and then to talk to me. "So what's going on?" he asks. "Well, he is bipolar and he is having a manic episode and he needs to leave" I say. I can hear Bo outside quoting the residential tenancy act and coming up with statements so confident that I hear his cop literally say "I don't know the law." Internal eye roll GREAT, I think. My cop then starts asking questions about leases and rental agreements and I know I am about three steps away from possibly getting zero sympathy if I continue to explain that this is a hippie house where these kind of agreements are not in place. "Kristen and Nando live upstairs, they own the house" I say. "Neither of them are here now but they are the ones in charge" and he asks for my ID and a few more questions meanwhile I hear Bo chuckling with the cop about how hard it is to have a wife and get her to listen and the cop says "Alright Bo well nice chatting with you" and he skips down the steps.

My cop could see the fear in my eyes and asked "Are you OK with him here?" "NOOOOOOoooooo" I cry into whimper. Wasn't this the whole point of calling you guys?! It wasn't for a little chit chat at 530am. My cop went on the porch to talk to his cop and Bo's cop says that they have no right to do much but still convinces Bo it was time to go for a walk. He squirms around but finally agrees and stomps in and gets his hat or something as he walked past the cop down the hallway he just stared at me with so much fire I could barely hold more than a glance. Even with the cop there I thought he was a flicker away from exploding in my direction. I locked the door and called Ellen and tried to go back to sleep. It's incredible how the body even in intense shock can still slow down enough that I drift off until I am awoken an hour and a half later by the metal hinge on the gate being opened on Bo's return. I gently pull aside the lace curtains and peek outside of the window and watch him clomp up the stairs. Not knowing what he would do next I curl up in bed and just cling to peace and quiet. I can hear him pacing around on the porch and part of me wants to reach out and see how he is doing but the fear inside of me is too great so I just wait silently. About 20 minutes later I hear a knock, two and then the front door gently opens. Oh geez. I dash to the bedroom door even though it is locked, to brace it shut having visions of him bombing in at full force. Rather, at 7am he picks up the phone and starts yapping away to someone about how terrible I am and how he's got it all set up and all I have to do is show up on Cortes and what's a guy gotta do to get some respect. My alarm bells just start ringing and I have already called the police, this guy is still freaking out, WTF am I supposed to do so I put on a warm jacket, a bra and some shoes, grab my purse and book it to the car. Jump in the bimmer and on my way to get away. To where though? The fucking car still won't shift out of first gear so I am nervous crossing even one lane of traffic until this thing corrects. I just start driving and find myself taking the route along Spanish Banks. By the time I am curling around the point at UBC the fuel changes from saying I have 136km left to only 32km left. Ef, are you kidding me!? Please don't let me run out of gas, please don't let me run out of gas. I don't know what to be more worried about, running out of gas or the fact that I have no idea where I am intending to go. At least for those 10 minutes I don't have to think about where I am going and can just focus on getting to a gas station.

I pull into the first gas station and have to reverse and adjust the car to line it up right. OK pumping gas now. It's $1.37/L looks like a screaming deal and my mind can't remember if thats the normal price or if it is more like $1.50/L. Anyways at least I am able to waste a few minutes pumping gas and not having to think about what is going on and what I am even doing there at this hour. I go to the washroom to kill time and I sit for what feels like forever and think to myself I might as well be sitting in a chair because my insides are so tight nothing is coming out of me. I catch my own eyes in the mirror and I see my paled out face, puffy bags under my eyes. Hopeless, I can see how frightened I look and I snap a photo to remember this low since I have been so forgetful lately.

I get back in the car and just start driving. Where the hell can I go? For some reason Richmond seemed like a good idea so I headed down Oak until a "613" calls and I pull over. It's Kristen calling in response to my 5am explanatory email. She quickly says "Alicia he MUST leave. That is your home and not his, he left and now he MUST leave." Fuck, OK and we go over some details and what to say and she tells me to call the police again. "They HAVE to protect you" she says. Ok, I can go with that. "911, police fire ambulance?" "Police." "Which district?" Blah blah blah till we get to "Do you have any guns in the house?" "NO!" I hate even thinking this way "Any large objects?" "Uh.. no?" Even though I am sure he could get creative very easily. "Any large animals or pets?" "No, no large animals." And I am shocked to find myself in this line of questioning. "OK mam, please stay on the phone, someone will come, where are you?" "King Ed and Oak" I say… why the hell am I at King Ed and Oak? Anyways "stay put" says the dispatcher, "we are sending a car your way."

About 15 minutes pass and I am still sitting in the car. Now I am feeling like I can't comprehend much more than my immediate environment. The police car drives passed me driving on the other side and we look at each other through our drivers windows. We both raise a hand to sort of acknowledge that we are meeting and I see it's my cop from this morning.

He gets out and I can tell he looks irritated. "So what's going on now" he says, sounding annoyed. "Well he came back, picked up the phone and he is still angry. I am afraid to be there, afraid to go back, he HAS to leave" and he says "Look, you can't just call me up and have us come over to sort this out. It doesn't work like that. This sounds to me like a domestic dispute that you two are going to have to sort out on your own."

Slap in the face.

"Sir you don't understand. He is bipolar." "That doesn't matter" he says "just because someone is bipolar doesn't mean anything." Oh jesus, I think. Now I have pushed the panic button and there is no ejection. Fuck, FUCK. Now what. "Look, will you PLEASE talk to the owner of the house" I plead with him. He really doesn't want to and says that he could basically be talking to anyone. While I can see he has a point I say "Look, I can't leave the house. He doesn't live there, has been gone for four months and.." "Why? Why can't you just leave him there? Don't you have somewhere else you can go?" He says.

Kristen's voice echoes in my head *Alicia this is YOUR home, he must leave.* "No! OK well fine I guess I could go to my parents but I can't leave the house alone!" I whine. "Why??!" he persists, "Why can't you just leave him there?" "Because Charlie's there!" I cry. "Charlie? Who's Charlie?" "Uh.....uh, well OK he is our *roommate*" "Can't Charlie protect himself!?" "NOOOOooooo" I cry and start crying and walk away.

I can see this is going nowhere fast. How do I explain in a nutshell the ins and outs of my hippy house to this rigid cop who is already annoyed with me. I dial Kristen and toss him the phone. "613?" he says "Where is she?" "Ontario" and he rolls his eyes. I can hear her directing him on the phone to remove Bo from the premises and see him just holding it away from his ear. "He is a guest" she says "and it's time for him leave." "When are you coming back?" he asks to try and quickly get out of the call. "Next week!" and so we continue.

We part ways and the cop says he will go back to the scene. Back at the house, Ellen has spoken to Bo who has agreed that if I bring back his food (in the bimmer) that he will go back to Cortes. Fine, so I call Kristen with the latest and I drive home and I can feel myself just trembling inside. Is this really happening? No, no no!! This can't be the end of the story. But those thoughts quickly fade to the overwhelming fear of Bo's hot, irrational, erratic, violent, scary and angry behaviour. The only goal in sight is peace and quiet.

I arrive home and he is standing in the driveway trying to direct me to reverse in. I make an attempt and he starts yelling at me some command or direction and I drop it into drive and pull over to a nearby corner. I can't even stand to be that close to him. I leave the car and we rotate positions, me heading to the house, him to the car. I can feel him staring me down as we rotate and I just look to the side and keep walking. The police are here and I can see them discussing their approach or more like discussing how they both think this is a total waste of time and there is nothing they can do.

The police come in and stand at the house entrance to the driveway with Ellen and I. We are mostly just standing around watching Bo pack his things from the bimmer to his work van. I feel glimpses of utter despair for the situation and even after being scared out of my wits I have flashes of being able to hold him and make everything OK. I feel his discomfort and rage and from experience in this situation I know that those come up when he is most vulnerable. These waves don't rise high because I have been up since 430am and I am still shaking from it all. He slowly moves the 10 packs of quinoa, four huge bags of rice and other basic survival things he has collected together. He takes the sourdough bread starter ceramic jar that we bought together. Seeing this pulls strongly at my sentiment because we had bought it together in one of the hopeful moments and I wanted to believe it was the kind of thing that years from now I could tell our own children where and when we bought it and how special and memorable this little trite object really was. As my heart strings pull he drops the lid which cracks hitting the sidewalk. My head snaps down, I just can't watch.

He shuffles things around a bit and finally closes all the doors. The moment is just unfolding before my eyes and I feel numb. He walks to the back of his van and says "Tell me when you've decided between me and Kristen's cunt" and I turn away to block out the rest of the vulgar. I imagine what he really means is I am freaking out so bad I will do anything to keep interacting with you so you will come with me… but I never really had developed good translating skills and tended to err on the side of love.

He pulls out of the driveway and our neighbour Doug runs up to the passenger window. He sends Bo off with some kind words and things to look forward to on Cortes. Watching this makes me feel jealous or something that anyone could still be nice to him after what he said or did. Good thing for neighbours.

With that, he tears off in that silver van. It's funny how your feelings can change about something through love. I remember the first time I saw that van. It was when we were first dating and I had reached out late at night. I think I probably said I was frisky but really I was lonely and I waited on the front stoop of my apartment and saw him pull up. My first reaction was, ugh, tacky, gotta change that and now watching him drive away that same van representing his livelihood. Filled to the brim with all of his tools and everything he owns. It represents the manifestation of a large bank account and endless hard working hours. Right now, it just represented Bo actually leaving. I would never have foreseen myself getting so emotionally attached to this silver van. Every time I took a walk since this all began I would collect the feathers that found me and I would tuck them into the wiper and it started a collection. Each time I had visions that one day he would come back and be so touched for the prayers and feathers but they simply went unnoticed. They may as well have been dried leaves for how he saw them but for me they represented months of pining, hoping, wishing, praying and unconditionally loving Bo.

We talked to the police for a while and they told me to get a locked door and a rental agreement. They basically reinforced that there is nothing they could do. Bipolar or not, the person has to help themselves and according to the law this burden is held by the family and friends who have to just watch the person deteriorate.

We wished them off well and thanked them (for not much) and I didn't know what to do with myself. Ellen invited me in and I agreed but figured I should check out the scene in our house upstairs before my imagination takes ahold of me. OK, nothing terribly destroyed. He has flipped up our plasma bed mattress and left things strewn about. Red fuzzy handcuffs that were left from my last apartment's finale *Bust Out* themed party were sitting on the bed frame. I wonder if he did that on purpose or what he could mean by that but not wanting to get into anything yet so I just walk away.

Sitting at Ellen's, she makes me a coffee. We both just can't believe what happened and we go over the details together, me reminding myself that he was scary and that was real. I am overwhelmed and have flashes of utter disbelief that he is gone and I am here. I am still shaking on the inside and start crying, feeling so sad for myself and the results of my efforts. I can't stop rocking, and fighting and moving. I look down at my right wrist, at those two strings I have been holding on to since June. Something snaps inside of me because for the first time ever the grey wool string I had held for Bo suddenly disgusts me. It feels gross and too close so without a thought I tear it off and throw it on the table. I can't take the other one either, why am I holding on to Easy- *get this off of me!* my mind says, and I yank, one finger, two fingers, three fingers pulling on this bracelet for Easy and my skin starts to tear before it does. I am pulling as hard as I can to finish this dramatic gesture and Ellen walks up with scissors and gently unchains me. I end with a whimper. Easy is strong and I am glad she proved that to me. She is safe and strong and he will be safe with her. Now me, here, alone, with no strings attached.

We calm down with some coffee and toast but it is hard to keep the emotions down. I return from the washroom to see my writs strings gone from the table. *Wait! I might still need those,* I think. *Maybe I want to cherish them? No, Alicia,* I think. *You knew you lost those at the right time now go with it.* Adjusting to the present moment starts hitting me and Ellen draws me a bath. It feels as though someone has just died and you don't know what to do because everything seems so insignificant under the circumstances but just like you keep breathing you keep moving. The bath helps, probably just as much as being in someone else's room. Other things to look at, no haunting memories. I stay there long enough to give Ellen a few minutes to settle down too. I return to some of my warm clothes and pull up at the table again. This time the waves are coming up much stronger and keep smashing into me with overwhelming despair. All my mind can say is *Noooooooo,* and Ellen encourages me to just let it out. I can feel myself shivering and collapsing from being pounded on the inside by these waves and Ellen pulls me into the bathroom to blow dry my wet hair. Let it out she whispers, just let it out, and I am sitting on the toilet rocking myself up and down. Twisting from the inside from all of the discomfort of my new reality. She combs at my hair with her fingers whispering that it is OK, everything is OK, let it out. And I do. I pull my knees in closer and while rocking put my hands to my face and reach down to the bottom of my despair that has been building for months and let out the loudest scream I have ever heard from myself. Part way in I can feel the world rattling from the sound but I continue anyways with all of my breath and I feel the hair stand up on my nearby neighbours bearing witness. Ellen shuffles me over to her bed encouraging me to try and nap or lie down for a few minutes. It is a good idea except that the scream has just cracked open a locked box inside me and my mind is still flooded. I can't stop twisting and scratching at my chest trying to make it easier to breath. Thoughts are not even clear at this point and all I want is to get out of my body, get out of this moment, get out of my own life. I can feel the tingling and numbness starting in my face and hands. I have lost my breath and have nowhere to go.

CHAPTER THIRTY-FOUR

BREAKING POINT

Looking back it's a blur as to how communication picked up following my meltdown and the police escorted departure but somehow it continued and was likely motivated by my unbridled optimism and inability to remember much due to sheer exhaustion. It was still a roller coaster ride.

October 28, 2011
Alicia Lindsay Boswell
To Bo
Dear Bo,
I am afraid I woke this morning with some new thoughts.

The way you were on the phone with me yesterday tells me you are still manic. The first step is for you and I to find a GP who can evaluate you and run some diagnostic tests and possibly prescribe a mood stabilizer. I have done research and it is extremely difficult to find a doctor in Cortes or in that area. I simply do not know a network of people outside of Vancouver who can help us find a doctor. Campbell River is the closest large city that may have something of help but even still, it would be a shot in the dark.

Part of our life means a future with a lot of appointments and a large support network of friends and family. Moving to Cortes takes both of those things away and leaves me isolated and alone to deal with your mania. I know enough now to know that is a bad idea and not something I am going to do.

My family and friends live in Vancouver and if you do not want to be here that is your choice and I accept that. It is important to me that my husband spends time with me and my family.

You have to make the choice if you are willing to trust those around you and seek help, or not. I am not going one step further in this relationship until the foundation is worked on and at this point all we have left is love.

I cannot convince you that you need help if you do not want to get help. On that note, I have been waiting but I do not know how much longer I will be able to wait. My life has been on complete hold waiting for you and fearing for your life for 5 months. I guarantee you that this is not a sustainable place to be and I am going to carry on with my life because you are an adult and you have to decide if you want to treat this disease or not.

Like two butterflies in a field I know that you are out there
.....and that is good enough for me because it is all that I have.
I love you and I let you go 5 months ago ....
hoping that you would find your way back... .. ..
....

It is clear by your actions that you would rather
be at the hands of your mania than in the arms and care of loved ones.

I love you, you are free.

The story of the butterfly

A man found a cocoon of a butterfly.
One day a small opening appeared.
He sat and watched the butterfly for several hours
as it struggled to squeeze its body through the tiny hole.
Then it stopped, as if it couldn't go further.
So the man decided to help the butterfly.
He took a pair of scissors and
snipped off the remaining bits of cocoon.
The butterfly emerged easily but
it had a swollen body and shrivelled wings.
The man continued to watch it,
expecting that any minute the wings would enlarge
and expand enough to support the body,
Neither happened!
In fact the butterfly spent the rest of its life
crawling around.
It was never able to fly.
What the man in his kindness
and haste did not understand:
The restricting cocoon and the struggle
required by the butterfly to get through the opening
was a way of forcing the fluid from the body
into the wings so that it would be ready
for flight once that was achieved.
Sometimes struggles are exactly
what we need in our lives.
Going through life with no obstacles would cripple us.
We will not be as strong as we could have been
and we would never fly.
Author Unknown

This is helpful: http://heretohelp.bc.ca/skills/supporting-family/family-toolkit
These people are helpful: http://www.mdabc.net/
Someone who will practice EFT with you: Shaun 604-...
Bye Bo... I love you.

October 28, 2011
Bo
To me

Your butterfly is on Cortez. Too bad you are acting like a caterpillar.

CHAPTER THIRTY-FIVE

BLACK

Fall was closing in and the OCCUPY movement had started and I was pleased to see that people were taking to the streets. With loads of people setting up camp at the art gallery it finally felt like the long awaited shake down was surfacing. Of course it was getting tainted by news coverage missing the message but I had never seen Vancouver erupt like that and welcomed the change.

Bo and I used to argue about the colour black. "Pass me my navy hoodie" he would say. "Your black hoodie, you mean?" I would reply. And he would insist that there is no way it was black and I would sometimes put up a fuss then acquiesce and say fine, "*faded* black" because he was right in the sense that if we were to compare a denser object like an iPhone that was 'black' it certainly didn't look the same as his hoodie or my faded 'black' jeans. I would try and get him to agree or understand that for ease of communication with people this navy/faded black thing is really just referred to as 'black' and that is the general consensus as we know it on earth. This didn't waiver his stance at all. He really didn't seem to care about convincing me it was navy or anything but insisted on making it clear between us that it was not black (black).

With a full degree in art under my belt I had a hard time letting that one go. Faded black really isn't the same as black, I could agree with that. I had a point as well about the consensus thing but we could argue until the cows come home about what colour something is from one persons eye to another. And I remembered how when we were first living together we used to sit for hours together flipping through paint swatches talking about colour and playing a game where we would take turns making up a room and each choosing a colour theme.

We were trying so hard to make things work still. Missing each other so much. We tried to clear the air with things like this:

November 1, 2011
Alicia
To Bo
Greatest fears
in order of panic level, my fears with you:
1. that you will commit suicide
2. that you will run away/disappear
3. that you will try and control me and isolate me from my family and friends
4. that being with you will stress me out so much that i become mentally unstable myself
5. that i will never really know "who you are" because you don't remember one mood from the next

November 1, 2011
Bo
To Alicia
1. Afraid you will react and not give us enough time to really iron out the last five months
2 Afraid to fail you are so important in my life.. I know all our energies have made a synergy and I want peace within us
3. Worried you won't give this place a chance

4 I have become more attuned and more sensitive, I need a little sensitive treatment or maybe I just need time and contact with you to be more in touch.

5 Afraid you won't give me enough time to feel my true intention in case my intention doesn't come through clear the first time.

November 1, 2011

Bo

To Alicia

Answer

Hope this helps.

1. that you will commit suicide

this won't happen… regardless I decided long ago my father took the easy way out and wood not do the same

2. that you will run away/disappear

not running now babe, I've been making more friends, being artistic and centering

3. that you will try and control me and isolate me from my family and friends

All I can say is I won't, I just want more of your time again… I love you, I won't trap you. I know as a man that if we are not in a place together willingly we will just come apart again.

4. that being with you will stress me out so much that i become mentally unstable myself

I have actually achieved an even energy, I am full of light these days but centered.   I think you will find my presence much improved.

5. that i will never really know "who you are" because you dont remember one mood from the next

I have always had this floating centre but lately like I said in answer to number 4; I have been feeling more focused and wholistic despite the pain I see, This is helping me know and keep myself in a new way… It is a revelation to me.

He followed this with a lovely email including the link to Blue Jay Lake, an organic farm in the centre of Cortes that he said he was saving for my arrival. Love Bo.

November 2, 2011
Chat with Matty

me: FUuuuucckkk

Matty: what's up?

me: charlie had a huge freak out this morning
he packed some bags and left

Matty: oh?
why did he have a huge freakout?

me: he came home at 10am and kristen asked if he was on drugs and started screaming at her and then at me

Matty: oh really?
perculiar

me: yeah...:(
i emailed Bo that i am not coming

Matty: oh okay, i'm glad

me: i feel ok about visitng for a week but i just dont like the feeling i have now
me going there would just be another round of chaos

Matty: i think so
i think it would send the wrong message

me: well what i think he isnt getting ...that is fundamental....is that i have my own life
he keeps thinking if we can "be somewhere" then we can start ...im saying it has to start now

Matty: hmmm
its all on thin ice i'm afraid

me: totes

CHAPTER THIRTY-SIX

THE FALL OF CORTES

Against all advice and previous planning, Bo had given me enough cues that he was holding steady for me to agree at the last minute to catch that flight and come meet him. He had booked me a flight that in one of our arguments I had told him to cancel. At the last minute, I fired off an email saying I was on my way and was blessed with good wishes from friends and family. I knew I was going into the storm again but Kristen handed me one of her pink birthday roses and I was out the door again with hope in hand. Her friend Mojave had said to me that if I am not attached to the outcome then I have nothing to worry about and I let that sink in.

I went through airport security holding for comfort the pink rose and the reminder that I had nothing to lose. Fear and excitement carried me through my flight and ferry over.

November 2, 2011

On the plane to campbell river, then to cortes. Bo picking me up. I am nervous as well. I am afraid of another explosion, another spin on the mary go round that has been all consuming. Afraid that I will lose who I am by getting closer to him. Afraid he will trick me. Afraid I am going to flip flop around again and get myself all tangled up. Mojave said "as long as you are not attached to the outcome you have nothing to lose." I really don't live with a lot of regret, meaning I already detach from the outcome of things I think. I really can't blame this human, she has gone alone for one hello of a ride. Let it go Alicia, You are human this time. It is ok. Live, be, love. Next stop- the rest of my life. I will follow you into the dark.

Fear is rooted in Love.

The plan was that I would ferry from Campbell River to Quadra and Bo would ferry from Cortes to Quadra so we would meet in the middle. I took refuge alone on the top deck of the ferry turning over and over in my head what was going on and what might happen as well as try and clarify how I was feeling so I didn't get lost in it all again. I had to keep my feet on the ground for this ring of fire.

Tears in eyes, clutching the pink rose to my heart and I walked off the ferry. I admit, I was sad but not exactly surprised to not see my Bo there waiting, reliably to pick me up…as he had done so many times. Like when he loved me every day by taking me to and from work. He would never say much more than a grumble if I ran late and he had to wait. But not this time.

Incoming text from Matty: "God speed friend!"

I walked through the parking lot and crouched down next to a jersey barrier. Fuuuck. Re-read Matty's text: "God speed friend!" I'm gonna need it, I think. Sitting on the ground in the parking lot holding a pink rose and my head is really starting to spin. Is this the fucking ending now? This is how it ends? Me crying in a parking lot alone? How could he ….and it's like as soon as I hear those words I let them fade into the back ground but rage and tears start surfacing and I sat there and cried for the next two hours until I finally dragged myself over to the only bar to try and figure out what to do. The local bartender spotted me and my teary eyes in a second and he offered his condolences for my screw up boyfriend in the form of setting me up in a hotel in Campbell River and suggestions of meeting up there later. Thanks but no thanks and I order my second beer and I emailed Bo at some point expressing my utter disappointment which put him into a frenzy where he tried to explain he didn't realize I was coming or something along those lines. I didn't know what to cry more for, the details of the situation at hand or the fact that I had truly lost the person I knew. Not keen to delve into the latter I chose to argue the details of the situation at hand. He showed up a ferry ride and island drive later and I felt that I couldn't keep myself away from him even though the feelings that were being expressed were nothing but anger and resentment. He let me get angry. Over and over and he told me he would let me get angry for as long as I needed and he sat calmly and took it. I was so angry I dunked the pink rose into the coffee he ordered. He still wasn't drinking alcohol and I hated everything now. He watched me dunk it, paused, and gently took it out. He shook the coffee off the rose and placed it on the table and followed with another sip of coffee. This made me even more furious so I grabbed the rose back and twisted the petals off with one fist and threw them at him. Before the last pink petal hit the ground I had caught myself smiling which then increased my frustration enough to crack a laugh and go out for some air and a smoke. Time was ticking now and I could catch a late ferry off Quadra back to Campbell River where I could easily get a hotel and scoot home but I also had Bo right in front of me and was torn again. I had spent so many cumulative hours dreaming of being with him, reuniting, having time together and we were there, but we weren't and I let the moment get the best of me.

After minimal deliberation we went over to the local hotel and Bo booked a room and I glared at him. I didn't know where to focus my frustration with everything. It was another one of the moments where on the outside I was getting what I had prayed for (reuniting with B) but I wasn't overly crazy on how it was feeling on the inside and was too overwhelmed and confused to sort it out. My anger was bubbling at the surface so I decided to take a bath to see if I could work through any of it on my own and turn shit into gold again.

He made dinner while I was in the bath. A vegan delight and I opened wine and told him I was going to have some. He probably knew I presented it as sort of check point to see his reaction and see if he could keep his rants and outbursts from shitting on my face and I drank my little glass of wine with ease and told him he looked like a bum. It wasn't the kind of language I normally used but I felt like a child nearing a tantrum who just couldn't get the words out. Calling him a bum wasn't the nicest thing in the world but I was angry! This guy posing as my Bo wasn't right! His hair was long and unclean and his face was retreating into his beard, long dirty hair and weird hats. I had gotten used to the unshaven hobo chic thing and was actually quite keen to find more about how a beard feels but his hands were filthy and nails were long and dirty and he had yellowing fingers from the tar from cigarettes. His clothes were different, dirty and baggy and the shoes were wrong again too. He seemed hurt for a quick moment to hear that I thought he looked like a bum because he walked into the bathroom to take a look. He walked out and told me he thought he looked good and that the yellowing fingers were adding character but he thanked me for keeping him in check and started rubbing off the colouring on his fingers and told me he would get rid of it if it bothered me that much. On the outside I laughed at the absurdity of my situation but on the inside I could feel the fractures in my heart deepening as I adjusted realities, again. Keeping things in perspective why did I even care if he wanted some yellowing on his fingers?! I was just so thankful that we had seen each other through this, thus far, and reminded myself about our independence ...

It didn't take much for us to be enamoured with each other again. Other than my seemingly sound mind we had very little holding us back from flying away together and as previously discussed, Cortes was going to be our place to start.

CHAPTER THIRTY-SEVEN

HEALING

By morning we were hip to hip again. I had no job or commitments for at least a little while so Bo and I could sit down for real and see what what left between us and if it could work. We lazily made our way back over to Cortes after stopping a place or two along Quadra picking up some bulk food along the way. Bo had moored Easy at the marina in Gorge Harbour at a beautiful spot. He told me all about the amenities and how comfy it was and how financially we would be fine for a little while at least. "If you want," he would follow. As if to avoid me freaking on him and his imposing ideas again. I admit, just a drive along the island, at island speed with B at my side and I wasn't seeing many stop signs ahead. I had dreamed of being able to spend some down time, walking, sleeping, healing and living the island life. Bo seemed to have the logistics figured out and there was no better place than Easy. So now it was just down to B and how he was doing.

Easy was one of only a couple boats on a huge dock that I imagine is packed come summer. A newly built kind of place with nice amenities with showers, laundry and a corner store that had enough aisles you could wander if you wanted to. The boat was nice and clean, Bo had said he spent all morning trying to get it ready hoping I would come. We were blissed just being with each other and sharing small affections that our hearts used to live on during the relationship we knew. Now was a new place and so far, so good. I slept a lot. For the first couple days I mostly slept. Winter was approaching and I was utterly exhausted by this point. I just wanted someone to take care of me for a little while so that I could relax again and not be so anxious and scared. It's crazy how the mind obsesses. It isn't really even logical sometimes. I had to remind myself for the first day or two that I was *with* Bo and didn't have to follow the thoughts of worry about him. Nonsense babble.

Going to town was fun. Like I said there really isn't much of a town except for two stores and a community centre near each other. He had talked to the people at the Co-op store and had his ban from the summer removed subject to future behaviour I imagine. We picked up lentils and veggies to cook up for dinner and had coffee and people watched as they watched us. We would walk or drive around the island sometimes in blissful silence and sometimes just picking each others brains and catching up. No subject was off limits at this point. I asked Bo about things like sexual abuse and if he was uncovering any trauma in that area, he declined. We could just as easily switch subjects and he was telling me about the fireplace he was building for Easy. He said he imagined me sitting in the v-berth for hours tending to this little fire, reading, sleeping and drinking tea. He had fashioned an old propane tank into the makings of a mini wood fireplace that would sit next to the v-berth. It was really awesome actually. Bo had cut up one of his old coffee tables and slotted it starboard in the v-berth so now we had this great little night table space and a fireplace on the way. We would snuggle at night and dream about it together and talk about how it would work.

One day we took a drive to meet the metal worker/welder that Bo had found to help him with our propane tank fireplace by welding the little door with sliding latch and exhaust tube. We walked into the guy's workshop and all of a sudden it was like my old Bo was back. He did the clearing of his throat that I used to hear all the time and used the deep manly work voice I used to hear him use all the time. They talked about measurements and details and it was music to my ears. Bo had finally found a place of balance! He was right! We were calm and collected and living on the island and it was actually an improved version of the old him. A healthier version in that he had taken out alcohol and we were eating vegan though I was not committed to that one yet myself. We walked out of the guys workshop and I was tearing up and shared my thoughts. B and I hugged each other tightly like the many times we have in the past; without words intwining our hearts.

Island life was not without some strife, however. Sleeping was still an issue for Bo and he was lucky to get four hours in a stretch if he could. He was also living on bottomless coffee at all hours and lots of pot, and I kind of followed. We would wake up at any hour of the night and talk. He would make me special teas in these little metal teapots he picked up earlier in the summer and I would curl up to the propane fire falling in and out of sleep. We also spent lots of time doing what we called bodywork. Bo was working on what he called "getting the gas out of his joints" or what looked to me like getting more range of motion and flexibility. We would stand and swirl our hips in circles and I would work on lengthening my spine. This was entirely unprecedented as far as the old Bo's stiff hips were known and I was loving it. I had always asked him to stretch with me and practice yoga. We would give each other hot rock massages with black rocks that we had collected one time with John on Bowen. They were kept on top of the fire place and they really did the trick. We could talk about new things like how the body stores emotional energy and how cleaning these areas removes the emotional shit. He could still see things energetically more than I felt I had capacity for. We got up one morning and wrote this together:

2am poem

Easy is like a dolphin, living in two worlds

Resisting water- and

Running to Ground;

Or tied at dock with seven lines, at night.

Waiting to be sailed...

To burn, to sink...

to be released...

She rests patiently for the seaweed to make its way home.

She thinks of the lives...

She burns across the water...

Souls on fire in the lake of life.

And is pleased to host the occasion.

Who is she...American Oak...

The hills of the Ozarks...In her shell. A hardwood grave of mahogany

in the jungle stranded in the aesthetics of time.

The mind follows, and with so many corners to look at the thoughts

get carried with the pulse of the waves.

The birds fly overhead looking for a difference...

Other than food...

-Alicia and Bo

And Bo kept writing.

Untitled

Whilst I while, protecting my honour and looking for respects...

The sports I deflect...

In a world of GnG gone Gun...

I am holding one...like time

Protecting my neck like more of a line...

I've seen this plan in Dasein...

People clueless to place and time...

People trying to survive...so materially...

We need a force field future..

To survive eternally.

I mean really...we all get it eventually.

Do you want to render your death materially?

Lo and behold we are walking through the valley of death...

Burning high test...

No stop sign, no rest...

The populace visualizes the world as flat and round.

The meniscus is overflowing and the dissonance of OM the only

sound.

Harmonic convergence to the loudest sound around.

Earthquakes, volcanoes and fertile new groups.

People are hungry. People are overfed.

-Bo

CHAPTER THIRTY-EIGHT

HEARING MY OWN SCREAMS

On a particularly bad night, Bo jolted up saying something, I forget what exactly, but something about me having a disease. He quickly started kind of laying into me and I was easy to catch fire. What is now a blur was then an early morning fight like we had never had before. I quickly yelled at Bo to leave, LEAVE! and he wouldn't and he would come closer or start saying more mean things and it went back and forth with pushing in the small galley of our boat. I don't remember feeling that scared but definitely trapped. I was screaming at the top of my lungs which I am sure carried over the water for all to hear pleading for him to leave and shut up and he was doing the same with his nasty rants. Nasty rants may be a difficult term to understand but honestly I think I turned my ears off because it was like being forced to watch a horror movie. Somehow he left and I sat with myself for a second and confirmed that what had happened was definitely out of hand so I changed my flight for that evening. I gathered my things, again saying goodbye to Easy having no idea what was going to happen now. I marched up to the little moorage village and Bo was coming towards me. I yelled more and ended up taking his van to make my way to the ferry to get the hell out of dodge. He insisted I stay and not act so rash. I took the van and after a turn or two realized I had no idea where to go. I had done the loops many times now but just as I did before with Bo I had not been taking a very active interest in my exact location.

So now I felt really stupid having been around so many times yet still lost and driving this huge van that is galloping along with Bo's entire belongings. We're talking tools, clothes piled and in a couple of suitcases, extra food stored under the benches, a printer, the footstool, more tools. It pleased me though to see the large Kent Crawford screen print he had given me for our anniversary balancing atop it all against one of the back windows. I quickly felt like I was moving around for nothing so I pulled the van over and started walking in the other direction. Only a bit into it I passed Bo and told him I ditched his fucking van down there and threw the keys at him. He insisted that this was not me and that he could see through it, channelling and seeing me having a tantrum at three years old. I boiled over with this and started in screaming at him with everything inside and then hit him in the chest a few times with my fists or maybe even kicked him. I didn't even know what I was fighting with, for, against… it was just boiling OVER. He just took it like a mirror, letting me witness myself. And then I shamefully marched off in the other direction. There was no way I could face this scene any longer having acted that way, abusively. I would have to just get myself out of there and I walked along with my huge duffel bag hoping for a ride as much as I was not hoping for a ride. Then along came Bo in a white car with a woman smiling like she was asked to reunite people who had lost each other and I glared as deep as I could. Bo got out and another yelling match ensued and turned into us sitting by the side of the road. He told me it was ok that we fought like that. That it was OK to get angry sometimes and that people can learn from these things. He said he had lost his cool, he knew that I had stored up anger, and wasn't surprised that I needed to let it out. He said he was pleased to discover he had no inclination to fight back after being hit. He said he could see me as three years old fighting with my Mom or something and I was just overcome with tears from every direction they come in.

I was exhausted. All the short sleeps and coffee and B still manic plus never really being able to relax. I had still not really gotten the resolving conversation that put things behind us, which only made me more convinced I must still be in it. My god no one else has ever turned a screaming match into seeing me when I was three before. I loved having that kind of stuff to chew on even though I was still on the fence as to his credibility.

Somehow we brushed our knees off and walked hand in hand again. We would always have to practice walking together because he would always take longer strides and faster steps than I. This time it gave me a sinking feeling because I figured it symbolized a lot between us. He would always insist on walking ahead of me and once said he thinks it might be because he was a dog before and likes to protect me. And sometimes he would catch himself up ahead of me and do a 180 and walk back to catch up with me and apologize. It can't feel good to have me buzzing off like that, he would say. We walked until he realized he didn't have the van keys and I asked him if he picked them up after I threw them at him. He said he didn't realize I had done that and I wondered how he would have dealt with that one if had I left! I walked us right to the grassy patch where I made the mental note of seeing the keys ricochet off Bo like one of those flash forward snapshots. We gathered our things including the blazer I had bought Bo one christmas and threw out of the van in rage sort of in protest of this new Bo. We piled our bits and pieces back into the van and rolled back to the marina. Waves would come over each of us in apology for what had happened but the ups still had some downs.

We tried everything to make it work including preparing our own written agreements which went something like this:

I Bo will respect Alicia feeling overwhelmed and not make her feel terrified.

I Alicia will respect that sometimes Bo feels terrified and I will tell him when I am feeling overwhelmed or hold his arm to remind him of above.

Alicia and Bo must remember that while there is a lot of negative Karma *in the world and it may somehow enter our sacred space from time to* *time we will push the negative away not dwell on it and instead focus on* *the positivity we share.*

Don't know why that was scratched out…oh, because it was followed by this…

This includes when Bo (or Alicia)'s thoughts are occupied with the devil or any of its forms.
We can be comforted by knowing the devil will die.
I, Bo and Alicia, will not let thoughts of the devil and all of its forms be brought up in conversation. Alicia does not believe in the devil.

Yep, was really losing composure by this point.

Bo will not mention the devil, "knowing the devil" or "having been friends with the devil" in conversations. The devil will cease to exist in his world.

Alicia and Bo promise to be mindful of stress levels for one another and do what we can to keep them low for ourselves and each other.

Bo was going in and out of this 'fear the devil things are black or white' stuff. He was mostly keeping his mouth shut when the negative stuff came out because it would irritate me like hell. The positive stuff usually surrounded anything about us and our new Cortes life.

Drumming night was a highlight. Pawl, his girlfriend and another guy put on this weekly drumming night in the community centre dance hall. It was like walking into a trance. It must have been a couple hours long and there were only about 10 of us give or take but everyone just danced, danced, anyway, anyhow, moving, swaying, jumping, clapping, jiving, bouncing, hands up, hands on the ground, flipping, stretching, spinning, spinning and the other direction spinning…all to the beat of the drums. It felt like the most healing thing in the world for Bo and I! I would occasionally glance over and see him doing some kind of chaotic break dancing. He was in a ZONE and then I would go back to mine. Mine was sweet and song like, very high up and light. After drumming we sat in a circle and shared a little. The girl who said Bo looked "at peace" when I first found him had come and sat across from me at the circle. I don't know if she remembered me but I think she did and I was joyous that we had come as far as we did. Not in the clear for sure, but in a better new place. Bo got up and brought over the raw balls of chocolate coconut oil etc. that he made, a new recipe to me. He walked around and had enough for everyone. There must have been more than 10 of us because he made quite a few. There was even enough for the guy who was sitting by himself on the corner of the stage. Pawl invited him to join the circle and he declined. Bo then stood up and told him it was OK, he said he was once like that before and that its ok to feel shy. This new Bo was surprising me left and right but I loved his speak up. The kind of honesty that can heal the world when passed on.

November, 2011
I love that man. He heals me and loves me and I heal him and love him. I want to take some time and be calm and clear. I want to spend time feeling centred. I liked the drum circle, and people smiling. Yep, going to give this one a go. I want to mediate on being afraid. I am beginning to see that I use that emotion or feel that emotion a lot. There is something I can do.

CHAPTER THIRTY-NINE

SWAN SONG

I had planned to go to a lecture by Temple Grandin with my sister and Mom at UBC the following Monday. I was using it as a check point or as an eject button, to see if I was getting lost in the chaos again. If what we were saying to each other was true, I could go back to Vancouver for the lecture, take some time to gather my things, return, and carry on as discussed. Bo reluctantly went along with it even though he expressed the terror of me leaving his side again. We assured each other it would be ok and enjoyed a walk along the beach where we had made our promises to each other in September. The beach was empty now, no one playing golf or sunning like last time. We walked for a while along the shore line, Bo wanting to go further, to always go to the furthest point he could see. I noticed it only in contrast to how I always seemed to be looking back. We agreed on a distant point and walked along peacefully at our own speeds. While I was standing next to Bo who worked on balancing some rocks, five swans and a black bird swooped in view. They landed gently on the water surface and we both beamed at each other for a second. My second was shorter than Bo's, though, because either my anxiety, my residual frustration or my total exhaustion was kicking in. Bo said "I can't believe you're not more amazed by that" and so was I. It was like the magic was wearing off, but something was shifting; maybe giving way to exhaustion. I don't remember what the black bird was but I think it was smaller. Maybe a black swan? but like I said I was exhausted. I wondered if they could represent us and our future family. And we kept walking back and balancing rocks.

Bo was cooperating nicely compared to the past and bringing me over to the Quadra ferry where we had met about ten days ago. We took our time and stopped at a few places here and there. He found a health food shop that was selling chic Norwegian long underwear that we agreed he could make good use of and certainly would enjoy the treat. He chose one in the colour blue, and although I had never seen his legs look so skinny, I smiled to see him taking care of himself. We stopped at a second hand shop and debated about getting a christmas tree stand. I found one and was so excited at the prospect of putting a tree up our first christmas tree on the dock. We had talked about inviting my parents and my sister up for the holidays and we could go spend a relaxing holiday nestled into the solitude of winter Cortes. As we stopped for a small lunch, I could see Bo's anxiety and rants bubbling up inside of him. He would get angry for a second, say things about not being able to go back, and that I was leaving him again. I would change the subject and it would be over for at least a little while.

I assured him that we were leaving things on a good page and that things would be fine between us. That I was coming back and it would be soon. I only wanted to go back to just clear my head and make sure I was feeling good about everything and get some things. We assured each other the entire way to the ferry and he walked me up the dock. We held each other and the fresh salt air, kissed and loved each other to the very last second and I grabbed a photo as a memory.

I almost deleted the photo because at first glance it looked nothing like how I felt we looked in that moment but held on to it regardless because the new Bo really hated getting his photo taken so even still it was a treasure.

In the end, Temple Grandin was great except for the fact that my understanding is she still believes in using loads of medication on animals and it seemed to me more about making the best of inhumane treatment rather than stopping it. The talk was followed by dinner with my mom and sister and I could feel myself slowly sinking back into some other reality that I had not been in while in Cortes land. It was like the ideas in my head were not being explained well enough and that I couldn't wholeheartedly even believe it myself. Family was supportive and faithful but wanted to see Bo looking ok with their own eyes before they could thumbs up me moving up there. A day or so after getting back to Vancouver, I had heard from family our friend Krazy Crow who explained that she was going to cut contact with Bo and wanted to explain herself. She said that he had been sending her vicious emails and rants lately, even while I was up visiting him. Krazy Crow said she couldn't participate with it anymore and was going to wish him to get help. My heart sunk. What I thought was a calm B was actually a B using a back door for his frustrations. I told Bo I was furious that this had been going on and that he was isolating me even more and making it impossible again. It was followed by the same old nonsense of back and forth phone calls and we worked things out somehow through the multiple failed gphone chats.

CHAPTER FORTY

RUNNING OUT OF GAS

November 20, (19?), 2011
Dream
find myself getting married. can't find Bo...or something. I am rushing around as people arrive, alone, scouring my closet for what to wear and then thinking about making my own bouquet, realizing how sad I feel about being alone and how I am getting married in a few hours and am totally unprepared. Can't find either dress I laid aside. Try one from my old vintage collection and it fits except that I can't breath and can't decide between not being able to breath or sit in the long cream dress or a short tulle dress with sparkles which just seems juvenile. As I look around I come across as sash used as window coverings and put it aside to use it in my hair. Can't decide on the dress and no one around me is even acknowledging the wedding. Something doesn't feel right.

     I was out for drinks with our friends Cailey and G and got word from Bo that he was on his way back into Vancouver. I was getting a little exhausted from this run around but at the same time was still enough in love and faithful on behalf of both of us that something could still work out. Things went downhill from the start. After a couple of awkward drinks I could see that both Cailey and G were keeping Bo at bay. I took this as a cue that B was not himself as they knew it at all and didn't want to get in over my head again. I had already seen him many times since he went mad and was used to his new hobo look but they weren't and it didn't feel like old times. But like old times he drove because I was drinking and he took me back to the hotel he had rented. It was nice inside and had a nice balcony which we smoked on and I suddenly hated. I asked him if he was aware that he had booked a room almost directly across the street from where we sadly said goodbye to our first child and he said he did know that and anger started rising in me. I couldn't tell if was another one of his attempts at pushing me into the dark spaces that hurt to heal them or if he was just a bold faced liar but I didn't like either.

He tried anything he could to smooth things over with us. He gave me the longest, best body massage he had ever given me that night. Only, when he was doing it I felt like he was manipulating things on or in me. It was like he could see and put his finger on the precise place that would make me flinch, jump or squirm. On the inside of my shoulder blades he kept trying to press onto both points and it was so intense that I would jump up and elbow him away from me and we would laugh and I told him to stop it because it felt like he was trying to pull at my wings or something. I told him it felt like that would be where I had wings or something and told him to stop it. I woke up when he did at 5am angry, and not able to explain why. It was just anger at everything, frustration with everything. He brought me coffee and breakfast in bed like he used to do but this time with a little heart chocolate and I was just angry. We made love in the morning and for the first time ever I didn't take pleasure in him and realizing that surfaced as even more anger as well.

I stomped around the city and followed Bo around for errands as usual. He picked up a new cell phone which I thought I would have been thrilled about but I couldn't shake my anger. When we were sitting for yet another coffee and he tossed out the idea of us going to city hall to "just make it official" and I thought, FUCK, something is NOT right here. Something just doesn't quite make my heart want to flutter, even though I couldn't say why. Nothing turned the mood around and I told him to just take me home because something he said set me off. I told him to pull over the car and let me out. We were only a couple blocks away he said and he accelerated from a stop sign. It was enough to trigger a previous experience I had from the pushy Montreal ex and I flipped into a person screaming for her life. Words like "stop the car" did come out but I imagine on the outside it was more like a cat trying to escape a pool because I was screaming from the depth of my lungs to get out of the car. I even grabbed the wheel at one point and had visions of running the car into another just to make it stop but Bo held it steady with wide eyes staring at my freak out. "I'm calling Deena," he said, "you need to make an appointment with Deena (my therapist) and I'm paying." "You did this to me!" I said.

He finally parked the car at the house he had invited me to stay with him in three years ago and I walked out slamming the door behind me. I don't remember what was said but my yelling was enough to bring Kristen on the porch to bring me in. I saw Bo see Kristen see Bo and he backed off. I walked into the kitchen and said something like "I can't take this anymore" and K said "well there you go, that's that then." And I paused to let it sink in for a second. Yes I had just said that I couldn't take it anymore, that was me. And fuck, its been a long ride! I took a long long hot bubble bath. By the time I had gotten out of the bath emotions were running high and both Kristen and I were feeling the pressure of some kind of attack. My thinking was as clear as mud and I started packing up a bag of my vulnerabilities. I used the big black POLICE duffel bag that Bo had bought for me and started packing the essentials in case I had to cut loose and run. Aside from my old computer and a photo album the bag consisted mainly of rocks, shells, dead bumblebees, feathers and other things I had collected and cherished unknowingly into an altar along the way. Again I couldn't help but simultaneously see the humour in my priorities and I hid the bag safely upstairs for safekeeping and decided to jump shit and take off to the parents.

My mind was racing as I drove the little Honda Civic my parents had lent me eastbound and played russian roulette with the gas gauge. I don't know what it is about stopping to get gas but I always put it off and would chose doing almost anything over going to a gas station. Anyways, the choice was taken out of my hands as I approached the crest of the hill on Grandview Highway and Boundary road. I followed one of my subconscious thoughts and signalled my way into the right hand lane just quickly enough that when she put-put-puttered dry out of gas I was thankfully in the curb lane and NOT in the intersection or highway onramp. FUCK no, as I restart her and get nothing. E is E in this car and there ain't no lights, dings or any other warnings than the little orange line pointing to the E and I'm out. Put the hazard lights on, e-break and walked over to the nearby tree to hide behind and call for back up, first in line- Mom. "I think I ran out of gas" and she called to make arrangements for my Dad to come to the rescue. We talked about whether or not I should walk down to the gas station a block away and get some gas or not so I headed that way to try that. They wanted to charge me $25 for the red container and I asked if I could just bring it back and she said no so I decided against it mostly on principal. WTF is this world about!?! The jerrycan is right there and they take the chance to squeeze rather than help. Fuck, so fine the car blocks Sunday traffic and I'll wait until my Dad arrives. I walked out of the gas station looking for a way to pass time and for a moment and forgot that it was my actually car that was causing the single lane hold up now blocks long and building quickly. The anxiety came back as swiftly as it had left and I called Kristen to laugh at my situation. "How poetic," said K.

I put his new number in my phone starting with an X which is what I sometimes do with numbers I don't think I'll need often also thinking Bo would get back to his old phone eventually once he was feeling better. I calmed down enough in a few days to encourage him to get meds. He said he would get some lithium and take it. I told him to prove it and things went back and forth like that and like this.

November 27, 2011

A: Take the pills and talk to me in a week. Calm. Sleep. You should know by now how much I love you. Let me go and the universe will take care.

XB: That's better! Thanks I do+ courage aye love 8

XB: Not crazy I we are metarsin people at the point like ashes TO STARDUST

XB: Starmagic I mean sõõn. U C U WILL § AB BA BA AB AGAIN № MM

Dec 2, 2011 5:56 AM
XB: Here. B
A: Where
XB: North ont .
A: I am so tired or crying all the time. I feel like I will never see you again.
 And I woke up dreaming you are with a waitress.
XB: Y no faith lady ?

CHAPTER FORTY-ONE

FULL MOON MANIA

Things had not improved in any sense. Now Bo was off the line and I had starting detaching from following his antics. He took off to Ontario after disappearing for a week. I was theoretically happy he was getting a visit in with his family which we had talked about doing during the good times but nothing really made me happy. I had been more in touch than ever with my intuition and had a sinking feeling about Bo. I told him point blank that I felt like I couldn't trust him and that I suspected he would take me around the universe like a dog chained to the back of a pickup and one day I would find out he was cheating on me and he would turn around and blame me for that too. I didn't even know where those thoughts were coming from but I was fearing the worst and it didn't take long to find out. Walls were breaking down. December felt a lot like shit because I found out that Bo had actually cheated on me with one of my friends, one of my guy friends, on our boat a while back a night where events unfolded that at the time I knew didn't feel right and when I confronted him he totally denied it. Now that was a hurdle even too high for me. In total rage, feeling like the biggest fool and I confronted him to which he said "oh like you never cheated" and I hadn't so I knew that was that. Yes I was a bit of a wild cat when we were first dating but had been fully loyal way past the expiry date of this relationship. That lovely breakthrough was followed by attending a fairly traditional christian wedding for my childhood friends and neighbour out in quaint Fort Langley. Luckily I had finally found a safe place to cry for a bit where no one would ask me about the source of my tears.

CHAPTER FORTY-TWO

CHRISTMAS

I was picking myself up again as best I could with winter setting in. Nando would be coming home soon so I wanted to get the bimmer out of the driveway but the battery was dead and in this car it meant that the automatic locks didn't open the door. It had happened once to Bo and I when we parked and went away for the weekend on Easy and we returned to find the car battery dead. We taxied home and got Bo's van and brought it back to jump but we couldn't open the hood because we couldn't get passed the auto lock doors. Anyways, in a flash he jacked up the bimmer, crawled under and was able to jump start it from under the hood. Cool, I thought as he explained it to me. Or stealing? I wondered… I gathered the gist of how he did it but not enough to help me jump the bimmer this time and I felt sad about not having Bo again. Or sad about regretting I wasn't more present during out times together. "I am just waiting for you to step into the present" he used to say to me all the time. My dead battery/auto lock problem was quickly solved by my Mother who googled to find a special turn key left pull up manual entry to bypass. "Of course there has to be a way to get in" said Mom. I could see the logic but was like a stubborn goat wanting to repeat what I had seen Bo do. And maybe dwell a while on not having him anymore.

Christmas eve this year was going to be Dad's choice for the first time since before I was born seeing as we had always celebrated with huge christmas eve parties. This included just me, my sis and parents having dinner at their place followed by gathering around the fire for Dad's reading of *A Child's Christmas in Wales* (true story). After a few drinks I was texting XBo and longing for anything to ease the rising pain inside of me. He wasn't making sense again and didn't pick up the phone when I called. Thanks God.

December 24, 2011
XB: Who is we and what does that mean. I am fit to carve 1 to 5 turkeys here u still in a daze? Dam intact?
XB: Up on potlatch road
XB: Glad I took the nightgown challenge.0this looks snl van by a river. Frozen 2 death.
XB: Looks like I found Christmas morning lies

By the following day we were sitting down for Christmas dinner, family guests included my Dad's cousin Jimmy and my Aunt and Uncle with his newly broken arm. Mom had pulled together another Norman Rockwell worthy masterpiece with all the trimmings and we were dishing out the plates and hunting down the bits and pieces from our Christmas crackers that always fly everywhere when snapped. There we were the Boswell family sitting with paper crowns and all Christmas day when what do we hear but a knock at the door. Our glances all feared what we found when my sister opened the door, a poor looking Bo. No one knew what to do and of course with all my heart I wanted this to be the scene at the end of the movie but it just didn't feel right. Something really didn't. I left the table and found Bo sitting in the TV room with my parents dog Winnie. He was sitting and gently petting her and I was freaking on the inside. I was overwhelmed and couldn't take more and more and more of this. And at the same time I love him and he needs help. And there is so much screaming of emotions in my mind just recounting that moment. He stood up and met me near the doorway. I reached out and touched him and told him that he wasn't ok. My eyes teared up and I told him that he was out of touch and couldn't even read the expressions on the faces of the people around him. I think I told him I loved him, I hope so. But he started getting angry and my sister said it was time to go and he started getting more angry and yelling that my Uncle was my real Father and other obscenities as the door closed. He drove off in his van and …it's Christmas… I thought. Thinking of him alone. I cried at the table and we all agreed that we had no idea what to do in this situation. My sister just said she didn't feel like he was better and that it would just aggravate everyone including him. She was probably right but a broken heart doesn't understand things like that.

CHAPTER FORTY-THREE

DETOUR NATURE HAIDA GWAII

So it's Boxing Day, and I am torn right down the middle and still possibly hung over. I know that it's super expensive to go up to Haida Gwaii for a week only but I also know how much fun it will be and really don't want to be stuck in Van for a New Years of Tears. I'm trying everything to come up with a decision including online I-Ching and magic 8 balls, which continue to tell me NOT to go or that it is a bad idea but I keep thinking that maybe they don't really understand the question. If I am leaving it would be tomorrow morning so deciding soon would be great. So I take the dogs for a walk and tell myself that by the time I get back I will have made a decision. Walk to decide. Walk to decide…

Walking along, weighing pros and cons with little Winnie and Isabelle mostly by my side, and I come around a corner to see a woman reaching with one hand to bring a cedar branch closer to smell. Her hand shakes the collected drops of water loose as she pulls the branch closer to her nose. I see her inhale it all and smile but she doesn't see me until Winnie runs up to her. "What a magnificent beast" she says as we walk closer to one another. And she ogled after Winnie's brindle pattern and her soft eyes for a few moments before turning attention to little Isabelle who usually dominates any attention paid to the girls. I liked this woman already. I don't even know how the conversation was opened but within minutes and without even knowing each others names we both disclosed the objections of our walk. Hers was to clear her head from a (possibly Christmas induced) blow up among family and I told her mine was to decide whether or not to go for this seemingly indulgent week in Haida Gwaii or not. With no more information than that she piped "GO! Always go, and deal with the money part later. It's just money" she said and then trailed into a story about being faced with the same thing that ended with a life changing trip. There was not an ounce of wavering in her dice which made it easier for me to be honest about the trip being partially/mostly about going up to see my piano man Dominic. I admit that I have a crush on him, or at least desire. She recounts a conversation about how urges often come from a primal place that has very little logic behind it other than basic human needs and desires. I like this response as it kind of gets me off the hook for any retained guilt and feeling free as a bird again. We stood in the woods for a while enamoured and quite chuffed with each other and the moment, trying to get in as many words as we could. Somehow I was helpful to her as we hatched out some of the details of whatever had transpired over the holidays in her world. The entire run-in was a bit of a blur but we ended up walking and talking for over two hours! By the time I got home my mind had been firmly made up and I booked to ticket to take off tomorrow. We loosely kept in touch and I learned later she played Noble Heart, one of my favourite *Care Bears* that I had grown up watching and no wonder she spoke straight to my heart. What luck!

That little week or so between Christmas and New Years is the best. It is like the last chance to get anything done before the year ends and it also lets you kind of see it coming and do whatever it takes to get things started on the right foot. With less than 24 hours to tie up loose ends of 2011, I decide to keep it simple and do little more than tell my nuclear people where I would be. I throw warm clothes into the "Detour Nature" duffel bag that Bo had bought me months prior when he was in a frenzy to move me/us out. Bag packed and

I'm in the taxi on the way to the airport. Total direction: North. The airplane surprises me with no bathroom, even though they warned me when I checked in. Though I was not desperate to go, I spent a good portion of the two hour flight thinking about how not having a bathroom make me a little stressed and how I can't remember the last time in life I was put in a place where you couldn't go to the bathroom for over two hours. Turbulence, turbulence then touch down at my little Masset airport. They call it an airport but really it is not much different than the portable I had as a grade four classroom. We march off the plane along the tarmac and into the portable airport and I am warmed to see my piano man's warm eyes, deerstalker hat, standing in contrapposto...and we share a hello and a hug. My insecurities rise up and I quickly start asking myself what I am doing here and hoping I have not made a mistake. We chit chat a little during this short drive to his farm but neither of us seem to have a good grip on the situation so we are making nice in the meantime. We had exchanged some hot emails and words but, as often happens, the reality of these fantasies can take on a different tone face to face, or at least until alcohol comes to the party. No sooner than dropping my Detour Nature bag by the wood fire does Dominic pull me in for a kiss and a feel up. My mind only fusses about for a minute before I give in and let my body take over. Yes, this seems a bit fast but let's be honest, it is what both of us want. It is kind of a blur but went something like shirt off and a carry/ lead up the ladder to his loft bed. It can be weird being intimate with someone who you have not seen in a long time. The mind can be as jazzed as it wants about it but the smells, tastes and touches still throw me for a loop, kind of like eyes adjusting to the sun and it is the beginning of a good trip.

I love being back "on island" as they say and Haida Gwaii holds me like a baby in a basket. I don't know why but the people, the size, the location and it feels like home there. I guess I am already naturally good at making a place feel like home but really, there is something there that pulls at my heart magnetically. That aside I spent the first few days sleeping my stress away. Seeing Bo on Christmas in such rough shape floats around in my mind but I quickly trip these thoughts away by reminding myself in my friend Andy's British accent that "everything will be juuuuust fine." One of the last one liners that hasn't seemed to lost its lustre yet.

Beach walks were calling my name and I was happy to watch Deelia frolic no matter how much snow, rain or win.

CHAPTER FORTY-FOUR

FORESTS, BEACHES, THE ODD PERSON

New Years came and went swimmingly. Dominic wanted to have a nap so I spent the evening with some new friends until we made our way over to the party. The party was announced to be down the road when, like any group, someone caves and decides to host the New Years party. I was really happy to spend the night in this place with electricity and loud music and lots of people. We rang in midnight by burning a home-made cardboard spaceship that the hosts had made. It stood taller than me and was filled with drawings and wishes that the kids and everyone had crammed inside. I was so charmed by the gesture that I ran out onto the snow with my camera in my bare feet and was pleased to not have one person squeal about how it must be cold. It's like there is more room to do what you want up there, without a fuss or a scene. Dominic was still holding steady keeping that he even knew me on the down low so I was buzzing from one flower to the next meeting people and having fun with yoga postures on the dance floor.

We walked home holding hands. No midnight kiss or much more than eye contact at the party but we're holding each other up on the icy walk home. I took my New Years beach walk this time with Deelia on North beach and thanks to hangovers and windstorm combined I miraculously had the place possibly entirely to myself. Winds so strong that they knocked me off my feet while I grinned as wide as can be.

CHAPTER FORTY-FIVE

PREPARE FOR LANDING

My indulgent New Years week of bliss was scheduled to come to a close. Dominic and I bickered for a minute because I didn't know what time my flight was at but with there being only one flight per day and him living there for the last five years I figured as the host he would know. Anyways, turned out we were early so we decided to drop my bags at the airport off and jet into town so I could say hello and bye to one of my favourite friends, his Mom. At her place I thought to check my email but decided to hold on to my calm bliss for just a wee bit longer.

We pulled back into the airport parking lot and the moment I had been dreading (saying goodbye to Deelia) was cut short when one of the flight assistants started walking toward me and asked if I was Alicia. "Ye...yes?" I reluctantly replied. "Call your mother" she said and I bolted for the door leaving my goodbye and Deelia behind. Concerned faces and hand gestures directed me to their office phone. I started dialling and one of the assistants grabbed my arm, took my eyes in hers and said "she wanted me to let you know that everyone is OK." Its the kind of moment that burns into the mind because you have no idea what will follow it. A death being the most obvious scare but with the "everyone being OK" detail I was confused and concerned at what could have prompted this call.

Ring ring, "Hello?"

"Mom!"

"Honey, it's ok, everyone is OK. It's just, well, Bo has been acting up and we are worried for you. He uh, he slashed our tires and Kristen's tires, he set the house on fire and I just got a call from Dad that he's plastering notes"…this is where I tuned out due to overload and was directed by flight people that it was time to go.

"Mom I have to go, they are boarding, should I just stay here?"

"No honey, we thought of that but who knows! We are worried he will try to come and find you. Ok, so I can pick you up, where is the south terminal?"

"Google it Mom, I have to go." and I rushed over to the ticket tearer fumbling to find my passport. It's ok, she said sympathizing with my frantic state. I took one look over at Dominic who had no idea what was said on the line.

"Everything ok?" he said with a slight grin.

"Noooo!" I whined shaking my head having no time to explain anything.

"Wait!" I said to the ticket tearer, "is there a washroom on this plane?" I was dying to go.

"Yes", she smiled and scooted me onto the tarmac to close the door behind. One look back at my piano man in the airport and we had come full circle. I had my week of bliss and had just picked up my shit again right where I had left it.

I spent the next two hours letting it all sink in and going over memories looking for clues or signs I had missed that this shit was going on. I remembered waking suddenly the day before without knowing why and wondered if I had missed the signs that this was all going down. I also nonsensically wondered if I caused this break by going away and feeling good. Tension filled into my entire body. Every crevice. I assumed high alert mode and defaulted everything into possibly suspicious, possibly a threat. Highly anxious and stressed I was building up inner strength getting ready to face whatever I was flying into, and also, if Bo was trying to hurt my family- he WOULD be stopped. United force, you name it. All kinds of thoughts.

Mom picked me up and by then my clenched jaw was as sharp as my heels in my rubber boots as I clomped through the airport. I was happy to be wearing my big puffy winter coat like a dog putting its hackle up I was puffed up to fight. We got to the car and just sat there for a minute. Mom wanted to tell me what the deal was but was finding it difficult to keep everything straight. She said it had been about three or four days waking up before dawn to these surprises. She started retracing his steps but stopped, took a breath and said "....the fire...they found gas" and her eyes teared up.

CHAPTER FORTY-SIX

POLICE AND FIRE

I was told the fire went something like this. Day after New Years and Ellen from downstairs wakes up at 4am. She doesn't know why but she hears this buzzing in her ears like she has in the past and it grabs her attention enough that she gets out of bed and makes coffee. She kind of laughs at herself getting up and making coffee at 4am but just goes through the motions and stays up for about an hour or so before deciding to try and climb back in bed. Only a few moments in bed and she sees flickering light coming from the alcove behind her TV that backs onto the crawl space under our front porch. She jumps up and runs outside to see roaring flames under the front porch, igniting with gusts of wind. Ellen calls 911.

"FIRE, FIRE! one nine zero six …Kitsilano come quick!"

"Hold on mam, address please"

"1906 I said, at …!"

"Ok mam, we'll transfer you to the fire department"

Three seconds take forever and she repeats the information and they try to keep her on the line. She is jumping from one foot to the other twisting the chord in her fingers to get off the phone and finally says "look I have to get off the phone, there are people sleeping upstairs!" and she hangs up and calls upstairs.

Ring, ring, "hello"

"Kristen Kristen, it's Ellen, quick get out there's a FIRE!" and Kristen and Nando rush downstairs to meet Ellen and Charlie with the garden hose and the neighbours garden hose making attempts at dousing the flames from either side of the porch. Nando tells me that it kept looking like it was going out but you still couldn't get anywhere near it because with only a bit of wind the flames would just kick up seemingly out of nowhere. With the heat and smoke combined no one could get close to the fire source so water was the best bet while waiting for the fire department.

Neighbours are trickling out and the lights and sirens arrive. As everyone is milling about Kristen and Ellen hear a crazy person yelling "Fire! FIRE! FIRE!" from the alley and they both agree that it sounds like Bo. I get the impression that the immediate danger was so pressing that no one even thought of following the voice until the flames had been dealt with. Lots of standing around in shock and horror and the fire marshal Mr. Messenger shows up to assess the scene. It seems that by default they assume that fires are not arson which Mr. Messenger tried to propose. He suggested that maybe a cigarette was dropped from the porch, landed into the woodpile beneath and over a few hours ignited itself. The theory lasted until the "accelerant" was found, a fuel cell for fondue that had been tucked down into the wood pile. They also found a canteen of gas and it is still up in the air as to whether this was part of the arsonists plan because Ellen says she would have heard someone moving the wood piles to place it underneath however no one can explain how else it would have gotten there. I know that gas itself won't ignite, just the vapours, and I learned that from Bo.

Messenger didn't conclude arson enough for a police report though he did say he suspected it, based on the accelerant that was found. The authorities stayed past dawn and Nando had the porch repaired by sundown, new locks, everything. Nando also hired a dump truck to come and pick up all the rubbish within a couple days. The fire had inspired some floor to ceiling spring cleaning in everyone trying to cope with the shock and everything from under the porch including the perfectly good BBQ was tossed into the dump truck.

From hearing the story I believe it was Bo. Kristen had always been open about her fear of fire, being in a wood house and all, and the fact that the house doesn't have a back door. It doesn't surprise me in the least that he would light the fire right underneath the only exit. Well that isn't 100% true because Bo actually built the house a fire escape ladder off the back porch upstairs which no one in duress even thought to use...still, we could have died.

My friend Matty says interesting things sometimes that seem to come from nowhere but the truth and when I relayed the story without hesitation he said he thought Bo knew I wasn't there. He was sure he had been watching the house and knew exactly what he was doing. I tend to concur. We talked and thought about this a lot, trying to figure out what happened or why.

CHAPTER FORTY-SEVEN

HOUSE ARREST

My family was very worried that Bo was so out of it he would try to kidnap me so they convinced me it was safer for me to stay at their house which I did for a few days. I set my bags down and reluctantly turned my phone on again to retrieve messages. There was a voicemail from Bo that sounded scary, he was ranting and said something like "is he finished yet or do I have to keep doing my work." It was enough to scare me because I didn't even know what he was talking about and I was so frantic I couldn't figure out how to get a copy of the voicemail off my phone other than to do a video of me playing the message which turned into a video of my dad getting home from work and walking into the kitchen with a glass of wine and animatedly reacting to the vicious words of Bo. I had to share it with the police and they ended up wanting copies etc. Kind of hilarious if you ask me but I guess you had to be there.

No one would let me go anywhere alone and we were checking in on each other frequently. My sister had just changed apartments in Kitsilano so she felt safe that he wouldn't know where she was. She told her work what was going on and they had a photo circulated to alert security if he was seen anywhere on site. Dad still went to work but called us if he made any step out of the commute and he installed even more smoke alarms both inside and out of the house. One day he was home alone and an outside smoke alarm went off. He had been sleeping and bolted out of the house grabbing the heavy duty fire extinguisher that was centrally placed in the kitchen. Turned out to be nothing but we all kept sharing these stories because we were simultaneously laughing at ourselves and the madness that surrounds. Laughing our way through adjusting realities was something we always did well as a group. Dad's work security had an ex-homicide cop as the top guy so he was all over the drama of this. He prepared an internal security memo to all staff describing Bo and using his drivers license as a photo. It was a striking photo in two ways. First of all he looked nothing like it now. He was covered in red scruffy hair and was gaunt in place of the round blond guy in the pic. Second, I was quickly reminded that when I had first seen his new pic I told him it looked like a mug shot. But not just a mug shot a scary one! Like I had seen in some of his other ID photos, he looked beyond tough, like jail tough. This was really getting crazy, I thought. A lot of stuff to explain away if he was to suddenly snap out of it.

I was happy to have time to spend with Isabelle and Winnie-too even though it was Mom and I who were hip to hip. We had a good time, meanwhile waiting to hear if the police had found him or not. The hunt was on for a white/beige Rav-4. He had ditched the van, we all concluded. My mind kept reeling at things just being cast away. The softest spot being for the Kent Crawford print that he had bought me for our anniversary, and built the frame for in blue wood. Mom and I visited antique shops and local thrift stores just looking around. We did have one day where I felt I was on a good flow, picked up a fab green riding coat, an empty mint 50's picture album and other little treasures. My parents and I seemed to make a quick agreement that we were all on our own agendas so there was no pressure to hang out or anything. They each carried on their weekday evening routines with tv shows, dinners and recorded tennis games and I spent my time by the gas fireplace in the living room. I would call friends and smoke a joint here and there and they let me be. It didn't take me long to gravitate toward the piano and start taking advantage of the house arrest. It was flat though, real flat so I called a piano tuner found on

Craigslist and he came the next day and I asked him to play a song when he was through. What a gem. He was really good and brought her to life. I wrote out by hand the Aria for Bach's Goldberg Variations and practiced playing it over and over and listening to Glen Gould's versions for days. House arrest was turning out to be just fine.

As I was saying, I was making the best of the time but emotions were still running high. My Mom and I had passed by 1906 to try and make a plan and it was all hands on deck. When I arrived I could hear a faint dog barking in the background from the new 'deterrent' that Charlie's brother Alex had installed that let out a barking sound every time you opened the front door and he was in the mix of setting us up with security like they use in the movies to come and sit watch outside 1906 for a while. Everyone was on edge, trying to carry on and puttering like normal but the vibe was tense. So tense that we didn't even really notice the non stop barking dog that was inevitable given the single door entry and busy house that we live in. We decided to call the police non emergency, so that I could give my own statement about what had happened, share the voicemail and also to see if my claim would get anywhere with getting Bo some help, and safety for us. The VPD sent over two nice cops in response to my call and Constable Prince Carino took the lead in questioning. We went over the main points and concerns with him and also provided them with a copy of our timeline statement that my Mom, Kristen and I had prepared about how this had all started and how long it had been going on. We all thought they would be happy to have some point of reference other than the stories and recounts we were spewing out considering the drama of the unfolding events. Prince Carino asked questions but still left it that there was nothing they could do since he wasn't actually being charged with anything.

As pleasant as it was being locked up like a princess the stagnation was starting to get old and we all wanted to feel safe again. We tried to lure Bo in with a trap by telling Charlie I was getting married as a trick, thinking he might be in contact with Bo. Nothing worked and I only mention it to point out how freaked out everyone was and the hair brained ideas that resulted. Emotions were running high.

Jan 6, 2011
Alicia Lindsay Boswell
To Prince Carino
IMPORTANT!! Re: voice mails from Bo dec 31 2011
Hi Constable Carino,

I just got word from my friend who works on the ferry that Bo went back to Cortes yesterday and I called the Quadra RCMP and Constable Neveau told me that he was arrested this afternoon. He said he is going to be held in Campbell River for the weekend and then will be brought to Vancouver on Monday or Tuesday to appear in front of a judge. I am still not clear as to why he was arrested or what may happen when he appears in front of a judge. When I reiterated what you had written about him being apprehended under the mental health act the RCMP didn't see any of that on file. Very confusing.

Please call me at your early convenience to discuss.
With gratitude,
Alicia 778 ...

A Facebook message from our friend Michael Rose:
This loving Buddha-boy immersed in his boat dreams is still at the core of the person who will stand and be questioned. Let us hold onto our warranted faith in his redemption and empowerment to be the loving mariner. May all be well. May all manner of things be well. And, without violating the free will of any sentient being, may all sentient beings find their heart's ease & make flower offerings to the sages when they have retrieved their balance. Swaha.

January 11, 2012
Alicia Lindsay Boswell
To Prince Carino
Hi Prince,

I really appreciate you getting back to me. I received notice that Bo is to appear at Main street this Friday January 13th at 2pm (court file 22..-1-K) and I want to make sure that the crown prosecutor knows that this is a mental health issue. I am afraid that either:

1. he won't show up, or

2. no one will see the background of his condition (mental health/possible charges in Ontario)

What happens in these cases? We all appreciate having the peace bond in place to keep our safety but still have strong feelings to get him help. I have prepared an email that I would like to send to the prosecutor with some background and some photos. Not too long, I promise. How can I find out who it is?

I imagine that going to court is not a good idea for any of us but how will we know what happens?

Please call me if it is easier. I bet you get the same questions all the time.

With gratitude,
Alicia

The stress was weighing on me to deal with the bimmer and do my part to clear out the driveway. I was emotionally attached to this little blue car that had taken Bo and I around so many times and have never sold a car on my own like this before but I didn't have the capacity to fix it and just felt like it was over my head to go down that route. Anyways, one morning I was whining about what to do again and K suggested making a sign FOR SALE so I brought out my pastels and did just that. It read: My boyfriend left and is no longer a girls car $1000 obo.

Dad said that was a dream price to ask but within a couple hours I had a bite and it was from a couple living just down the street. Skippity do and we charged up the battery and took her for a spin. The old bimmer drove without any of the problems I had experienced and even though I had informed them and the husband didn't argue on the price and said we were both getting a good deal.

January 11, 2012
Chat with Cailey

me: hi honey

Cailey: hey babe
So Emerson got a text message yesterday from an unknown number "Cailey think you're a real asshole".

me: what was the number?

Cailey: unknown
as in blocked

me: hm. not sure
Bo's court date is friday

Cailey: haha - not sure. who the hell else would send that message?!
else*

me: well yeah
and now he can't contact me or anyone 1906 or my parents
he may just leave the province

Cailey: or try to drag the rest of us in...

me: he has an order to "keep the peace"
so anything outside of that can be held against him

Cailey: good to know
so forgetting about him. How goes it?

me: i fainted last night

Cailey: say whaat?
when/why?

me: yeah. never happened to me before
about 11pm ...just stood up wanted to go to bed and the whole room went black
michael, charlie and rithea were here thank goodness

i just held onto the counter and walls and tried to go to the bathroom but could barely walk because my balance was all off it was crazy. i couldn't hear anything either...like my ears were plugged

Cailey: Wow - that sounds like what happen to G in Amsterdam probably combination of stress and not eating properly

me: it was crazy

i guess I'm pretty exhausted

Cailey: I can imagine. Lots of stress and probably a lack of sleep.

me: i felt like i had been sleeping not bad

Cailey: well stress takes a pretty big toll on the body

January 11, 2012
Chat with Tara

me: morning t

Tara: hey you! are you okay??

me: i fainted last night!

Tara: !!!!!!!!!

me: entire room, black

Tara: what happened?

me: i grabbed the counter and tried to walk to the bathroom but i couldn't hear anything
i couldn't hear anything in my ears for about 5 minutes
nothing happened i just stood up from the table at about 11 pm

Tara: are you eating

me: yeah totally

Tara: iron?
low?

me: no idea

Tara: weird

me: nothing out of the ordinary

Tara: maybe you should go to the doc

me: i doubt there is anything they can do

Tara: sigh, well at least it would be documented if something further were to happen

me: i imagine it is just built up stress. although my first thought was that something happened to Bo.
ugh.

Tara: ugh
do you know what happened with his court appearance?

me: friday at 2pm

Tara: ah

me: they released him sunday

Tara: i see.

hm. I thought they might hold him.

me: they told me the definitely would hold him because he had an outburst with the bailiff and then the next day they let him go

Tara: what kind of outburst?

me: the cop called it a problem with authority

Tara: that's an understatement
 how are your parents doing?

me: ok i thin
k

Tara: has your dad recovered from the slander
?

me: yeah i don't think it went very far
one of his notes said dad comes home drunk and rapes his daughters
which was enough to know it isn't true bc dad never goes out and drinks
he and my mom are nearly inseparable!

Tara: i mean, it was clearly ridiculous

me: well for anyone who knows any of us it is

Tara: man...
so how goes day to day?

me: oh well. I've been writing
painting
playing piano

Tara: that sounds nice

me: it is nice i mean who could complain about doing that?! I've also been baking bread every second day or so

Tara: also nice!

Meanwhile my piano man sends me a sneak peak of his new album that he had been working on while I was visiting him. It is called *Piano Songs* and he used my photograph of his strong beautiful hand playing piano. Delightful.

CHAPTER FORTY-EIGHT

JANUARY 12TH, 2012

The New Year certainly was off to a smashing start. K had postponed her India trip a few times and decided at the last minute to go for it leaving Nando and the gang back at 1906. Nando had also postponed his return flight to the Philippines in order to see how things unfolded with Bo etc. He called in Pawl from Cortes to come down and spend a bit of time with Charlie and I after he left. I was thankful because Pawl is advanced in marital arts and just his presence did allow me to relax more than I otherwise was. Any noise or twig breaking could rise me with a startle. Pawl mostly kept to himself and did his city things and I started reading Moby Dick. Me reading Moby Dick and Bo in Whaletown made me chuckle, grasping at anything to lighten the mood. Pawl helped in that sense with his incredible stories about the traditional ceremonies that he does in the woods with friends. Getting tied to a tree for days and things like that.

January 12th, 2012 was a big day for me. You see, in case you had been wondering, I guess I did have some hints or clues that something wasn't quite right with Bo during our relationship. Despite the romance experienced in the when we were first together, I set the date of January 12th, 2012 as the day I would decide if it was working or not. I had set the date about a year prior when I was getting confused and overwhelmed with his seemingly irrational anger. We had just returned from an epic new years with our friends Cailey and G at some hot springs where we rented an RV and camped in luxury and excess. By nightfall, we got home and he was angry at me again. I felt like I was bending over backwards trying to make things work and still not understanding what it was that was causing it. Always wondering how I could improve or how I could get us back on the right track. Looking back now, maybe I wasn't the source of the problem? And wow, who would have known that on that day I had noted over a year ago that I would end up writing a pleading letter to the crown prosecutor hired because of...well, you know the story.

January 12, 2012
Alicia Lindsay Boswell
To Joanna
re: Bo..., File 22...-1-K
Joanna,
I wanted to give you a brief background on Bo as I understand you see hundreds of people in a day and probably have no more than a few minutes on each case, if that.

For the two years that Bo and I lived together he was a hardworking finishing carpenter who specialized in design and installations in high end homes in and around Vancouver. He had his own business, occasionally employed other people and had all of his own tools and work van. He supplemented this by investing in the stock market and in June 2011 his bank account was over $80,000. We spent nearly every weekend on our sailboat either working on it or sailing. We had an active social life and regularly visited with family and friends.

Since June 2011 Bo showed all the signs of a mental problem (manic bipolar is my best guess):
- not sleeping more than a couple hours a night
- increased irritability
- increased energy and firm beliefs in his 'psychic powers' (never referred to before)

- delusions eg. Lions Gate Bridge collapsing, our house falling into a sinkhole,
- paranoia eg. if he uses a cell phone a plane flying over head will crash
- isolating himself (I found him this summer living on the beach on Cortes Island, he did not even know what day it was)
- throwing away electronics because they "interfered" with his visions
- blowing through his money (had gone through about $50,000 by the end of September)
- not eating- his regular weight was about 170 lbs
- escalating dangerous and violent behaviour (Dec/Jan slashing tires, setting the house on fire see report by Prince Carino VP 11-... and investigator Bryon London)
- extremely poor judgement
(eg. he abandoned our sailboat in the summer and it sank, in December 2011 he flew to LA and ditched a rental car on the side of the road in Washington and they are now pressing charges, RCMP spoke with him about yelling at children that he would kill them on Cortes Island in July 2011) All of the above would NEVER have happened to the Bo we knew.

He has a history of these manic episodes, which I was not previously aware of, and has come out of them in the past on his own however this episode has lasted twice as long (8 months of full mania) as any previous one and his condition is only getting worse. I believe the only doctor he has seen was in his hometown in Ontario and he was prescribed Lithium once. I was told that there is police documentation from his previous episodes as well.

At this point he has isolated himself from almost all family and friends through his dangerous actions and threatening behaviour. His friends include lawyers and other hard working professionals which you would never know given his current mental state and near homeless condition. I believe he has gone through almost all of his money and that he has sold his van and tools making it that much more difficult to recover from this.

I understand that there are limitations with the mental health act however Constable Prince Carino has written a report indicating he will be seen by a doctor for his escalating dangerous behaviour over the holidays (VP file: 17...). I think it is also notable that mental illness runs in Bo's family and his father committed suicide when Bo was young.

I could go on forever but I think you get the point. I speak on behalf of all of his family and friends when I say that we all LOVE and MISS him very much and have his mental and physical health as our primary concern and we fear that if he does not get the help that he needs he will end up in jail, living on the street or worse, to follow on the path of his father.

With gratitude,
Alicia Boswell 778....

ps. Photos attached include the following:
pic#1 Bo's bank account in June 2011 (when his episode started) The last time I was able to check (September) he had about $20,000 left and had racked up a new credit card.
This reads: Canadian Cash $79,199.92
Infinity Account $4,045.75
pic#2 Bo baking May 2011, in the kitchen he designed and built in 2010/2011
pic#3 Bo and my dad (Bo plastered notes my Dad's work on January 2, 2012 with notes saying he is a child rapist and "die" see Vancouver police report by Bryon London)
pic#4 Crabbing with our friends on Gabriola
pic#5 Bo, May 2011, one of the last photos of him before this mental break
pic#6 Bo and our close friends
pic#7 Bo and I out sailing

January 16, 2012
realized that sitting on the boat all alone was probably not that great.

I was finally able to put myself in his place and could see how sad it was. Just as sad as me in this room. Funny when perspectives shift.

One night Ellen and I had been visiting her place downstairs when I caught a glimpse of a flashlight shine through her window followed by a knock on her door. Opened the door and there are two VPD officers standing there. You know how people's knees give out when they get shocked, well I was feeling like that. Or like the many women whose husbands were away at war and never returned. They asked us who we were and if they could come in. "Is he dead" I said before partaking in any further social graces, wondering if I would remember this moment forever. "Dead?!? No." he said shaking his head and continued to tell us that Bo had been calling the police to tell them he was going to kill Kristen and they wanted to know if we knew if she was safe or not. "She's in India" I said and wouldn't be back for at least a little bit and the officers looked relieved as if they could easily tie up that loose end. "But wait, he called YOU to tell you guys he was going to kill Kristen?" I asked. "Uh, could have fooled me but aren't the police the last people you want to tell something like that to?" I asked them if this in addition to EVERYTHING else that had been documented could be used to get him help, get him medical attention. No, unfortunately they continued. It would have to be up to a judge and only if he is an immediate danger to himself or others. And, for the record, we can take from this that calling the police to tell them that you are going to kill someone apparently doesn't even qualify. We wondered if the hospitals were full? If the case was too expensive for the health care system to pay for? Why does no one care that this man was a fully functioning member of society for years? Why doesn't anyone else care about bringing Bo back.

January 18, 2012
Alicia Lindsay Boswell
To Prince Carino
Constable Carino,
I just received a visit from two vpd constables that wanted to inform me that Bo made some threats towards Kristen. I don't understand

why he is still not being apprehended under the mental health act? Is it clear now that he is a threat to others?

I know that we have a peace bond but it does not address the attention that he needs. He is supposed to appear in court again this Friday. Please let me know

Alicia 778...

Not all of us were as remorseful however. Cailey texted me early in the morning to say that Bo had come to her apartment early in the wee morning hours to deliver a note. She wondered if the conditions the police had put in place aka the peace bond covered a stunt like this.

January 19, 2012
Chat with Cailey

me: it is a form of him contacting me indirectly

Cailey: of course - he knew the first person I would tell would be you

me: the emphasis is that this is breaking the peace bond
do you know if he asked about me?

Cailey: the concierge didn't say
I can ask
poor guy was so uncomfortable
middle aged asian man

me: the police are coming and probably will call you

Cailey: yea, they have my number - the woman I spoke to was pretty good

me: i'll call someone good if they arrest him and get him HELP for fucks sake

Cailey: yea fair enough

me: so he was at your place between 7-730 this morning?

Cailey: yes

me: ok good to know

Cailey: I asked if they knew what he was driving but he had not seen

me: no cameras?

Cailey: probably - would it help? I think he parked on the street and walked around to the front door

me: if they have a camera of him doing it YES

Cailey: calling concierge right now

me: your phone?
you called me

Cailey: sorry - meant to dial the concierge
they have video

me: get a copy

Cailey: they have it there - but the police will have to come by to view it
she said anytime

me: ask them to give you a copy
better than getting it lost in the wrong hands
there are file numbers up the wazoo here and no one cares
they have bigger fish to fry and this is only going to get worse before it gets better

Cailey: ok - i will ask for a copy.

me: fucking HELL

Cailey: yea...

me: there is nothing anyone can do

I've come to realize this really clearly
even if we get the police to act and arrest him or something...
he will be out in no time

Cailey: yea
him getting help is the only long term solution

Cailey: that or we all move out of the country

me: or he kills himself

or gets killed

Cailey: do you think he would hurt himself?

me: yes

Cailey: ugh

me: seems like the only solution to me
like having a rabid dog
there is no help out there for any of us
including him
I'm the eternal optimist but I'm telling you, there is no help
he doesn't want it. therefore nothing

Cailey: Yea that is the tricky part
not sure at what point people are institutionalized

me: could be court ordered after a criminal offence
which is why I'm more than willing to be the bait
for fucks sake i just want him to get help

Cailey: what point does this qualify as criminal harassment?

me: harder to prove i think
but it is breaking the peace bond
this is NOT keeping the peace

Cailey: not so much
what's tomorrow's court date about?
surely the death threats are an offence

me: he called the police to give them
i have no fucking idea

Cailey: are you sure you are safe there?

me: where am i safe?

Cailey: where he does know where to find you

me: if i run to the far corners and he finds me there he will get
off by saying it was a coincidence we were both there

Cailey: How would he find you if you were somewhere
completely unexpected?
Like New West or Maple Ridge

me: honestly i would rather not modify my life anymore

Cailey: fair enough

me: if something happens let it be on the police
and the whole system

Cailey: ugh - don't say that

me: i can be another example of how the system lets us down

Cailey: fucking hell

me: c I've been in this long enough to know there are no other solutions
i swear it has to be blood or something else on that level for this to go anywhere
he is NOT getting better
and the system tells me "there is nothing we can do"

Cailey: that's pretty evident

me: so fine

Cailey: someone smashed in the window of the hair salon under my office - I wonder if it was him

me: no!!

this morn??

Cailey: it was in the middle of the night - I think Monday
they assumed it was a robbery

but I don't think much was missing
meeting an Officer in 10 mins
at the Waves by my office

me: one is here now to meet with me
let me know how it goes
he was just at my dads work 10 min ago

Cailey: jesus
what was he doing there?
I am just back to my office - we went and picked up the evidence and went over the video footage
was there a no-contact or no go to your Dad's work?

me: not on the paperwork i have

Cailey: shitty

me: ah shite
ok dad called the prosecutor and was told they are filing another
warrant for his arrest as we speak

Cailey: great

January 19, 2012
Alicia Lindsay Boswell
To Joanna

Joanna, I understand from the court docket that Bo appeared last Friday and is to appear again tomorrow. Some updated information:
-Last night I was visited by two vpd constables who came over to advise us that Bo had called them to give death threats against Kristen (owner of 1906). She is currently out of the country but Bo doesn't know that and I am still living at 1906 and therefore scared because the last time he threatened to kill her he set the house on fire, January 2, 2012 (VP 18…)
-I received a call last night from Bo that was just a hang up and from a number that is untraceable.
-this morning between 7-730am Bo went to my best friend's house and left more terrible notes like he did at my father's work (VP 44…)

There is nothing PEACEFUL about this behaviour. He has contacted me directly, and now through going to my best friend's house, indirectly and last night the police were looking for him from their concern over the death threats he has given.

Please when is this going to stop?!?

January 20, 2012
Chat with Cailey

me: hey honey
the warrant is out

Cailey: that's good

me: yeah, thats all i know

Cailey: no mischief in the midnight hours?
well hopefully he shows up to court today and they can pick him up then...

me: nope, all quiet
i bet jail would be mighty hard for Bo
not being able to move or go out
i on the other hand would probably be able to handle that part no prob

Cailey: I doubt they will be able to keep him long
Hopefully they get him into psychiatric care.

me: well its friday again
last time they kept him till monday
what a challenge c...i mean...half of me says this monster has to cease, desist or die...and then i just can't even imagine the terrible things that happened to him as a child
the universe really came up with a doozy this time!

Cailey: yea it a terrible cycle.
best case scenario is he gets some help - otherwise it is a tragedy.

me: he has to want help
that is the integral link
if he puts his mind to healing he will do it

Cailey: well he won't be in the mental state to make that decision for himself until the courts intervene, imo

me: but at this rate ...well who knows now.
yeah i agree
he needs a boost out of this

Cailey: Fingers are crossed, to say the least

me: i can't believe he wrote his note on the RV flyer!?!
haha
wtf?!?
thats a lot of effort

Cailey: oh no - it is better than that

me: ?

Cailey: he convinced my concierge - a middle aged asian man - to write the note for him

me: what?!?

Cailey: oh yea

me: as if to be leaving a message?

Cailey: exactly

me: his arrogance is wonderful fuel for my anger

Cailey: the note was something like this:

7:20AM - Hand delivered with the message for Cailey: "Less Threesomes".

me: the concierge guy hand delivered it?!?!
WTF LOL
lol

Cailey: No - he was saying the flyer was hand delivered by Bo with the following message

me: oh i get it
holy SHIT
sorry i don't know if it is funny for you yet

Cailey: yea - you can see him in the video trying to convince this guy to do it

me: oh shit

Cailey: it's pretty funny

me: poor concierge guy
im lol

Cailey: he was so embarrassed when i asked him about it

me: of course

Cailey: threesomes
lol

me: he doesn't know what to think

Cailey: oye

me: I'm still lol at the scene
and the 'hand delivered' detail

Cailey: it's completely wacky
a fucking RV flyer
wtf

me: Canada dream????

Cailey: yep

me: oh SHIT
lol

Cailey: where did he even get that?
me: thats what i was thinking

Cailey: like did he go all the way to a rental place to get that - just for me
wtf

me: or it cold work like he found it somehow and then thought it was a sign for him to pass on a message to you

Cailey: what does that even mean?

me: less threesomes?

Cailey: haha

me: thats an odd one i hadn't heard him ranting about that at all come to think of it

Cailey: yea - not sure why he would feel the need to concern himself with my sex life

me: because his is an arrogant asshole
who quite obviously accuses others around him of things that bother him on the inside

Cailey: well he seems to think he is on some sort of mission to rid the world of what he perceives as sexual perversions

me: yes that is about right

Cailey: yea - that is very evident. G said that is textbook for this kind of thing

me: why the hell isn't it common knowledge then
would have made it way easier for me to bob and weave his shit in the last 7 months
instead i hung myself out to dry

Cailey: who knows

me: meh. I'm content with it. I'm WAY stronger now

Cailey: anyway he better not show up at my place again - I will fucking freak out.

me: just call the police

Cailey: isolated incident - ok... but if this becomes a pattern... ugh

me: yeah. I've dreaded that loads
i may have a crazy Bo guy doing shit like this for the rest of my life
anyways. not there yet

Cailey: Fuck - i'd move
yea, thankfully. Hopefully we can 'nip it in the bud'.

me: what does g think
re: nipping possibility

Cailey: honestly - I don't know. He has kind of gone from compassionate to protective of me over the last 24 hours...

me: of course
i just mean does he have a take on if the situation can be rectified
or is Bo a lost cause

Cailey: I don't think he thinks anyone is a lost cause

me: good idea

Cailey: but I don't know - he'd have to speak for himself on this one - he is much more knowledgeable than I am on this

me: less threesomes

Cailey: ugh

me: well he didn't say none

haha
just less
wtf

Cailey: bhahahahahah

me: WTF

lol

Cailey: honestly I am just glad it happened at home residence and not my work.

me: totally and we are all listed now so less likely it will occur again

Cailey: fuck - i sincerely hope so

me: smear campaign on us all
and my dad :(

god now you can really imagine that :(

Cailey: fuck my heart totally goes out to him - like I said, so glad it did not happen at my work... I can't even imagine...

me: if it gets worse and i have to testify criminally i will remember to include the fact that i couldn't have a job or things like that because he would do these things!

Cailey: I am surprised he has not made an appearance at your Uncle's to be honest

me: less threesomes is one thing...makes you look like a sex kitten..but calling him a rapist of his daughters?!?
My Uncle is on the list now too
he was proactive about it

Cailey: Yea - that is on a whole other level for sure. Fuck.

Good on him.

me: it has to stop
i want to get on in my life and add some new things

Cailey: no kidding - talk about being held hostage

me: oh MAN. i just used a deodorant that i used to keep on the boat. the smell...so sad

Cailey: take the good memories for what they are

me: yeah. they were good.
there were things about Montreal i missed when i left and then they were filled with even better things here...so...

Cailey: and they will be refilled again

January 20, 2012
Alicia Lindsay Boswell
To mom, lal, alexis, tara, andy, cailey, G, nando
I just had a nice phone call with Joanna, the prosecutor, who told me that Bo did show up today and was very calm when he was arrested. When given a chance to speak she said he didn't really make much sense. They have put him in jail now and between now and monday he will have a quick evaluation to see if he is even competent to appear in court. If he is not, then they will put him in a mental facility until he is. If he is deemed competent he will be released and then appear again in the court and the judge will order him to abide by many more conditions than previously set. The new conditions will include a peace bond for everyone else as well as to have a comprehensive psychiatric evaluation and Joanna also said that their conditions will include for him to be detained for the evaluation. There is also an option that he would appear in front of the judge again and the judge releases him and gives him another chance to behave under the new conditions but this would include psychiatric appointments as well.

Rest assured my lovelies that if anything happens over the weekend I will let you know but as of now our Bo is in jail.

January 23, 2012
Chat with Cailey

me: morning honey

Cailey: hello my dear
how was the weekend?

me: fairly uneventful
Bo is to appear in court in 10 min
don't know why or what is going on, no one has contacted me
looks like he is being released

Cailey: I was told the crown is asking for psych evaluation

me: thats what they told me
but now it shows he is being released, i think
likely the kind of thing that someone looks at and says, well he
is better than the other guys we are keeping so release him

Cailey: I think is more a "we can't prove he broke the law" thing
You can't lock someone up for just being crazy

me: yes they can

Cailey: If that was the case I would have had G's ex locked up
years ago...

me: 'rogers orders' they call it
Cailey: I think it has to be pretty severe
be pretty

me: yeah
well i think Bo is feeling good

Cailey: Not sure honey - but I think they are doing everything they have legal grounds to do. I know it's frustrating and we'd all like to see more done,

me: I'm used to it
it doesn't really make me angry anymore
it just is what it is

Cailey: hopefully he abides by the new orders
and seeks out help

me: who knows
im super blue today

Cailey: sorry love

me: haven't cried in a few days

Cailey: not sure if that's good or not
but must slowly move on
put this behind you - it

me: it is inevitable

Cailey: it's controlling your life

me: yes it really is
being afraid all the time
or people telling me i should be afraid

Cailey: there is not good reason to go through life with fear...
there are a 1000 ways to get hurt or die everyday - we be cautious, not afraid.
fear is paralyzing, caution will move you forward

me: im not scared of Bo now
everyone else has been since xmas
anyways.

Cailey: you should focus on healing your wounds and finding something fulfilling

me: yeah everyone keeps talking about that
'where's your passion? what do you love' etc etc

Cailey: well it's forward
people want to see you move forward

me: it is inevitable that i will
but so far i don't have a passion that i love enough to move me in much direction

January 23, 2012
Alicia
To Mom and Alexis
just got a call from jail to confirm that they do still have him. he is set to be seen by a judge today and they will call me to let me know what happens.

January 27, 2012
Tomorrow is Bo's birthday. I won't let my heart break about it because that will only keep him as a person I am sad about. Let this year bring new enlightenments and peace. Pawl has been here a few weeks. He is a real treat. Endless stories and adventures long passed. He is really calm and equally strong. His drum playing give such a nice vibration and even though he is quite loud and sounds like a sack of potatoes when he comes down the stairs I find hearing his voice through the walls quite soothing. Like the puttering of Charlie.

Having his birthday and court appearance line up was enough to really get my attention and I decided it was a good time to cut the story. I was now counting eight months since he first left and I had no sign of him improving or even wanting to improve, in fact I could see pretty clearly that we were a far cry away from making any amends. Only he can help himself I reminded. The butterfly has to build his own strength.

I didn't know how I would spend his birthday except that I would take a walk down to the beach. I had thought about it the night before and always wondered what gifts could be waiting for me when I got there. There was nothing at first, but in the darkness and stillness I walked out into the water in my wellies and noticed I was sharing the quiet sea with a great blue heron. We stood together and after a few minutes I gently walked as close as I could before it would slowly pick up one leg and I took one step back. We stood there for a while. I noticed that it would lift one leg up just a few seconds before I could even hear people along the path. The things we can't sense. And I watched him pierce into the water after what looked to be a whole fish that he then somehow gobbled, fully almost all at once. And we stood there more. Wave after wave washing over my green rubber boots. This ocean that was the place of so many of my memories and now tears. I let the waves wash over my feet until I was cold allover and thanked the heron and walked myself home.

FOUR STAGES

DR. MICHAEL BECKWITH

BY US	THROUGH US
Gain control	Give up control
Life supports our manifestations	Become a channel, life flows and guides us

TO US	AS US
No control	Co-creating
Life is doing something to us	One with ALL life

CHAPTER FORTY-NINE

ONE YEAR LATER

Two butterflies in a field, my ass. I forgot to mention that one of the things I did the first week he left was I put an apple left over from my lunch on our desk and used it as a focal point thinking for sure by the time this apple rots he will be back. Well let me tell you that apple slowly wrinkled and lasted over a year on that desk and no, he didn't come back. I took it as a symbol of my loving heart. Also kind of scary how long an inorganic apple can sit without even looking aged or wilted!!

I was down at the ocean for my regular beach walk, sitting watching the waves when my phone barked. It was the prosecutor calling, the latest prosecutor, to tell me an update on Bo. My latest hope was that he may be looking for work on Bowen, from an ad that K came across. It said boat access sites in the ad so I was optimistic about his recovery and maybe Easy's as well. This solace was quickly ripped from my clutches by the prosecutor's cutting words. "He really smells," she said, pausing "And I've been doing this for 20 years, working at Main street!" If you know anything about Vancouver's homeless population, the east side, and main street, we are talking about the cream of the crop of those down and out.

"He babbles," she said. And I paused to encourage details. She couldn't tell me much but she said it was horribly vulgar, talking about sexual things among judges, rape, disgusting things, and he believes the crown has been funded by old money, "the Rothchilds?" I asked having read some David Icke just that morning "Yeah, like that," she said. "It is really sad" she continued. "Welcome to my world," I replied and we sighed and chuckled for a second.

The prosecutor said that because he doesn't qualify for jail or criminal charges she was trying to get him legal aid. "If this thing goes to trial," she said "it will be a total gong show."

"Which is exactly what he wants," I followed.

"Yes, we try and give them a platform", she said (now referring to him as them, as in mentally ill? I assume?) "It's better to let them say what they want to say in here, where we have a bailiff, with a gun! No really, we gave him at least 10 minutes to say what he wanted to say but it was so vulgar the JP had to stop him."

What a waste of a process and everyone's time. And we talked about what a trial would mean and I clarified that there were no criminal charges and I thanked her for the call. Joanna the first prosecutor seemed to take the lead on Bo's case. I corresponded with her about any details that came up with Bo and finally Kristen got her on the phone to confirm that in fact yet again that there was absolutely nothing that we could do to help get him medical attention. We expressed our fear that he would hurt himself and how much damage has been done already, but alas, nothing we could do I was told.

As I write this, approximately one year since he first went mad, he has been in and out of jail multiple times including a month in Ontario for going into a coffee shop in his hometown and ranting obscenities then later tearing a table off the wall in the courthouse. I believe he is currently out but no one from the authorities have contacted me. I regret that we as family and friends were not more involved in what happened to Bo in the courts in Vancouver. In fact we were told not to come to court, that it would be only disruptive, when I said I wanted to come down and speak with the judge myself. A number of us wanted to go. Who knows what it could have done. Now it is sincerely out of my hands. I do appreciate one's right to free will and Bo's ability to get respect from authorities for "his choices," as they kept telling me.

I don't have an answer to any of this any more than I did when I started. If a person doesn't want to take medication or participate in what people call 'normal' society then they won't and that is their choice, really. But at the same time what measure of health is it to adjust to a sick society? Cancer killing people you know everywhere, an environment depleted, greedy kind of sick society. I know too many people who slave through their jobs. We can't be thriving. Being in debt is one kind of jail but there are lots of other kinds too. Mostly just jails you have in your mind of how you think you should be or how you think others think you should be. It's all mostly nonsense because if you think about it, everyone is slaying the same dragon so who's really noticing anyways. As I learned through Bo, you can go far on the outstretches and people still love you and will give you a chance. K said something once like you have to kick off a hundred hands before you crash because people generally do want to help and I agree. Like that nice woman on Gabriola who drove me to see our boat Easy whose contact info I lost but anyways. Paying it forward helps. Getting the ball rolling, especially on a rainy day. One of my favourite past times is walking down at the beach and picking up the garbage I see. It never fails. It's fun to watch how things come back because they do if you can pay attention.

It's been a year now of listening to the Black Keys or Glenn Gould's Goldberg variations and Alan Watts, thinking and writing this away. Sometimes there are rainy days, given I still don't know where Bo is. I was hoping that by the time I got to this part of the story that I would be closer to that magical answer, solution or something to tell you it was all worth it. I haven't got there yet and much of my time is spent in sadness. I feel overwhelmingly shocked when I think back to how much I have lost, we have lost in this year. I am especially sad when I think about all of the petty quibbles I was part of that took away from what in hindsight was a time of my life. Sailing, Bo and Alicia. I knew it felt good but still let stupid shit get in the way. I suppose that is a lesson in itself, for the next time of my life. Everyone says it will happen, that we weren't together that long and that I will have a happy fulfilled life, or something like that. I can feel a really strong wall in my mind that doesn't let comments like that seep very deep. I feel like people don't understand how empty I am inside. How hard the space is to fill. I don't discount the option of finding someone else that will fill my heart like I dream but it's like the options are dwindling. Where is the online dating site for people who can see and travel to other dimensions? Or at least fathom them. In the sad times I feel like I am watching myself go through this life. Who is watching? Me, or part of me is watching my physical body go through the motions. And so many motions there are! Or watching life go through me.

One of my more recent pet peeves is needless space filler. For example, driving with someone to a place and spending the entire drive thinking about whether there will be parking or not. Yeah basically dialogue surrounding things that may or may not happen in the future, like hopes. Hopes? I hope it will be sunny, I hope it will be good, I hope it will be worth it. What kind of a response can anyone even give to that other than…we'll just have to wait and see! And even that is driving me nuts. It's one of the default responses we need to just move past. Yes, we will ALWAYS just have to wait and see so can't we come up with a more original line? I tend to probe that kind of conversation now to explore or uncover and connect it with underlying issues like anxiety. Trying to help or something and point out to other people that their mind is living in the future with that moment, instead of the present. It's like the future and past have taken over living in the now. Or maybe we never knew now? I don't think I knew it as well as I know it *now*. I used to think that my thoughts were my now until I could see the difference between me and my thoughts. Now I can see my thoughts as clues or clouds drifting by and I can choose which ones to look at or follow. I say clues because they certainly come from somewhere and often observing or listening to them has given me much inquiry into what is beneath or motivating such thoughts. Who cares right? At least that seems to be the message I get when I try and talk about this kind of thing. Usually with most it's followed by a pause and an "…anyways" and yet I am dying to share a message. Or maybe I am just dying to put all the shit I went through to some use, I don't know.

I watch people, they look happy, walking along and carrying on and I wonder what I am missing. How are they so happy? Are they so happy? Why am I the only one having problems with these kinds of questions. It only took me two apartment moves to decide I would never paint a wall I don't own because the effort at the end didn't seem worth it. Conserving energy is my game? Efficiency? Some people tell me I sound depressed which could be partly true but what feels true is that I am different. I see things differently than I did and can no longer be swept up with 'things' as I used to.

If our Facebook accounts show enough cool stuff in the time-line then we feel alive or if we have vacation plans in the future then we feel alive, but NOW gets missed under both preoccupations. Bo told me once that the rhodo was the only thing that could get him out of bed in the morning once when he was healing from depression. When he told me he said the blooms were pink. When I finally saw it bloom in real life they were so clearly purple that we never figured out that one. Putting it all together in hindsight my best guess was that Bo is either partly colour blind or he really does see things different than they seem.

Some of the ironies in all of this include that I have taken on a lot of the drastic changes that Bo went through when he first went mad. Including not eating meat, not drinking alcohol, spending my days doing body work, walking the beach and meditating. I can see now that a lot of what he said did come true. The stuff that he was saying in the beginning more than the last stretch with the fire and everything. He was trying to entice me to come live at up at Cortes by suggesting we start a body work class. I remember the rejection in my head at his suggestion just because he sounded so nuts! I could probably do some kind of body work class with all of my fitness background but with what certification and who was Bo to teach body-work? He had the stiffest hips and lower back around. That is, until he spent his summer "getting the gas out of his joints." He used to hate it when I would crack my knuckles then came back from his astral travels trying to encourage me to swivel my knees around in circles and he did the same. I can take flexibility with the best of them but his knee rotations made even me squirmy. The irony of all that being that just less than one year later I have wholeheartedly taken on the Ashtanga yoga practice now doing my own knee twisting into full lotus many mornings a week.

Imagine if you can, crossing someone who smells, in ragged clothes, limping and or pushing a cart and imagine how it feels to have your first thought be "is it him? Is this my love?" As you try to look, but not look, deep into the eyes and not trying to provoke but dying to get close enough to know. The perspective has changed my life, probably for the better. I like to believe that by responding emotionally and practicing being open rather than closed off we are adding more love to the world. Now my peering and gazing are often followed by smiles. Now, I am really looking at someone, rather than glazing over or pretending to look through them. Like autopilot mode where I think we acknowledge the other person perhaps, but mostly wash them into the background or atmosphere for our own comfort.

Eye contact can hurt the most. Especially with animals humans claim are *property*. My mind has flipped. I look at a homeless person or a street dwelling addict with interest.…..curiosity……compassion…. Love.

You could be my Bo. You could be my missing butterfly.

Do you believe me that since he left I was fingers crossed that when I wrote this we would be sitting together on our boat and that I could tell you it can be done guys! Don't turn your back and give up! Don't discriminate! Well we are not together, this is true. But do you think I regret it in any way? The things I learned with and from this man have changed me deeper than I could have previously imagined. I feel like I see more beauty in the world. And can see closer to the edges than ever before.

It seems when you are up the only place to go is down and vice versa. or better yet, you only know when you have hit the top when you start sliding to the bottom and only know you have hit the bottom when things start coming back up. But doesn't it seem inconsequential to qualify it either way because the variation is inevitable so why bother? Doesn't it kind of seem like getting upset about the sun setting? Is this just forced detachment through trauma and exhaustion?

The story starts where you want it to start because once you grab hold of the ride you realize that it has always been there. It goes far and wide in directions that you cannot even fathom because we are in human bodies and many of us don't know what that means. That we are having a human experience. And we move as ONE. You can go backwards or forwards as much as you want, because it just keeps going. Even after you die, it just keeps going.

CHAPTER FIFTY

FEED THE EAGLES

I sat with my depression for a while on this. Many months of slowly losing touch with friends, smoking pot to numb my pain, staying at home which was 1906 still and mostly and keeping up only a slight pace in life by working on and off for my uncle which got me out of the house. I cried almost every day just feeling shattered inside and unrelatable to anyone. Activities and people that I used to find fun just didn't fit anymore, it was as though I was dwelling in a deeper realm that made it impossible to relate to my old self but still completely unsure of who this new self was, especially after having chased Icarus for so long, without him I was lost.

Almost daily I would nearly force myself to walk down to the beach if that was the only thing I did and other than that much time was passed with Kristen and I at the table in the kitchen and just chat for hours. She was a good friend who just allowed me to be and helped me make sense of the changes I was going through. One particular day she brought down her rudraksha mala. Not the regular kind but a very special kind and asked me to hold it and what I thought of it. I really liked them but the only thing I felt at the time and shared with her was that it felt like hers, her energy. My beach walk the next day was a particularly rainy and windy day but still I went. Within the first stretch of low tide beach I found a rudraksha seed of my very own! Excited and feeling magical I enjoyed my beach walk all the way to Jericho and by the time I got there I was pretty soaked but I reminded myself how many times I had stuck with it when we were sailing and I felt encouraged to take the same beach route back rather than tucking into the houses out of the wind. On my journey back I found nine more rudrakshas scattered along the stretch of beach. 10 in total, nice ones and they did feel like mine. I said thank you to the beach and my spirit guides. I was living mostly in the magical realm.

One day Cailey, who had stuck by my side through and through, made yet another attempt to help me out of depression by inviting me for a girls weekend in Tofino. Her plans had fallen through with G because his daughter had advanced to provincials for soft ball and he was the coach so she was scrambling to switch gears. I am sure I complained about the cost or feeling like I didn't deserve a weekend away since I was barely working but a few days prior to leaving she told me she had ran into their friend Donny at a pub who mentioned he had a place in Tofino and was actually going to be up there the same weekend and had a suite where we could stay. This cornered me out of excuses and I recalled how strongly I felt Tofino beaches were heaven on earth. I remember thinking this was a fork in the road where I either sink deeper to the bottomless pit of sadness and depression or pick my socks up and say YES to life again. Cailey told me later that even she didn't think I was going to make it but I packed my bag and when she gave me that last pick up phone call on their way to the ferry I said YES. We arrived quite late and it was dark with an address in hand set up to meet this guy Donny. I had a vision in my head that he was an older cowboy type from Alberta and we would be bothering him by arriving so late and he would be fast asleep in reclining chair or something. We turned into the complex which ended at a T, she said "right or left?" ... "left!" I said and we turned, nope not finding the address and I asked to get out to pee which felt like the middle of nowhere it was so dark but it was in fact in some-one's driveway but it gave me just a few seconds to take a look at the stars, something told me to take a second. Meanwhile Cailey made a call to Donny to clarify directions which by process of elimination were to go right and as we approached she said "there he is!" And he had walked out to meet us in the driveway of his Jensen's Bay home. He was far from fast asleep and had a fresh ice filled cocktail in hand as we drove past him and parked the car in front of a bumping and Botiful house. The girls stepped out and I remember taking a breath or two from the front seat wondering if I was ready to have fun again after retreating for so so long. Donny walked up and opened my car door and I will never forget it.

The second our eyes met I felt a fire ignite from the depths of my belly all the way up through my eyes. It startled me for a moment and I brushed it off thinking maybe this was just the Tofino air reminding me how much I love Tofino except no. My girls and his boys all made cocktails and headed over to the beach for late night glow in the dark bocci. Smelling the ocean and being back to my heaven of south Chesterman was overwhelming and I ran straight into the ocean in my clothes with Cailey. Donny picked me as his partner for bocci and he made a point of emphasizing the word every time he said it, PART-NER. It made me laugh. We danced around each other and smiled and flirted for the entire weekend. He was SO hot. So hot that I held onto my heart thinking he probably had a string of girls he flirted like this with. It was the Canada Day long weekend and on July 1st we all piled into the boat and he drove us up a river and we floated out of it, we saw dolphins, he caught fish and fed them to the eagles right before our eyes, we went to the ocean front hot springs which are the most stunning I have ever seen, we took the outside route back and a huge humpback whale breached right next to us- I was screaming and jumping for joy and we barely got back by dark pulling back into the driveway just in time to see the Canada Day fireworks as if they were meant just for us. I was getting sparks for Donny but wasn't sure if they were reciprocated because on our last night he leaned in seemingly to give me a kiss but missed or chickened out and ended up kissing my eye. I remember asking myself something like if I could I fall in love with this guy and having another DONG moment where my inner voice said louder than I have ever heard it before "YOU CAN HAVE IT ALL." It was so striking I looked over both my shoulders as if someone was there next to me and said it. It didn't make any sense to me at the time because I lived in the city and he lived in Tofino but I learned just moments before we had packed up to leave that he actually lived in Maple Ridge and this was just his vacation home. We exchanged numbers and before we had even reached the ferry we had exchanged texts... magic was in the air. It became known as "the weekend so good we made t-shirts" which Cailey and I designed in yellow with a logo of an eagle swooping in like they did right beside us under the logo Feed the Eagles.

The group met up the following weekend off wreck beach on his boat and Cailey and G's boat to distribute the t-shirts. It felt amazing to be back on the water again and I was getting my life force back. As sunset was falling the two boats pulled around to Coal Harbour for a nightcap and Donny was going to spend the night tied to the Coal Harbour dock. Any confusion of mixed signals was cleared with his invitation that I could join him if I wanted and oh boy did I want to. The girls each extended an invite that I could crash with them but the temptation was too much for this Girl on a Boat and I said yes to Donny however it came with the provision that we wouldn't be doing monkey business all night long and I wanted to actually get some sleep which he agreed to with a cheeky smile. He followed through and we cuddled all night in the cuddy on the squeaky coal harbour dock. By morning I woke with the thought that I better figure out if there was chemistry here because I had never dated someone that much older than me and as fun as I was having I didn't want to string him along if it wasn't in the cards. I jumped him, it was in the cards and in fact I have never had such co-sensual, equally pleasurable sex with another man let alone right out the gate. Cailey and G came down to meet us on the dock with coffees and we chatted for a while before taking off up Indian Arm. We ended up finding a place near a waterfall that had no cell reception and checked out completely for the next day and a bit, just us enjoying each other and meeting each other. As the weekend was coming to a close we pulled into Deep Cove and checked our messages again. Both of our friends and family had left inquiries as to where we were and we both laughed at how we had just checked out completely and loved it.

CHAPTER FIFTY-ONE

DNA

That night on the boat brings me to the present which has been years where somehow I stopped 'writing' and started living. Over the years in that 21' Bayliner named DNA we have travelled the entire coastline and most islands from Seattle up through Desolation Sound, the Broughton's and up to Nimmo Bay spending a roughly estimated 4000 hours on the ocean seeing orcas, whales, dolphins and bears often boating with our friends- Cailey and G and Wilson and his girlfriends. Something we all enjoy so much that we ended up making up our own group entitled the Royal West Central Maple Ridge Yacht Club comprising so many stories over the years that they require their own book.

I'll just say one of our boating adventure weekends took us to Steveston for a little 'staycation' since Donny and I crammed in as much boating as possible even if it we only had a few days to spare. Upon docking and heading up the ramp a wood mast caught my eye along the way. My heart started racing and sure enough as pretty as I remembered her, there was Easy, sitting pretty still with the red heart and all!! Memories came flooding back and joy that she was alive took over. I left a note saying I was a previous owner and received a call a few days later from her current guardian. We had a nice exchange comparing notes and his family had a wood boat yard on the Island so she was heading back there to be primped back up. Delightful she was safe and cherished with loving hands.

I checked in with my therapist Deena somewhere along the way and she put it well, that I "went shopping in a different store" in choosing Donny. His family was definitely an unanticipated bonus and we have been close since we first met and have now spent years sharing so many good times, laughs and holidays. His oldest son had two boys by the time we met and it has been such a pleasure to watch them both grow into teenagers. He since re-married and had another baby boy Ryan with the lovely and psychic Rosalie who had her own two boys, suddenly making them a full Brady bunch. Donny's middle daughter Leanne was with her partner Jay since before we first met and I was lucky enough to be at their wedding, be part of the wedding and named as their first son's Grinisha, my very own made up Grandma name. Donny's youngest daughter Mariah and I grew quite close since we met when she was still in high school and we lived together for a while learning and growing and aligning as earth loving Virgos. She is heart centred, stunning and embodies peace together with her fiancé the calm and confident Clay. Before meeting any of them I had been following what is sometimes called 7 Thunders Destiny Cards previously introduced to me by Pawl. It lines up birthdays with the traditional deck of cards with personalty archetypes and is said to have originated out of Atlantis. What caught my eye was that my birthday puts me in the group of seven said to be born with fixed or semi-fixed natures and who do not have karma cards like all the others who are said to 'owe someone' and 'someone owes them.' I don't really know what it all means but I was intrigued because it is said the group of seven often will find themselves surrounded by each other. Pawl also falls within the group of seven as the Ace and I quickly learned so do both of Donny's daughters, and of course baby Ryan who shares my birthday.

CHAPTER FIFTY-TWO

THE RETURN OF BO

It would be nice to really say the 'return' but for me I wonder sometimes if he ever left. It was more like he slowly disappeared and that I was left with his things, his life and expected to just carry on. Then again there was always that chance he would land on his feet so I kept stuff like his old passports and of course all of his tax records and various items I found like stones and this turtle that seemed magical or sentimental. I guess I hadn't exactly started things with Donny with a clean slate. It was more of a whirlwind so he ended up being witness and an active participant to my healing which often took the form of me lashing out or acting out repressed pain in his direction. It was a wedge between us somehow because I had lost a limb or so it felt. Without healing the pain I kept trying to justify it and explain it, dying for someone to understand my position or what I had gone through in losing him. He did his best and certainly gave me the time of day but it was a rocky road for a while trying to be in love with someone who was broken. It was as if I had a loose thread that led to a second storyline that was going on in the background, keeping me from being in the present moment and truly enjoying it to the hilt. We tried living together here and there but as painful as it was at times I bless him for setting healthy boundaries against a co-dependent relationship. He simply wouldn't go there as familiar as it was to me and most. By 2017 he was leading up to retirement and likely selling his Maple Ridge home and I had taken an apartment on my own after bouncing around between leaving some stresses of 1906, my parents basement and a year or so in the ridge with him. It was the opportunity I needed to regroup, reset and get myself healed again. Part of this included tying up these loose ends which began with an email sent to the abyss of Bo's old account, basically wondering if he was dead or alive.

February 6, 2017
Alicia
To Bo
Hi

I just have to say hi... I wanted to let you know that I think of you a lot, almost every day and lately lots of people have been asking about you and sending hopeful wishes that you are well. So much to say and still a blank... my life and my experience of living life was changed irreversibly through you. Rabbit hole. And I am also very sorry for the mistakes that I made, so many mistakes.
I just have to tell you that. I don't even know if you are alive... but I thought I would try. And also wish you a happy belated birthday
Love Alicia

Finally one day I jolted upright upon receipt of a response.

February 25, 2017
Bo
To me
Hi Alicia,
I got the email above from your email account.. just this is not out of the blue.. I am alive. Don't worry I'm a good distance away (I'm presuming) and no threat to you. Im sorry I didn't reply sooner.
Thanks for the kind birthday wishes. Whatever mistakes you made, I made more. I'm so sorry for the impact my mental health has had on your life. The psychosis you encountered was not my first episode.

I think my third. I was in complete denial of my disorder trying to pretend I could just live normally. It took me forever to come out of the psychosis and the crash was very brutal. I sought help and took medication and see a psychiatrist now, nothing I object to really, I have also taken to eating a ketogenic diet which seems to help even out my energy. I'm very sorry. I really hope your ok.

Bo

We stayed in touch by email most of the year, on and off just sharing niceties like old friends. I was thrilled as you could imagine just to hear the old Bo back again. It sounded just like him and he was taking full responsibility for his mental illness. Nothing romantic picked up from it but it was still love and healing for both of us I am sure.

My birthday present that year from Cailey was a ticket to go with her to her Mom's new house in a tiny town of Mexico in December. As the flight drew near Bo mentioned he was going to be in Mexico at his usual spot which we had visited together so many years passed. Hmm…. After my flight down my computer just suddenly died and I had absolutely no cell reception which I like to think was divine intervention because as our trip finally was coming to a close it suddenly came back and I impulsively shot off an email to Bo to let him know I was also in Mexico and that Cailey and I were heading to Merida en route to the airport which was somewhat halfway between our two locations. *Oh god what have I done* I thought but the temptation for a happy ending was just too much. Bless Cailey for her support and we checked into our Merida hotel, chose a restaurant to meet at him, emailed the details and hit the streets in my new linen dress feeling shaky as a spooked bird. It was time to get a drink to calm the nerves and as we wandered looking for a spot this tourist guide guy came up to us with some nice hellos but then followed it by looking at me and saying "you have to forgive him." DONG Yep just like that he was speaking to my soul. Stunned and amazed we went for some drinks in one of their beautiful squares and he came by after to invite us to his store. Let's just say it was kind of a blur, not drunk exactly, just highly emotional and we ended up meeting healers and/or tourist traps but I didn't care at the time. We each got spiritual readings followed by something like trust falls and all I remember was one guy telling me I just had to let it go, let it go I kept trying, he eventually picked me up and hung me nearly upside down over his shoulder bouncing me to let it go. The healing was followed by the invitation to purchase very overpriced stones which we declined in favour of a stunning embroidered poncho and it was getting time for our dinner reservation.

CHAPTER FIFTY-THREE

KUUK

I couldn't miss the humour in the name of the restaurant we chose to meet at in Merida, Kuuk. It had rave reviews and we were treating ourselves to a night out but even still Cailey and I were quite aw struck when the taxi dropped us off at this stunning floodlit heritage mansion with a double curved staircase and shiny luxury cars lined up outside. Not your typical Mexico having just come from the small town plastic tablecloth and chair, fluorescent lighting scene, this felt like home again. A stunning restaurant with tiny tables set up for private conversations and service that was of the highest rate. We sat and ordered a bottle of bubbles, classic Cailey and Alicia, and we took it all in. She asked me many times if I was OK as we waited for our guest and I truly was. At this point we had nothing to lose and at the minimum a lovely dinner ahead of us. He walked in over my left shoulder and I paused for a moment to read the expression on Cailey's face before turning to look at him myself. There he was, in the flesh, alive and well, Bo. The man I spent oh so many of my life hours holding on to, missing, loving, hating and trying to let go of. We each hugged and smiled and it was honestly just like old times picking up the thread from 2011 where we left off seven years ago. Wow. I was all too consumed by it all to really eat much but they did. I remained guarded of course, not divulging too much personal information although so much seemed normal again.

I mostly let the bubbles carry me through the night felt overwhelming gratitude for the moment and to my dear friends Cailey and Bo who had both seen me through so much. Our laughter and fun times walked us out the door and I paused for a moment asking Cailey to take our photo on the staircase of this beautiful mansion. This will be the happy ending I thought! He made it! He is alive and well! He recovered! We are still friends!!! And part of me wondered how much of this was real and how much of it was me just desiring to live out a fairy tale.

The three of us frolicked through the town fuelled by tequila shots as long as they would stay open that night. We even Facetimed G who was pretty much knocked off his chair to see the real Bo again. Surprise!!! We had a chance to finally reflect together on what had happened years ago and he said to me "you stayed way longer than you had to, you went above and beyond." Coming from the strong and healed man in front of me I couldn't have asked for more in that moment. The last words he said to me before we parted was "do you feel safe, are you OK?" I took it deeply as in 'safe in life' and YES I did. I wasn't broken anymore and I was safe and finally I knew he was as well and assured I had done everything I could have, and more.

CHAPTER FIFTY-FOUR

IT JUST KEEPS GOING

And so how do you like that for an ending? Seven years later I wish I could stop the tape at the staircase photo and say all was well, but no. Days later I had a dream of Bo going mad. In the dream it was as though it happened overnight. We were in a large apartment full of old heavy wood Chinese furniture and I was trying to get him medical help but he was resisting and wouldn't take my word that he needed.

After that Mexico meeting, we kept in touch by email and even on the phone a little but within two weeks he was starting to sound weird again and I was crushed. By his birthday at the end of January he was clearly out of his mind. Fuck. He started calling family and friends again and sounding like a crazy person. It was as if I opened Pandora's most locked box that he had successfully put away and my joy was quickly extinguished to watch this happening again. Donny was supportive and understanding having been along the ride for my healing for so many years.

The resolution, though not ideal necessarily, was much quicker this time around after my parents received threatening phone calls and contacted the police. There were precedents in place by now and the police went straight to his house in Ontario and he was charged with death threatening and shortly after we were advised of his court date and that he had secured a lawyer.

I poured my energy into an 18 page document of Bo's history and sent it to the courthouse only to learn it was inadmissible and it would have to go through his lawyer who I prayed would be able to help get him the proper care.

I can't remember all of the steps that followed but the final result was that he was charged with death threats, probably went to jail for a bit and asked to not be in contact with me and a short list of family and friends who were also targets. I don't know if he was offered any mental health care. He was banned from coming back to BC and there was to be in place an order of no contact for a year. His lawyer added one final request which was that everyone on the list, including myself, not to contact him indefinitely. Fuck. Many months later I got a message from his parole officer leaving her contact info and that is basically how all of it was left, for better or for worse.

CHAPTER FIFTY-FIVE

HAPPILY EVER AFTER IS A STATE OF MIND

It's been so many years now since we were set to sail off and the only resolve I found is that there is no resolve. I am still in Kits and Tofino and I've spent much of the last eight years enjoying many water adventures with Donny. I've found that life just continues along like a wave of the ocean, "it's ongoing" as he would say. There is no point that you get to where you can tie a ribbon on it and 'ta-da' your work is done and you can rest. The pleasure only seems to come if you enjoy it as it keeps coming. I wonder sometimes if you speeded it up enough if our lives would look like the stars... some shooting quickly through, some twinkling for years on end. I'd say I'm the twinkling kind, a slow burn but who knows.

The healing path also never ends but there certainly is no going backwards in what we learn. For me it was an evolution of consciousness learning through my love. Now I realize I had more choice in the storyline than I ever thought. Finally empowered as a creator on this earth. Bo was right about a lot when he first went mad. Our society is sick in many ways and it is up to those with light to spread and share the love, peace and harmony that is our natural state. The universe is expanding through us.

I've maintained my *Girl On a Boat* life that started way back when to the tune of learning how to surf, another ongoing process with no destination point. Each effort brings a smile to my face that stretches ear to ear. I love being on the water in any form but as much as I love snowboarding and our summer boating adventures it is much simpler and therefore appealing plus I can practice year round. Just me, my board and the ocean. A meditation in itself that keeps me humble, grateful and joyful to be alive.

2020 was the year of 'unprecedented' and 'cancelled' and I must admit it partly felt as though much that Bo had seen in his earlier visions was coming true. Goodbye to the *Little Pink Houses* North American dream as we fall deeper into riots, separation, death and denial. Years later I can confidently say I am grateful that my dream bubble burst, as painful as it was, it has made this year much more palatable. We are at the boiling point now, the darkest before the dawn and these times will be followed with a great resurgence of love and freedom and oneness, I suspect more than our written history as humans has ever known. As everything unraveled for me those years ago, it became clear that the pain of things falling away were ultimately bringing me closer to the only thing that is permanent: love. And the only way to really experience love, without the conditions attached, is to just sit with yourself and connect from within. I am working on practicing it often, an hour at a time.

I didn't know what to make of this melodrama except I just kept collecting material as it grew. One day our yacht club crew boated over to Bowen for a weekend and were taking a small morning walk "Oh look a monarch butterfly!" I pointed to Wilson, "oh and another one!!! Aahh…two butterflies in a field… that was always my idea of love."

"That's a good name for a book" said Wilson. And I sit, writing this as I literally watch the tides come and go from Heaven on Earth in Tofino after many coastline journeys, with love in my heart, signing off for now.

FOUR STAGES

DR. MICHAEL BECKWITH

BY US	**THROUGH US**
Gain control	Give up control
Life supports our manifestations	Become a channel, life flows and guides us
TO US	**AS US**
No control	Co-creating
Life is doing something to us	One with ALL life

CHAPTER FIFTY-SIX

2020
IT IS WHAT IT IS

Well wouldn't you know it the story kept going. A proverbial fives minutes before I wanted to wrap this all up I guess the universe had other ideas and a fairy tale ending again wasn't one of them. I was happy to end on a high note that I had found love and peace from it all but during one of my trips back to the city having spent most of this year in Tofino, right there in the middle of the Toyota dealership I receive a long email from Donny. Scary long, so long that I jumped to the end before reading it and the last line read "You will always be in my hart." FUCK. An email? Not even spell checked? It was entitled Bright Star and it was his letter 'letting me fly' and chasing his own freedom.

I breezed over the details of our relationship earlier and within the highest highs of fun, love connection and travel of course it was not without strife. Since Montreal I suppose I have been still searching for home, the sense of home that I left when I left my parents house and even with mixed signals Donny's words were always "Babe, earth is your home, your heart is your home" which I never fully understood. I would say, "OK yes I get that but where do I send my mail or put my stuff?" In all the years we lived together on and off in Maple Ridge, at 1906 and in Tofino it was never for long enough for me to actually call it home before he would put my stuff in a box and basically send me on my way or take off on his own. I was constantly building *our* life as quickly as he would tear it down. "What about *us*?" I would inquire, "Just worry about *you*" Donny would say. I guess I was still processing a lot and facing my own delusions. Confused- but I grew into it, understanding the strength in interdependency vs. the detriment of codependency. It was a painful journey with intermittent discord though I would say still with strong love, each of us facing our fears. Lately it seems as though a healthy relationship if seen as a Venn diagram wouldn't be two circles overlapping (as I previously believed for so long) and more like two circles just close enough to touch. Khalil Gibran put's it much better though it is still a bit of a learning curve for me.

Making our way to our last boating trip I was cueing up a song, choosing among a playlist that I hadn't heard in a while so I paused to hear one of them in my mind before deciding if it would fit to play next and the silent moment was broken by Donny breaking into the exact opening beats that I had just silently recalled. My jaw dropped and I asked him what he was singing and he said he had no idea and when I played him the song we both gawked at each other. He had just read my mind without even knowing it. The most confusing part in accepting his email was how congruous it always felt when we were together in groups or with family and the energy we shared physically and obviously psychically. We usually slept with feet touching and moved together in such great sync, cut from the same cloth. That part always felt like a free flow of love but what can I say... here we are, two butterflies in a field.

The lockdown global pandemic changed my life just like everyone else's and I write this from only seven months in having know idea yet of what the long term effects of this will be. I had spent the last seven years or so working various jobs at Emily Carr University that came to an abrupt halt with the entire establishment locking its doors and moving online. My role of studio technician faded to black but being blessed enough to fall into the catchment of the CERB financial benefit it seemed like a gift from heaven above. Forfeiting the community at Emily Carr was a great loss as I had finally found a place I felt that I could exist in and be respected as a sensitive person meanwhile being inspired by art and creating while critically analyzing our world at hand.

Ashtanga yoga has been there for me as another supportive community for about 10 years and it also faded to black as they had to lock the doors and move online. My deeply dedicated teacher Geoff, despite intuitive reluctance, quickly and smoothly transitioned to a zoom platform to keep us connected and it was like a life raft holding us together and connecting unlike ever before. An ashtanga room is generally silent except for our breathing so it was the first time I actually got to talk to people whom I had been intermittently practicing with for years. It is no replacement to have an instructor try and teach from a zoom room but we adapted as best we could. I had finally built myself back up to a full Ashtanga practice of primary series three to four times per week and by early pandemic I recall waking up for practice being very tired, not wanting to do my full series catching myself wondering if was just being lazy and telling myself that I literally had nothing else to do the entire day so no excuses for not completing my practice and I pushed myself. I enjoyed it and journaled later that day that my lower back had opened up so much I felt such freedom, more than ever before!!!! By that evening my lower back had seized up and for days following I had to hold onto the wall just to walk. It was relieved after some rest and I gave it a month or so of very light practice only doing the minimum essential postures. After what I deemed was the appropriate amount of time to rest I decided to start incorporating hard core ab workout routines and only got one day in before it seized up even worse than before. In Tofino there are limited health care practitioners even at the best of times but under global pandemic times no physio, massage, acupuncture or anything was open across the province for months. Donny helped me with heat and ice and a stretching routine but things were not improving. In fact I could barely sleep more than an hour before being woken up by sharp pains and I could not feel my left leg for a few days. Panic started to set in I guess and about three days in I couldn't even sit long enough to take a pee without cringing in unbearable pain. The only thing that gave a few moments of relief was lying with towels propping me up in the bathtub with epsom salts so I tried that again and was finding myself getting shortness of breath. I used my hands to cover my face as I could feel I was not breathing in enough air. My hands started to feel tingly and the pain was increasing. Mere moments later my legs started getting rigid and I couldn't feel them anymore as they stuck straight out of the edge of the tub. Quickly following this my fingers flattened then curled up into my palms and I couldn't feel my arms or legs anymore and thought I was going to black out so I started screaming for help to Donny who was asleep nearby. DONNY!!!!! DOONNNYYYYY!!!!! He tore in the bathroom and covered my mouth likely completely confused as to why I was screaming and I yelled at him that I can't feel my arms and legs and showed him my curled up hands. CALL 911 I screamed and he frantically fumbled to wrap his head around what was happening. He said there was no 911 to call but that he would help me and he left the bathroom to make some calls. I sat there for an unforgettable moment feeling my entire energy body rush to my centre, my trunk, my heart core and with everything felt a rush that I WANT TO LIVE. It was so quick but it was one of those moments you make a deal with God. Donny quickly returned and said he had called the neighbours and they were going to come by to help get me to the hospital. He leaned over and pulled me out and onto the floor at the foot of the bathtub and my circulation quickly started to return together with mobility but the pain was still tremendous and neither of us knew why that had just happened. Donny dressed me on the floor and carried me like a hero to our friend Billy's truck who was waiting and took us to the hospital.

Luckily global pandemic conditions meant I didn't have to wait very long to get a bed in their emergency room and they reassured me that this sounded like a bad case of sciatica and tried pain medication which still left me writhing to which they inquired further and reluctantly was administered a shot of morphine. Now let me tell you... WOW. I can see why that is highly addictive and very reluctantly given. Within minutes I was lifted out of the torture, smiling and able to walk and I felt as high as a kite! Ready to take on the world!! The back pain started recovering from that moment but it's been a couple of months now and I still don't quite feel like myself. Physio and needles have helped and I am gently returning to my physical body and movements but it was quite a shock. My mobility is returning but I still feel cautious and it struck me to my core.

So I'll be honest this Donny email is still fresh and combined with everything else this year it did knock me off my feet big time. In a different way though, than I have ever experienced. I was witnessing my emotions of loss and sadness rather than being fully consumed by them. What will later be known as *The year of cancelled*. I didn't want to talk about it with anyone or make a story about what had just happened with his email because I admit he has walked in and out of my life a few times over the years… so who knows. The love is still there, my heart knows it. Realizing at the same time what I love so much is the connection I have with the present moment through loving him, and the loving connection I have with myself that I found through loving him. Lately I have returned to my childhood room and experienced many hours lying in bed staring at a familiar blank ceiling learning that I don't need the vehicle of the relationship to feel that love all on my own within my own heart and experience. That the real stability, the real infinite universe is within me. Realizing that both of us are just fingers on the same hand and examples of the universe trying to see itself. Learning, growing through all life forms, no guilt, blame, shame just love. Ceremoniously taking his picture down no longer would change anything. Arranging things in the outside world thinking it would change the inside has lost it's pizzazz.

Recent reflections revealed to me that since all of our human emotions have been scientifically charted on a scale[3] rather than trying to spend so much time identifying each emotion or figure them out the entire chart can be basically summed up like similarly to math: positive, zero and negative. Quite simply the entire negative region could be summed up as fear- it's always a fear of something! And the entire positive region could be summed up as LOVE! Some could maybe say PEACE but I find LOVE speaks to me at this moment so I will go with that.

---

[3] Well explained in David R. Hawkins, Letting Go: The Pathway of Surrender 2012

Basically nearly every moment of every day our choice really only comes down to fear or LOVE. It might sound easy or too simple but it certainly was not for me. I have passionately spent much of the last 10 years or more trying to figure out how to swim through my own emotions. Swimming felt like the best analogy because once I realized I had a choice I started building my skills and choosing a happy loving life. As Donny would say "I want to ENJOY my life, what's the alternative?" Sometimes I just couldn't see it as an option but I kept at it. Learning that anger is actually closer to positive than depression was a good lesson even though generally people would discourage the step because it makes them uncomfortable.[4] Gaining a sense of direction in how the emotions are related seemed to help and I tried so many things including ignoring, suppressing, distracting, exploring, allowing… all of which required effort of some kind.

Which brings me to where I am now somehow understanding that I am not my emotions. Who is the "I" that is even asking the question? It's like it is just happening, unfolding as I walk with life. I defer to an Alan Watts quote as he puts it so well:

"Your skin doesn't separate you from the world; it's a bridge through which the external world flows into you, and you flow into it. Just, for example, as a whirlpool in water, you could say because you have a skin you have a definite shape you have a definite form. All right? Here is a flow of water, and suddenly it does a whirlpool, and it goes on. The whirlpool is a definite form, but no water stays put in it. The whirlpool is something the stream is doing, and exactly the same way, the whole universe is doing each one of us, and I see each one of you today and I recognize you tomorrow, just as I would recognize a whirlpool in a stream. I'd say 'Oh yes, I've seen that whirlpool before, it's just near so-and-so's house on the edge of the river, and it's always there.' So in the same way when I meet you tomorrow, I recognize you, you're the same whirlpool you were yesterday. But you're moving. The whole world is moving through you, all the cosmic rays, all the food you're eating, the stream of steaks and milk and eggs and everything is just flowing right

[4] Abraham Hicks on YouTube

through you. When you're wiggling the same way, the world is wiggling, the stream is wiggling you."[5]

Alan W. Watts

---
[5] Alan Watts on YouTube

CHAPTER FIFTY-SEVEN

LOVE

A few days later after receiving the email I headed up to Squamish to return a paddle board to friends who forgot it in Tofino and I had enjoyed a particularly good morning meditation. One of the best things to come out of the lockdown year is that I have had the time and space to explore this realm unlike ever before and I have been setting the timer for an hour upon waking and just lying there. I don't quite have the strength yet to regularly do this even sitting up as I had practiced in yoga all these years but it still works. So I just lie there now, staring at the ceiling and allow it. Inspired lately hearing things like "it's kind of like going to the toilet for your emotions."[6] Thinking of the universe as the master operator that removes the cavity's or toxins and all I have to do is sit there, release and allow. Nothing required. Not attach to stories or make up new stories or think there is a bottom to get to.... allow. Feel. Breath. Heart. Listening to the sounds, inner and outer sounds, witnessing. That particular morning as the tears were flowing and I found myself scratching at my chest as though it was a prison cell I wanted to get out of and it occurred to me that yes, this year has been fucked up, so many losses all around...
......but if I cannot find peace lying in this comfortable bed on this

[6] Kyle Cease on YouTube

calm day with no actually present impending issues, doom or gloom, family and friends have their health, I have my health, my pup Isabelle is alive and well…. if I can't do this for even one hour how could I possibly be more happy or peaceful anywhere else with this running in the background? How could I ever be happy if I can't be happy in THIS moment…. And I sat with that…..perplexed… Letting the tears flow….. and something shifted, a tiny shift but I can only describe it as feeling like when the clouds part and the sun hits your face… a warmness from within and I felt myself start to smile…. And I said out loud somewhat surprised… "this feels good." And I felt the warmth flow through me in a totally new way without any identifiable circumstances to attribute it to.

From there my day had a nice flow to it that started off leaving later than I had planned and just barely missing a large chunk of rock that fell onto the road along the sea to sky highway- score! Followed by a nice visit with friends and I had some sadness they might ask about Donny but when Isabelle and I arrived their kids were already so excited we ended up just having a nice visit not even touching on the subject.

It was raining when I left the city that morning but just as we arrived in Squamish clouds parted to blue so I asked my friends about finding a local hike but ended up getting distracted and not getting the directions. When Isabelle and I left somehow we drove around and pulled over to a small hike that ended up being just the one they had recommended! At one point on our return I had somehow gone much further and we had walked past my parked car but I ended up singing along the way back and coming up with the beginnings of a new song. Upon arriving back to the car literally a moment after closing the door it started to rain and then pour! I had the thought to take myself out for lunch since Isabelle would be ready for a sleep anyways and it wasn't too hot to leave her in the car so I set my intention to a veggie burger and a beer treat. I went to the first place a quick internet search revealed and arrived to see that my lunch of choice was actually featured as their special! I enjoyed my meal, worked on my song a little and asked my heart if I should have another beer or not, trying to think less and feel more, inspired by the morning's heart shift... it felt like a yes so I went up and ordered another beer which was much larger than what I had in mind from what was given with the lunch special but when the server handed it to me and told me the price was $7.77 I felt DONG... Ok, some kind of message coming through with group of seven always on my radar. So I happily sat with my beer and only moments later suddenly walking towards me catching my attention from across the parking lot was Jay! I can't believe my eyes so I subtly wave to see if he sees me and he does. Like magnets we are brought together and he says that Leanne and their son Harvey are here as well that they stopped to order lunch on their way to Whistler! We shared niceties for a few minutes before Jay took Harvey to the car while Leanne ordered leaving her and I time to talk. I don't know what Donny has told her yet but I learn quickly he has told her, probably told all of his kids some kind of explanation because she asks me how I am doing and I start crying. She stands up and gives me the strongest, longest, biggest most needed and most illegal global pandemic hug and I hug her back with her not yet born but already much loved baby girl pressed between us. Losing a relationship is more than just that relationship, and this is years of so many memories, growing, laughter and love that we have shared. We sit back down and across the table from me with her teary warm green eyes and stunning smile she holds my hand and says "no matter what happens nothing has to change with us, you're family and you'll always be Harvey's Grinisha. Too much time has passed and we are too bonded to let anything change between us." And I cry, I crumble and I hold my heart. "It would be my honour" I reply with profuse thank you's and gratitude. And just like my morning meditation I feel clouds parting in my heart and it occurs to me all this time with all my struggles in love that was all I wanted to hear, that I belong, that I am loved, that someone in addition to the family I was born into loves me, like how I love the world. My chosen family, and tribe. What a gift. I have grown to love them as my own family and together, regardless of the journey between Donny and I, we could keep the spirit of love I felt so strongly with him alive and present, undoubtedly. When I got back to my car I looked down and chuckled out loud to see a sticker hiding in my hair- a shiny yellow smiley face.

On the drive back I pulled over to Porteau Cove and decided it was time to unload some weight. Donny and I always collected stones and rocks along all of our boating adventures and somehow among all the moves I ended up with most of these once highly treasured items. By now it felt like I was just dragging around bags of rocks, memories, lost dreams and what if's and it was time to let go and allow. I kept the shells and maybe a choice stone or two and released the many bags of sand and rocks back home, the ocean, while the gentle laps of the waves kissed my ankles, with gratitude.

The universe bringing us together that day showed me we really are one. Love doesn't go nowhere, it attracts more love. I am love. And what I have embarked on seems like a critical piece of the puzzle that any love actually starts with opening the heart first to self love. What gifts would I have missed that day had I been walking around like a sad wet hanky consumed by my own emotions as I was for so many years?

And love doesn't extend just to humans! It's all for all of life. There is so much hate right now on earth (which is actually fear of the other) it is unpalatable. It is a crossroads of choosing love or choosing fear. It seems obvious that choosing love and peace is the only way through but if you watch the news it won't appear so. There is a mainstream program that is set on polarizing and dividing humans against one another and it is for control. There is a myth underlying our culture that we are separate from our universe and that effort and control are required or else chaos will reign. Man versus nature, us against them. Control. This is fundamentally not the truth and at this time we are being called to rise above and discard this flawed belief. This is what my heart tells me. Even for one of my biggest triggers-clean oceans and cancelling pipelines, love truly is the way. We won't get any progress by yelling, arguing or defacing, only through living a well loved life can we hope to inspire others to choose a similar path meanwhile not being attached to the outcome because really, we just don't know and gratitude for this moment is the best we can do. We don't know the future and any speculation of such is essentially missing this moment, now. Distractions and emotions kept me in the past or future for so much of my life and I learned slowly that one of my attractions to love was that it brought me into the present moment, little by little challenging me to grow and listen to my heart.

The global lockdown is uniting us as one on earth and the loss of life as we knew it is eliminating distractions leaving us to face ourselves, now it just comes down to what we do with it. I've heard it put that "change is painful because our mind measures what we will lose but it can't see what we will gain."[7] As humans we only move as fast as our weakest and we are one with a collective consciousness.

My offering in sharing this is with the intention to increase peace and love on earth for all life, based on the lessons I have learned so far. My only wish for my human family is courage to smile and listen to our own hearts, where all of the answers reside.

---

[7] Kyle Cease on Youtube

CPSIA information can be obtained
at www.ICGtesting.com
Printed in the USA
BVHW030850231120
593766BV00006B/2